Efficient Minds: Mastering Memory Management in Operating Systems

Table of Content

Chapter 1: Foundations of Memory Management

- Defining memory management in operating systems.
- Importance of efficient memory handling.
- Historical perspective on memory management evolution.
- Understanding the central role of Random Access Memory.
- How RAM influences system performance.
- RAM's connection to overall system speed.
- Exploring the process of memory allocation.
- Differentiating between static and dynamic allocation.
- Memory allocation's impact on program execution.
- Unveiling the concept of virtual memory.

Chapter 2: Dynamic Memory Allocation

- Defining dynamic memory allocation.
- Importance in managing varying memory requirements.
- Comparison with static memory allocation.
- In-depth exploration of allocation strategies.
- Pros and cons of first fit, best fit, and worst fit.
- Choosing the optimal strategy for specific scenarios.
- Understanding fragmentation challenges.
- Techniques to minimize fragmentation.
- Compaction and its role in handling fragmentation.
- Identifying causes and consequences of memory leaks.

Chapter 3: Memory Paging and Segmentation

- Defining memory paging and its purpose.
- The role of page tables in mapping memory.
- Benefits and challenges of memory paging.
- Understanding memory segmentation principles.
- Advantages and disadvantages of segmentation.
- Combining paging and segmentation for optimized memory use.
- Contrasting paging and segmentation approaches.
- Situational suitability for each method.
- Hybrid models for advanced memory organization.
- Introduction to page replacement strategies.

Chapter 4: Cache Memory Optimization

- Definition and purpose of cache memory.
- Types of cache memory and their functions.
- Cache hierarchy and levels of caching.
- Explaining the concepts of spatial and temporal locality.
- How these concepts influence caching efficiency.
- Strategies to leverage locality for optimization.
- Direct-mapped, set-associative, and fully associative mapping.
- Advantages and disadvantages of each mapping technique.
- Choosing the right mapping method for specific scenarios.
- Overview of cache replacement policies.

Chapter 5: Memory Protection and Security

- Significance of protecting memory from unauthorized access.
- Preventing data corruption and security breaches.
- Balancing security with system performance.
- Understanding privilege levels in operating systems.
- Implementing access control mechanisms.
- Securing critical system resources through privilege management.
- Introduction to ASLR as a security measure.
- How ASLR mitigates risks of memory-based attacks.
- Challenges and considerations in ASLR implementation.
- Explaining buffer overflow vulnerabilities.

Chapter 6: Parallel Processing and Memory Management

- The role of multitasking in modern computing.
- Parallel processing as a key aspect of system efficiency.
- Challenges and advantages of concurrent memory management.
- Understanding shared memory systems.
- Implementing memory management for shared resources.
- Optimizing performance in shared memory environments.
- Overview of distributed memory architectures.
- Coordinating memory across multiple processing units.
- Scalability and challenges in distributed memory management.
- Techniques for managing concurrent access to shared resources.

Chapter 7: Real-time Memory Management

- Understanding the demands of real-time systems.
- The critical role of memory management in meeting deadlines.
- Balancing efficiency with predictability in real-time environments.
- Techniques for partitioning memory in real-time applications.
- Guarantees and limitations of partitioned memory models.
- Adapting partitioning strategies to specific real-time requirements.
- Impact of scheduling on real-time memory management.
- Deterministic and non-deterministic scheduling algorithms.
- Ensuring timely access to memory resources in real-time scenarios.
- The role of memory locking in real-time applications.

Chapter 8: Future Trends in Memory Management

- Overview of new and future memory technologies.
- Non-volatile memory and its impact on system architecture.
- Evaluating the potential of emerging memory innovations.
- Integrating machine learning techniques in memory management.
- Adaptive memory allocation based on usage patterns.
- Enhancing efficiency through intelligent memory optimization.
- Quantum implications on memory storage and retrieval.
- Memory management challenges in quantum computing.
- Preparing for the integration of quantum principles in memory technologies.
- Decentralized approaches to memory management.

Introduction

In the fast-paced and ever-evolving landscape of technology, where the significance of every nanosecond cannot be overstated, the mastery of intricacies within memory management in operating systems emerges as a pivotal factor for achieving optimal efficiency. The immersive journey through the intricacies of memory handling unfolds in "Efficient Minds," a comprehensive guide meticulously designed to cater to both novices stepping into the domain and seasoned professionals seeking a profound understanding of this critical domain.

This journey through "Efficient Minds" is crafted with the intent to unravel the complexities inherent in memory management, providing a holistic guide that traverses the entire spectrum of knowledge, from foundational principles to advanced strategies. The objective is clear – to empower readers with a nuanced and comprehensive understanding of the intricate world of memory management.

As we embark on the exploration of the eight chapters lying ahead, each segment serves as a meticulous dissection of various facets of memory handling. The journey commences with the fundamentals, ensuring that even those new to the domain can establish a solid foundation. Concepts like the central role of Random Access Memory (RAM) in influencing system performance and the historical evolution of memory management provide context to the intricacies that follow.

Moving forward, the guide delves into the dynamic realm of memory allocation, differentiating between static and dynamic methods and highlighting the profound impact on program execution. The exploration of virtual memory unfolds, introducing the concepts of paging and segmentation as foundational elements for optimizing system resources. This initial phase sets the stage, ensuring readers are well-equipped to navigate the more advanced topics that lie ahead.

The subsequent chapters progressively dive into dynamic memory allocation, allocation strategies, and techniques for minimizing fragmentation, providing readers with an in-depth understanding of memory optimization. Concepts such as garbage collection become integral components, striking a balance between efficiency and system overhead.

Memory paging and segmentation take center stage in the third chapter, providing insights into the mapping of memory and evaluating the benefits and challenges of these foundational concepts. The guide skillfully navigates through the intricacies of page replacement strategies, offering practical considerations in implementing these techniques with real-world examples that bring theory to life.

Cache memory optimization, explored in the fourth chapter, emerges as a critical aspect of achieving system efficiency. Spatial and temporal locality concepts are dissected, shedding light on strategies to leverage these concepts for optimal caching efficiency. Cache mapping techniques and replacement policies are explored in detail, along with the challenges of maintaining cache coherence in multiprocessor systems.

The exploration of memory protection and security in the fifth chapter underscores the importance of safeguarding memory from unauthorized access and corruption. Addressing privilege levels, access control mechanisms, and the implementation of security measures such as Address Space Layout Randomization (ASLR) and buffer overflow protection, the guide emphasizes the critical role of secure coding practices in mitigating risks.

As the journey progresses, the sixth chapter navigates the intricate relationship between parallel processing and memory management. Multitasking's role in modern computing, shared and distributed memory models, and the challenges and advantages of concurrent memory management are dissected. The guide provides insights into optimizing performance in shared and distributed memory environments, emphasizing the importance of concurrency control and threaded memory management.

Real-time memory management, explored in the seventh chapter, sheds light on the unique demands of systems that require instantaneous responsiveness. Techniques for partitioning memory, scheduling in real-time systems, and the role of memory locking and pre-emption control are unveiled. The chapter addresses challenges and solutions in garbage collection for real-time systems, ensuring that memory management aligns with the stringent requirements of real-time environments.

The concluding chapter, "Future Trends in Memory Management," takes a forward-looking perspective. Emerging memory technologies, the integration of machine learning for intelligent memory optimization, quantum computing's implications on memory, and decentralized and blockchain-based memory systems are explored. Ethical considerations in adopting future memory technologies serve as a guiding principle, ensuring responsible innovation and mitigating potential societal impacts.

In essence, "Efficient Minds" is not just a guide; it's an immersive journey through the intricate landscapes of memory management in operating systems. With its comprehensive coverage, practical insights, and forward-looking approach, this guide serves as an indispensable companion for those who seek mastery in the dynamic and ever-evolving world of memory management.

Chapter 1: Foundations of Memory Management

Defining memory management in operating systems.

Memory management is a critical aspect of operating systems that involves the coordination and organization of a computer's primary memory, also known as RAM (Random Access Memory). The primary objective of memory management is to efficiently allocate and deallocate memory space to various processes and applications running on the system, ensuring optimal utilization and preventing conflicts. Operating systems play a pivotal role in this process by overseeing the allocation of memory resources, tracking their usage, and resolving potential issues that may arise.

The memory management system operates on the fundamental principle of dividing the available memory into distinct partitions, each serving different purposes. One key component is the kernel space, reserved for the operating system itself, its essential data structures, and device drivers. On the other hand, the user space is allocated for running applications and user processes. This partitioning helps maintain a clear separation between system-level operations and user-level activities, facilitating a more organized and secure environment.

To effectively manage memory, operating systems employ a variety of techniques, with one of the most common being virtual memory. Virtual memory allows the operating system to use a combination of RAM and disk space to create an illusion of a larger, contiguous block of memory than physically available. This technique enables efficient multitasking, as the system can temporarily swap data between RAM and the disk, allowing more processes to run concurrently without being limited by physical memory constraints.

Memory allocation strategies are crucial in determining how the operating system assigns memory blocks to different processes. Two main approaches are used: static and dynamic allocation. Static allocation involves pre-allocating fixed-sized blocks of memory to processes during system initialization. While this method is straightforward, it may lead to inefficient use of memory if processes do not fully utilize their allocated space. Dynamic allocation, on the other hand, allows for more flexible and efficient use of memory by assigning blocks as needed during runtime. Various algorithms, such as first-fit, best-fit, and worst-fit, are employed to optimize the allocation of memory based on the characteristics of the processes.

The tracking of allocated and free memory is a critical aspect of memory management. Data structures like page tables and linked lists are used to maintain a record of allocated memory blocks, their locations, and their current status. This information helps prevent conflicts, such as attempts to access unallocated memory or overwrite data in use by other processes. Additionally, these data structures play a vital role in facilitating the efficient retrieval and deallocation of memory once a process has completed its execution.

Memory fragmentation poses a significant challenge in memory management, and two main types—internal fragmentation and external fragmentation—must be addressed. Internal fragmentation occurs when allocated memory is larger than necessary, leading to wasted space within a memory block. External fragmentation, on the other hand, arises when free memory is scattered in non-contiguous chunks, making it challenging to allocate large contiguous blocks of memory to processes. Operating systems employ various strategies, such as compaction and memory compaction, to minimize fragmentation and enhance memory utilization.

In a multi-user environment, the operating system must also implement protection mechanisms to prevent unauthorized access to memory areas. Access control lists and permissions are employed to define and enforce the level of access that different processes have to specific memory regions. This ensures the security and integrity of the system by preventing unintended interference between processes and safeguarding critical system data.

Furthermore, modern operating systems often incorporate features such as demand paging and swapping to optimize memory usage. Demand paging involves loading only the necessary portions of a program into memory as needed, reducing the initial memory footprint. Swapping enables the operating system to temporarily transfer less frequently used portions of a process from RAM to secondary storage, freeing up valuable memory for more active processes.

The evolution of memory management techniques has been influenced by advancements in hardware architecture and the increasing demands of complex applications. For instance, the transition from single-core to multi-core processors has necessitated the development of memory management systems capable of efficiently handling parallel execution and shared memory spaces. Symmetric Multiprocessing (SMP) and Non-Uniform Memory Access (NUMA) architectures have become prevalent, introducing new challenges in designing memory management systems that can effectively harness the benefits of parallel processing.

In conclusion, memory management is a foundational aspect of operating systems that plays a pivotal role in ensuring the efficient and secure allocation of memory resources to processes and applications. The complex interplay of memory allocation strategies, fragmentation mitigation, protection mechanisms, and support for advanced features like virtual memory and demand paging underscores the critical role of memory management in the overall performance and functionality of modern computer systems. As technology continues to advance, memory management will remain a dynamic and evolving field, adapting to meet the changing demands of increasingly sophisticated hardware and software environments.

Importance of efficient memory handling.

Efficient memory handling is of paramount importance in the realm of computing, as it directly impacts the overall performance, stability, and responsiveness of an operating system. The efficient management of memory resources is a fundamental aspect that influences the ability of a system to execute tasks, run applications, and handle concurrent processes seamlessly. As computer systems have become more complex and the demands of software applications have increased, the significance of optimal memory handling has only grown.

One primary reason for the critical importance of efficient memory handling lies in the limited physical resources available in a computer system. Random Access Memory (RAM), which serves as the primary working space for active processes, is finite. Any inefficiency in memory usage can lead to underutilization of this precious resource, hindering the system's ability to execute multiple tasks concurrently. In contrast, efficient memory handling ensures that the available RAM is allocated judiciously to running processes, maximizing the system's multitasking capabilities and overall responsiveness.

Furthermore, efficient memory management directly impacts the speed of program execution. When applications have quick and unhindered access to the required memory, they can execute operations with minimal latency. On the other hand, inefficient memory handling, characterized by frequent page faults, swapping, or excessive fragmentation, can introduce delays and result in sluggish performance. This becomes particularly pronounced in resource-intensive applications such as video editing, gaming, or scientific simulations, where rapid access to large datasets is crucial for smooth operation.

The reliability and stability of an operating system are heavily contingent on its ability to manage memory effectively. Inefficient memory handling can lead to a variety of issues, including system crashes, freezes, and unresponsive behavior. Memory leaks, a common problem in poorly managed systems, occur when processes fail to release allocated memory after use, gradually depleting the available memory and compromising system stability over time. Robust memory management practices, on the other hand, involve vigilant tracking and timely release of memory, minimizing the risk of memory-related errors and system instability.

The concept of virtual memory underscores another dimension of the importance of efficient memory handling. Virtual memory allows the operating system to create an illusion of a larger memory space than physically available by utilizing a combination of RAM and disk space. This enables the concurrent execution of numerous processes without the need for extensive physical memory. Inefficient virtual memory management can lead to excessive swapping between RAM and disk, resulting in performance bottlenecks. On the contrary, a well-designed virtual memory system optimizes the use of both RAM and secondary storage, enhancing the system's ability to handle a diverse range of applications and workloads.

In a multi-user environment, where multiple users or processes share the same system resources, efficient memory handling becomes even more critical. The operating system must ensure fair and equitable distribution of memory resources among competing processes to prevent one user or application from monopolizing the available memory. This requires sophisticated memory allocation algorithms that consider the dynamic nature of resource demands and adapt to changing conditions, fostering a balanced and responsive computing environment.

Moreover, the economic implications of efficient memory handling are significant. In the realm of cloud computing and data centers, where resources are allocated dynamically based on demand, optimal memory management directly translates to cost savings. Cloud service providers must efficiently allocate memory resources to virtual machines to meet the varying needs of different workloads. Inefficient memory usage not only impacts performance but also leads to increased infrastructure costs as more resources are required to support the same level of service.

Security considerations further highlight the importance of efficient memory handling. In a computing landscape rife with security threats, vulnerabilities related to memory can be exploited by malicious actors to compromise system integrity. Buffer overflows, a common type of memory-related vulnerability, can be mitigated through effective memory protection mechanisms implemented by the operating system. Secure memory handling ensures that processes cannot access unauthorized memory areas, preventing potential security breaches and safeguarding sensitive data.

As technology continues to advance, with the advent of new architectures, hardware capabilities, and increasingly sophisticated software applications, the role of efficient memory handling becomes even more pronounced. The shift towards parallel processing, exemplified by multi-core and many-core architectures, necessitates memory management systems capable of effectively harnessing the power of parallelism. Innovations such as Non-Uniform Memory Access (NUMA) architectures introduce new challenges that demand adaptive and intelligent memory handling strategies to ensure optimal performance in diverse computing environments.

In conclusion, the importance of efficient memory handling cannot be overstated in the realm of operating systems and computing at large. It is a linchpin that influences the performance, stability, and security of a system. As technology continues to evolve, the need for sophisticated memory management systems becomes increasingly pronounced, necessitating ongoing research and development to address the challenges posed by emerging hardware architectures and the demands of modern applications. A well-tuned memory management system is not merely a technical necessity; it is a foundational element that underpins the seamless functioning of computer systems, enabling them to meet the ever-expanding expectations of users and the demands of contemporary computing environments.

Historical perspective on memory management evolution.

The evolution of memory management in computing spans several decades, reflecting the continuous progression of hardware capabilities, software demands, and the quest for more efficient and versatile computing systems. The early days of computing, characterized by room-sized mainframes and limited memory capacities, laid the groundwork for rudimentary memory management techniques. During this era, programs were often written in assembly language, and memory allocation was a manual process, with programmers responsible for avoiding conflicts and ensuring optimal use of the available memory.

The advent of batch processing systems in the 1950s marked a significant milestone in memory management evolution. These systems allowed users to submit jobs to the computer, which would then process them sequentially. Memory management in batch systems primarily revolved around partitioning the available memory to accommodate multiple jobs concurrently. Fixed partitioning was a common approach, where the memory was divided into fixed-sized partitions, each allocated to a specific job. This method, while simple, suffered from inefficiencies as it often led to wasted space due to varying job sizes.

The 1960s saw the emergence of time-sharing systems, introducing a shift towards interactive computing. Memory management became more dynamic, as time-sharing systems needed to allocate and deallocate memory rapidly to support the quick switching between multiple users. Dynamic partitioning, as opposed to fixed partitioning, gained prominence, allowing for more flexible memory allocation based on the actual size of the program.

The development of virtual memory concepts in the late 1960s and early 1970s represented a transformative leap in memory management. Systems like the Atlas Computer introduced the concept of demand paging, where only the portions of a program needed for execution were loaded into memory, minimizing the initial memory footprint. However, it was the introduction of paging and segmentation by systems like the IBM System/370 and the Multics project that paved the way for more sophisticated virtual memory systems.

Paging involves breaking down the physical memory into fixed-size blocks or pages, and the program's address space is similarly divided into pages. This enables the operating system to load only the necessary pages into memory, swapping others to secondary storage as needed. Segmentation, on the other hand, divides the program's address space into logical segments, each representing a specific type of data or code. Together, paging and segmentation allowed for efficient use of memory, reducing the limitations imposed by physical RAM.

The 1980s witnessed the rise of personal computers, leading to new challenges and opportunities in memory management. Early personal computers had limited memory, often measured in kilobytes, necessitating creative solutions to manage the constraints. Operating systems like MS-DOS relied on simple memory models, such as the Real Mode, where programs had direct access to hardware, and memory protection was minimal.

The advent of 32-bit processors in the 1990s brought about a paradigm shift in memory management. Extended memory architectures became prevalent, allowing for larger address spaces and more efficient memory handling. Operating systems like Windows

95 and Windows NT introduced protected mode, providing enhanced memory protection and preemptive multitasking. The concept of virtual memory became more ingrained in mainstream computing, enabling the efficient execution of complex applications that required more memory than physically available.

The late 1990s and early 2000s witnessed the proliferation of 64-bit computing, further expanding addressable memory space. This transition addressed the limitations of 32-bit architectures, which had a theoretical maximum addressable space of 4 gigabytes. With 64-bit architectures, systems could potentially address exabytes of memory, providing the foundation for handling the escalating memory requirements of modern applications.

Parallel processing and the advent of multi-core processors in the 21st century presented new challenges and opportunities for memory management. Symmetric Multiprocessing (SMP) and Non-Uniform Memory Access (NUMA) architectures became common, requiring memory management systems to adapt to the intricacies of shared memory spaces and varying access latencies. The concept of memory affinity, where processes are scheduled to run on specific cores with proximity to their assigned memory, emerged as a strategy to optimize performance in these environments.

The rise of virtualization and cloud computing in the 2000s introduced further complexities to memory management. Hypervisors and virtual machines necessitated advanced memory management techniques to efficiently allocate resources among virtualized instances. Technologies like Transparent Page Sharing (TPS) and Memory Ballooning became essential in optimizing memory usage within virtualized environments.

Contemporary memory management systems are characterized by a combination of these historical developments, incorporating virtual memory, demand paging, and advanced algorithms for efficient allocation and deallocation. The evolution of memory management has not only been driven by hardware advancements but also by the demands of increasingly sophisticated software applications, ranging from resource-intensive video editing software to complex scientific simulations.

Looking ahead, the future of memory management is likely to be shaped by emerging technologies such as persistent memory, which blurs the line between traditional RAM and storage, offering faster access times and non-volatile characteristics. As computing continues to evolve with the advent of quantum computing and other transformative paradigms, memory management will remain a dynamic field, adapting to the unique challenges and opportunities presented by each technological leap. The historical perspective on memory management underscores its central role in the evolution of computing systems, showcasing its resilience and adaptability as it continues to play a pivotal role in shaping the landscape of modern computing.

Understanding the central role of Random Access Memory.

Random Access Memory (RAM) stands as a linchpin in the architecture of modern computing systems, playing a central and indispensable role in the execution of tasks, the smooth functioning of applications, and the overall performance of an operating system. Its name, "Random Access," underscores its distinctive feature of providing rapid and direct access to any memory cell, irrespective of its location. RAM serves as the primary working space for a computer's active processes, holding the data and instructions that are currently being used or processed. This volatile memory is distinct from the long-term storage provided by hard drives or solid-state drives, as it loses its contents when the power is turned off. The criticality of RAM lies in its ability to provide high-speed data access, enabling quick retrieval and manipulation of information that is essential for real-time computing.

In the realm of computer architecture, RAM acts as a bridge between the processor and the storage devices. When a program is executed, the operating system loads portions of the program and its associated data into RAM, allowing the processor to swiftly access and manipulate the information. This dynamic and rapid access is crucial for the efficiency of computing operations, as the processor can quickly retrieve and modify data without the delays associated with accessing data from slower storage media. The speed of RAM is measured in nanoseconds, making it significantly faster than even the fastest solid-state drives, and this speed differential is a key factor in determining the overall responsiveness and performance of a computer system.

One of the primary functions of RAM is to facilitate multitasking – the concurrent execution of multiple processes or applications. In a multitasking environment, various programs are vying for computational resources, and RAM plays a pivotal role in ensuring that each running process has the space it needs to function smoothly. Each open application or process requires a portion of RAM to store its code and data. Inadequate RAM can lead to performance degradation, as the system may need to constantly swap data between RAM and slower storage devices, introducing delays and hindering overall responsiveness. Ample RAM, on the other hand, allows for efficient multitasking, enabling users to seamlessly switch between applications and work on complex tasks without experiencing a significant slowdown.

Efficient memory management within RAM is essential to harness its capabilities fully. Operating systems employ various strategies to allocate and deallocate memory dynamically, adapting to the changing requirements of running processes. The allocation of memory to processes involves dividing the available RAM into distinct partitions, with each process assigned a specific portion. This process is intricate, with the operating system continuously monitoring the status of memory blocks, tracking their usage, and ensuring that each process has access to the required resources. Memory management algorithms, such as first-fit, best-fit, and worst-fit, are employed to optimize the allocation of memory, taking into consideration the dynamic nature of program execution and the varying sizes of memory requests.

An understanding of RAM's role in the broader context of memory hierarchies is crucial for appreciating its significance. Computer systems typically feature a hierarchy of memory, with different levels of access speed and capacity. Registers, located directly in the processor, provide the fastest but smallest storage for immediate data manipulation. L2 and L3 caches, situated closer to the processor than RAM, serve as intermediate storage that can quickly supply data to the processor. RAM, positioned between the processor and long-term storage, serves as a larger but slightly slower pool of accessible memory. This hierarchical structure is designed to optimize data access, ensuring that the processor can quickly retrieve frequently used data from the fastest available source.

The concept of virtual memory further enhances the capabilities of RAM, allowing the operating system to extend the apparent size of the available memory beyond the physical limitations of the RAM modules. Virtual memory combines the capacities of RAM and secondary storage, such as hard drives or SSDs, creating an illusion of a larger, contiguous memory space. In situations where the physical RAM is insufficient to accommodate all active processes, the operating system can temporarily swap out portions of the less frequently used data to the secondary storage, freeing up space in RAM for more immediate needs. This enables the efficient utilization of available resources and supports the execution of larger and more complex applications.

RAM's significance becomes particularly pronounced in resource-intensive tasks such as video editing, 3D rendering, scientific simulations, and gaming. These applications often involve the manipulation of large datasets and demand quick access to data for real-time processing. In such scenarios, having an ample amount of high-speed RAM is crucial for ensuring a smooth and responsive user experience. The absence of sufficient RAM can result in performance bottlenecks, leading to sluggish operation, delays, and even application crashes.

The reliability and stability of a computer system are intrinsically tied to the robustness of its memory subsystem, with RAM being a focal point of this subsystem. Inefficient or faulty memory can lead to a myriad of issues, including system crashes, freezes, and data corruption. Memory errors, such as bit flips or corruption, can occur due to various factors, including hardware defects, electrical interference, or cosmic rays. Error-correcting code (ECC) RAM, designed to detect and correct such errors, represents a specialized form of RAM employed in critical systems where data integrity is paramount, such as in servers and high-performance computing environments.

Security considerations also underscore the importance of RAM in the overall system architecture. RAM is a potential target for certain types of cyber attacks, particularly those that exploit vulnerabilities related to memory. Buffer overflows, for instance, involve injecting malicious code into a program's memory space, potentially leading to unauthorized access or control of the system. Modern operating systems implement security mechanisms within RAM to mitigate these risks, employing techniques such as address space layout randomization (ASLR) to randomize the memory addresses of key system components and make it more challenging for attackers to predict or manipulate their locations.

The evolution of RAM technology over the years has been marked by a continual quest for higher capacities, faster speeds, and improved energy efficiency. From the early days of magnetic core memory to the advent of dynamic random-access memory (DRAM) and the more recent developments in DDR4 and DDR5 Synchronous Dynamic RAM (SDRAM), advancements in RAM technology have been instrumental in pushing the boundaries of computing capabilities. The transition from traditional hard disk drives (HDDs) to faster solid-state drives (SSDs) has further elevated the significance of RAM, as SSDs, while faster than HDDs, are still significantly slower than RAM.

Looking to the future, emerging technologies such as persistent memory hold the potential to redefine the role of RAM in computing. Persistent memory combines the speed of RAM with the non-volatility of storage, offering the prospect of faster boot times, quicker application launches, and enhanced data durability. This evolution aligns with the ever-growing demands of modern applications and workloads, where the boundary between traditional RAM and storage is increasingly blurred to create a more seamless and responsive computing experience.

In conclusion, Random Access Memory stands as a cornerstone in the architecture of computing systems, facilitating rapid data access, enabling efficient multitasking, and serving as a pivotal component in the broader memory hierarchy. Its central role in memory management, coupled with its impact on system performance, responsiveness, and stability, underscores its significance in the ever-evolving landscape of computing. RAM's journey from early manual memory management to the sophisticated virtual memory systems of today exemplifies its resilience and adaptability, as it continues to be a critical enabler of the diverse and demanding computing tasks of the contemporary era.

How RAM influences system performance.

Random Access Memory (RAM) exerts a profound influence on system performance, serving as a dynamic and pivotal component that significantly determines the speed, efficiency, and overall responsiveness of a computing system. At the core of this influence lies RAM's role as the primary working memory for active processes, providing high-speed access to data and instructions that are currently in use. The sheer speed of RAM, measured in nanoseconds, stands in stark contrast to the relatively slower access times of other storage mediums, such as hard disk drives (HDDs) or solid-state drives (SSDs). This speed differential is a critical factor in the ability of a system to swiftly retrieve and manipulate data, shaping its capacity for real-time computing.

One of the primary ways in which RAM influences system performance is through its role in facilitating multitasking. In a multitasking environment, where multiple applications or processes are concurrently active, RAM plays a central role in ensuring that each running program has the space it needs to function seamlessly. When a user launches an application, the operating system allocates a portion of the available RAM to store the program's code and data. The speed at which RAM can provide this space is crucial for enabling smooth and responsive multitasking experiences. Inadequate RAM can lead to performance degradation, as the system may need to continually swap data between RAM and slower storage devices, introducing delays and hindering overall responsiveness. Ample RAM, on the other hand, allows for efficient multitasking, enabling users to seamlessly switch between applications and work on complex tasks without experiencing a significant slowdown.

The impact of RAM on system performance is particularly pronounced in resource-intensive tasks and applications that involve the manipulation of large datasets. Video editing, 3D rendering, scientific simulations, and gaming are examples of activities where the demands on memory are substantial. These applications often require quick and frequent access to large amounts of data for real-time processing. In such scenarios, having sufficient RAM is crucial for ensuring a smooth and responsive user experience. For instance, in gaming, where high-quality graphics and rapid scene rendering are paramount, the availability of ample RAM ensures that the system can quickly load and store textures, models, and other graphical assets, preventing lag and providing a more immersive gaming experience.

Efficient memory management within RAM is another critical aspect that influences overall system performance. Operating systems employ various strategies to allocate and deallocate memory dynamically, adapting to the changing requirements of running processes. The allocation of memory to processes involves dividing the available RAM into distinct partitions, with each process assigned a specific portion. This dynamic process is intricate, with the operating system continuously monitoring the status of memory blocks, tracking their usage, and ensuring that each process has access to the required resources. The efficiency of memory management algorithms, such as first-fit, best-fit, and worst-fit, plays a crucial role in optimizing the allocation of memory, taking into consideration the dynamic nature of program execution and the varying sizes of memory requests.

Furthermore, the concept of virtual memory enhances the capabilities of RAM and influences system performance significantly. Virtual memory allows the operating system to extend the apparent size of the available memory beyond the physical limitations of the RAM modules. This is achieved by combining the capacities of RAM and secondary storage, such as hard drives or SSDs, creating an illusion of a larger, contiguous memory space. In situations where the physical RAM is insufficient to accommodate all active processes, the operating system can temporarily swap out portions of less frequently used data to the secondary storage, freeing up space in RAM for more immediate needs. This dynamic utilization of virtual memory is essential for efficiently handling large and complex applications, ensuring that the system can effectively manage its resources and support the execution of diverse workloads.

The hierarchical structure of memory in computer systems further underscores the influence of RAM on overall performance. Registers, located directly in the processor, provide the fastest but smallest storage for immediate data manipulation. L2 and L3 caches, situated closer to the processor than RAM, serve as intermediate storage that can quickly supply data to the processor. RAM, positioned between the processor and long-term storage, serves as a larger but slightly slower pool of accessible memory. This hierarchical organization is designed to optimize data access, ensuring that the processor can quickly retrieve frequently used data from the fastest available source. The efficiency of this memory hierarchy is instrumental in determining the overall speed and responsiveness of a computing system.

The reliability and stability of a computer system are also intimately tied to the robustness of its memory subsystem, with RAM playing a central role in this subsystem. Inefficient or faulty memory can lead to a myriad of issues, including system crashes, freezes, and data corruption. Memory errors, such as bit flips or corruption, can occur due to various factors, including hardware defects, electrical interference, or cosmic rays. Error-correcting code (ECC) RAM, designed to detect and correct such errors, represents a specialized form of RAM employed in critical systems where data integrity is paramount, such as in servers and high-performance computing environments. The reliability of RAM contributes significantly to the overall stability of the system, ensuring that it can operate smoothly and handle complex tasks without encountering unexpected failures.

Security considerations further emphasize the importance of RAM in the overall system architecture. RAM is a potential target for certain types of cyber attacks, particularly those that exploit vulnerabilities related to memory. Buffer overflows, for instance, involve injecting malicious code into a program's memory space, potentially leading to unauthorized access or control of the system. Modern operating systems implement security mechanisms within RAM to mitigate these risks, employing techniques such as address space layout randomization (ASLR) to randomize the memory addresses of key system components and make it more challenging for attackers to predict or manipulate their locations.

The evolution of RAM technology over the years has been marked by a continual quest for higher capacities, faster speeds, and improved energy efficiency. From the early days of magnetic core memory to the advent of dynamic random-access memory (DRAM) and the more recent developments in DDR4 and DDR5 Synchronous Dynamic RAM (SDRAM), advancements in RAM technology have been instrumental in pushing the boundaries of computing capabilities. The transition from traditional hard disk drives (HDDs) to faster solid-state drives (SSDs) has further elevated the significance of RAM, as SSDs, while faster than HDDs, are still significantly slower than RAM.

Looking to the future, emerging technologies such as persistent memory hold the potential to redefine the role of RAM in computing. Persistent memory combines the speed of RAM with the non-volatility of storage, offering the prospect of faster boot times, quicker application launches, and enhanced data durability. This evolution aligns with the ever-growing demands of modern applications and workloads, where the boundary between traditional RAM and storage is increasingly blurred to create a more seamless and responsive computing experience.

In conclusion, the influence of RAM on system performance is multifaceted and fundamental, shaping the speed, efficiency, and overall responsiveness of computing systems. Its role in providing high-speed access to data, facilitating efficient multitasking, supporting dynamic memory management, and enabling the use of virtual memory highlights its centrality in the architecture of modern computers. RAM's impact is evident in various aspects of computing, from resource-intensive applications to the stability and security of the overall system. As technology continues to advance, the role of RAM remains pivotal, reflecting its continual evolution to meet the demands of contemporary computing environments.

RAM's connection to overall system speed.

Random Access Memory (RAM) serves as a linchpin in determining the overall speed and responsiveness of a computer system, establishing a critical connection between the processor, storage, and various active processes. At the heart of this relationship is the role of RAM as the primary working memory, providing quick and direct access to data and instructions actively utilized by the processor and applications. The speed at which RAM can deliver this information is pivotal in shaping the overall speed of the system, creating a dynamic interplay that significantly influences the user experience.

In a computing environment, the processor, or central processing unit (CPU), is the powerhouse responsible for executing instructions and performing calculations. For the processor to operate efficiently, it requires immediate access to data and instructions, a role that RAM fulfills admirably. RAM stands as the bridge between the processor and the slower storage devices, such as hard disk drives (HDDs) or solid-state drives (SSDs), ensuring that the processor can swiftly retrieve and manipulate the data it needs. The speed of RAM, measured in nanoseconds, is several orders of magnitude faster than the access times of traditional storage media, establishing it as a crucial component for real-time computing.

One of the primary ways in which RAM influences overall system speed is through its role in facilitating multitasking. In a multitasking environment, where multiple applications or processes run concurrently, RAM ensures that each active program has the space it needs for efficient execution. When a user launches an application, the operating system allocates a portion of the available RAM to store the program's code and data. The quick and direct access to this information allows the processor to seamlessly switch between active processes, enabling users to work on multiple tasks simultaneously. Inadequate RAM can lead to performance degradation, as the system may resort to constantly swapping data between RAM and slower storage devices, introducing delays and hindering overall responsiveness. Conversely, sufficient RAM allows for efficient multitasking, preventing slowdowns and ensuring a smooth user experience.

Efficient memory management within RAM is another crucial factor that determines overall system speed. Operating systems employ various strategies to allocate and deallocate memory dynamically, adapting to the changing requirements of running processes. The allocation of memory involves dividing the available RAM into distinct partitions, with each process assigned a specific portion. This dynamic process is intricate, with the operating system continuously monitoring the status of memory blocks, tracking their usage, and ensuring that each process has access to the required resources. The efficiency of memory management algorithms, such as first-fit, best-fit, and worst-fit, plays a pivotal role in optimizing the allocation of memory, considering the dynamic nature of program execution and the varying sizes of memory requests. A well-tuned memory management system enhances the overall speed of the system by minimizing delays associated with memory allocation and deallocation.

Furthermore, the concept of virtual memory significantly contributes to the overall speed of the system and its interaction with RAM. Virtual memory allows the operating system to extend the apparent size of the available memory beyond the physical limitations of the RAM modules. By combining the capacities of RAM and secondary storage, such as hard drives or SSDs, virtual memory creates an illusion of a larger, contiguous memory space. In scenarios where physical RAM is insufficient to accommodate all active processes, the operating system can temporarily transfer portions of less frequently used data to secondary storage, freeing up space in RAM for more immediate needs. This dynamic utilization of virtual memory optimizes the use of available resources and supports the execution of larger and more complex applications, contributing to the overall speed and efficiency of the system.

The hierarchical organization of memory in computer systems further accentuates the impact of RAM on overall speed. Registers, located directly in the processor, provide the fastest but smallest storage for immediate data manipulation. L2 and L3 caches, situated closer to the processor than RAM, serve as intermediate storage that can quickly supply data to the processor. RAM, positioned between the processor and long-term storage, serves as a larger but slightly slower pool of accessible memory. This hierarchy is designed to optimize data access, ensuring that the processor can quickly retrieve frequently used data from the fastest available source. The speed of RAM plays a pivotal role in maintaining the efficiency of this hierarchical structure, influencing the overall speed and responsiveness of the system.

The influence of RAM on system speed becomes particularly apparent in resource-intensive tasks and applications that involve the manipulation of large datasets. Activities such as video editing, 3D rendering, scientific simulations, and gaming demand quick and frequent access to substantial amounts of data for real-time processing. In such scenarios, having ample and high-speed RAM is critical for ensuring a smooth and responsive user experience. For example, in gaming, where high-quality graphics and rapid scene rendering are paramount, the availability of sufficient RAM ensures that the system can quickly load and store textures, models, and other graphical assets, preventing lag and providing a more immersive gaming experience.

Reliability and stability are also intertwined with the influence of RAM on overall system speed. Inefficient or faulty memory can lead to system crashes, freezes, and data corruption, directly impacting the stability of the system. Memory errors, such as bit flips or corruption, may occur due to hardware defects, electrical interference, or other factors. Error-correcting code (ECC) RAM represents a specialized form of RAM employed in critical systems where data integrity is paramount, as it can detect and correct such errors. The reliability of RAM contributes significantly to the overall stability of the system, ensuring that it can operate smoothly and handle complex tasks without encountering unexpected failures, further influencing the perceived speed of the system.

Security considerations also play a role in understanding the connection between RAM and overall system speed. RAM is a potential target for certain types of cyber attacks, particularly those that exploit vulnerabilities related to memory. Buffer overflows, for instance, involve injecting malicious code into a program's memory space, potentially leading to unauthorized access or control of the system. Modern operating systems implement security mechanisms within RAM to mitigate these risks, employing techniques such as address space layout randomization (ASLR) to randomize the memory addresses of key system components and make it more challenging for attackers to predict or manipulate their locations. The efficiency of these security mechanisms contributes to the overall speed of the system by safeguarding against potential threats and ensuring the integrity of the data stored in RAM.

The continuous evolution of RAM technology over the years reflects the ongoing efforts to enhance overall system speed. Advancements from the early days of magnetic core memory to the development of dynamic random-access memory (DRAM) and subsequent improvements in DDR4 and DDR5 Synchronous Dynamic RAM (SDRAM) have played a vital role in pushing the boundaries of computing capabilities. The transition from traditional hard disk drives (HDDs) to faster solid-state drives (SSDs) has further heightened the significance of RAM, as SSDs, while faster than HDDs, are still significantly slower than RAM. The pursuit of higher capacities, faster speeds, and improved energy efficiency in RAM technology continues to shape the landscape of computing, contributing to the ongoing quest for enhanced system speed and responsiveness.

Looking toward the future, emerging technologies such as persistent memory hold the potential to redefine the connection between RAM and overall system speed. Persistent memory combines the speed of RAM with the non-volatility of storage, offering the prospect of faster boot times, quicker application launches, and enhanced data durability. This evolution aligns with the ever-growing demands of modern applications and workloads, where the boundary between traditional RAM and storage is increasingly blurred to create a more seamless and responsive computing experience. As technology continues to advance, the role of RAM in influencing overall system speed remains central, reflecting its continual evolution to meet the demands of contemporary computing environments and user expectations.

Exploring the process of memory allocation.

Memory allocation, a fundamental aspect of computer systems, involves the dynamic assignment and management of memory resources to programs and processes during their execution. This intricate process is essential for optimal system performance, as it ensures efficient utilization of the limited and precious resource that is Random Access Memory (RAM). The journey into the realm of memory allocation begins with the initiation of a program or process. As a program is launched, the operating system is tasked with allocating a segment of the available memory to accommodate the program's code and data. The first step in this process involves determining the size of the memory block required by the program, which is influenced by factors such as the size of the executable file, the data it manipulates, and the requirements of any dynamically allocated structures during runtime.

The traditional method of memory allocation involves dividing the available memory into fixed-sized partitions. In this scenario, each partition is assigned to a specific program or process, and the program's entire address space must fit within the allocated partition. This approach, known as fixed partitioning, though simple, suffers from inefficiencies as it can lead to wasted space in partitions due to varying program sizes. Fixed partitioning is reminiscent of the early days of mainframes and batch processing systems, where manual intervention was often required to allocate memory partitions for different jobs.

The evolution of memory allocation strategies led to more dynamic and flexible approaches, with the advent of dynamic partitioning. In dynamic partitioning, the available memory is treated as a single, large pool, and programs are allocated memory as needed. This method eliminates the wastage associated with fixed partitioning, as memory is allocated based on the actual size of the program. However, dynamic partitioning introduces the challenge of fragmentation, both external and internal. External fragmentation occurs when free memory is scattered throughout the address space, making it challenging to allocate contiguous blocks of memory. Internal fragmentation, on the other hand, results from allocating more memory than needed, leading to inefficient utilization.

To tackle the issues associated with dynamic partitioning, sophisticated memory management algorithms come into play. One such algorithm is the first-fit algorithm, which allocates the first available block of memory that is large enough to satisfy the program's requirements. While straightforward, this method can result in external fragmentation, as it may leave smaller, unused blocks scattered throughout the address space. The best-fit algorithm aims to minimize external fragmentation by allocating the smallest available block that meets the program's needs. However, this approach can lead to inefficient utilization of memory, as it may leave behind larger free blocks that are difficult to utilize. The worst-fit algorithm allocates the largest available block to a program, intending to leave smaller free blocks for future use. Despite its intention to reduce external fragmentation, the worst-fit algorithm can result in inefficient memory usage and larger amounts of fragmented space.

The challenges posed by external fragmentation led to the exploration of paging and segmentation, more advanced techniques in memory allocation. Paging involves breaking down the physical memory and program address space into fixed-sized blocks or pages. These fixed-sized pages facilitate efficient allocation and deallocation, as they eliminate the need for contiguous memory blocks. When a program is executed, its pages are loaded into available page frames in physical memory. Paging introduces a level of indirection, as the operating system maintains a page table to map between the logical and physical addresses. This mapping allows for non-contiguous allocation of memory, reducing external fragmentation. However, paging introduces the potential for internal fragmentation, as the last page may not be fully utilized.

Segmentation, another approach to memory allocation, divides a program's address space into logical segments, each representing a specific type of data or code. Segments can vary in size and are allocated independently, allowing for flexibility in accommodating different aspects of a program. Segmentation helps mitigate external fragmentation, as each segment can be allocated as needed without concern for contiguous space. However, segmentation introduces challenges related to managing variable-sized segments and the potential for internal fragmentation within each segment.

The combination of paging and segmentation results in a hybrid approach known as demand paging. In demand paging, only the portions of a program needed for execution are loaded into physical memory. This minimizes the initial memory footprint and enhances the efficient use of RAM. When a program accesses a portion of memory that is not currently in physical memory, a page fault occurs, prompting the operating system to bring the required page into RAM. Demand paging aims to strike a balance between efficient memory utilization and minimizing delays associated with loading pages into memory.

Virtual memory, an extension of demand paging, further revolutionizes the memory allocation process. Virtual memory creates an illusion of a larger, contiguous address space than physically available by utilizing both RAM and secondary storage, such as hard drives or SSDs. This allows systems to run programs that require more memory than the physical RAM can accommodate. Virtual memory introduces the concept of pages, where portions of a program are swapped between RAM and secondary storage as needed. While virtual memory provides flexibility, it also introduces challenges related to page faults, excessive swapping, and the need for efficient page replacement algorithms.

Efficient memory allocation strategies also consider the requirements of multi-user environments, where multiple users or processes share the same system resources. Memory must be allocated fairly and equitably to prevent one user or application from monopolizing the available resources. Sophisticated memory allocation algorithms and policies are employed to address the dynamic nature of resource demands in multi-user environments. Techniques such as time-sharing and fair queuing aim to distribute memory resources based on priorities, ensuring a balanced and responsive computing environment.

The advent of 64-bit computing architectures further impacts memory allocation, as it allows for larger addressable memory spaces. With 64-bit processors, systems can potentially address exabytes of memory, providing the foundation for handling increasingly complex and memory-intensive applications. The transition to 64-bit computing addresses the limitations of 32-bit architectures, which have a theoretical maximum addressable space of 4 gigabytes. Larger addressable spaces open new possibilities for memory-intensive applications, enabling them to access and manipulate vast datasets more efficiently.

The intricacies of memory allocation are further influenced by advancements in hardware architectures, such as symmetric multiprocessing (SMP) and non-uniform memory access (NUMA). SMP systems feature multiple processors, each with its own cache and memory, sharing a common address space. NUMA architectures introduce a hierarchical structure of memory access times, where access to local memory is faster than access to remote memory. Memory allocation algorithms must adapt to these complex architectures to optimize performance and minimize latency associated with memory access.

In conclusion, the process of memory allocation represents a dynamic and critical aspect of computer systems, shaping the efficiency, performance, and responsiveness of programs and processes. From the early days of fixed partitioning to the sophisticated techniques of demand paging, virtual memory, and beyond, the evolution of memory allocation strategies reflects the continuous pursuit of optimal resource utilization in the face of varying program sizes and system demands. The exploration of algorithms, such as first-fit, best-fit, and worst-fit, alongside the integration of paging, segmentation, and virtual memory, underscores the complexity and depth of the memory allocation landscape. As computer architectures advance and applications become increasingly memory-intensive, the quest for efficient memory allocation strategies remains a key focus, ensuring that systems can effectively harness the capabilities of modern hardware to meet the diverse and evolving needs of computing environments.

Differentiating between static and dynamic allocation.

Static and dynamic allocation represent two distinct approaches to the management and utilization of memory resources in computer systems, each with its characteristics, advantages, and limitations. Static allocation, also known as compile-time allocation, involves reserving memory for a program during the compilation phase, before the program is executed. This allocation is fixed and predetermined, with the sizes of memory blocks and their addresses specified at compile time. The key advantage of static allocation is its simplicity and efficiency. Once the memory layout is determined, the program can directly access the allocated memory locations without the need for runtime adjustments or complex memory management mechanisms. This efficiency makes static allocation suitable for scenarios where memory requirements are known in advance and remain constant throughout the program's execution.

Conversely, dynamic allocation, or runtime allocation, adopts a more flexible and adaptive approach by allowing memory to be allocated and deallocated during program execution. Unlike static allocation, the size and structure of memory blocks are determined dynamically at runtime based on the program's evolving needs. This dynamism is particularly advantageous in scenarios where memory requirements are uncertain or vary dynamically, such as in applications that handle variable-sized data structures, user input, or complex data processing tasks. Dynamic allocation is particularly prevalent in modern programming languages that provide mechanisms like pointers and dynamic data structures, enabling programmers to allocate and release memory as needed.

Static allocation has certain inherent characteristics that influence its use and applicability. The fixed nature of memory allocation at compile time means that the program's memory requirements must be known and specified in advance. While this predictability can lead to optimized memory usage and fast access times, it imposes limitations on the adaptability of the program to changing conditions. Additionally, static allocation can result in wasted memory if the reserved space is not fully utilized during execution, as the allocated memory remains dedicated to the program even if it is not actively in use.

Dynamic allocation, on the other hand, offers greater flexibility and adaptability. The ability to allocate and deallocate memory at runtime allows programs to respond dynamically to changing conditions, making it well-suited for applications with unpredictable memory requirements. Dynamic allocation is particularly advantageous for scenarios where the exact size of data structures is not known in advance or when dealing with variable-sized datasets. However, this flexibility comes with added complexity and overhead. The need for runtime memory management introduces the possibility of memory leaks or fragmentation, where allocated memory may not be released properly, leading to inefficiencies or even system instability.

One of the key mechanisms for dynamic memory allocation is the use of pointers. Pointers are variables that store memory addresses, providing a way to access and manipulate data at runtime. Dynamic allocation is often associated with the use of the heap, a region of memory separate from the program's stack that can be dynamically managed during execution. In languages like C and C++, programmers can use functions like `**malloc**()` and `**free**()` to allocate and deallocate memory on the heap. These functions allow for the creation of data structures with variable sizes and lifetimes, offering flexibility that static allocation cannot provide.

However, the power and flexibility of dynamic allocation come with certain responsibilities. It is the programmer's responsibility to manage the allocated memory properly, ensuring that it is released when no longer needed to prevent memory leaks. The absence of automatic memory management, as seen in languages with garbage collection, places the burden on the programmer to explicitly free the allocated memory. Failing to do so can lead to memory leaks, where portions of memory are not returned to the system, gradually depleting available resources.

In the realm of dynamic allocation, memory fragmentation is a notable concern. Fragmentation occurs when the memory space becomes divided into small, non-contiguous blocks, making it challenging to allocate larger chunks of memory, even if the total available space is sufficient. Fragmentation can be classified into two types: external fragmentation and internal fragmentation. External fragmentation arises when free memory is scattered throughout the address space, making it difficult to allocate contiguous blocks of memory. Internal fragmentation occurs when allocated memory is larger than needed, leading to inefficient utilization of the reserved space.

Various memory allocation algorithms are employed to address the challenges posed by fragmentation. One common approach is the use of linked lists to manage free memory blocks on the heap. Each block of free memory is associated with a data structure containing information about its size and location. When a program requests memory, the allocator traverses the linked list to find a suitable free block. While this approach helps mitigate external fragmentation, it introduces overhead due to the storage requirements of the linked list nodes.

To address internal fragmentation, memory allocators may employ strategies such as memory pooling or slab allocation. Memory pooling involves preallocating fixed-size memory blocks and grouping them into pools. These pools are then allocated to specific tasks or data types, reducing internal fragmentation by ensuring that allocated memory closely matches the required size. Slab allocation is a technique where memory is divided into slabs, each containing blocks of a specific size. This approach is particularly effective in managing objects of varying sizes within the same pool, minimizing both internal and external fragmentation.

The choice between static and dynamic allocation depends on the specific requirements and characteristics of the application. In systems where memory requirements are well-defined and constant, static allocation offers simplicity and efficiency. Embedded systems, real-time applications, and certain performance-critical scenarios often benefit from the deterministic nature of static allocation. However, in environments where memory needs are dynamic, unpredictable, or involve variable-sized data structures, dynamic allocation provides the necessary flexibility and adaptability. Modern programming languages and frameworks often leverage a combination of both static and dynamic allocation strategies to harness the strengths of each approach in different parts of the application.

In conclusion, the differentiation between static and dynamic allocation represents a fundamental aspect of memory management in computer systems. Static allocation, with its fixed and predetermined memory assignments at compile time, offers simplicity and efficiency but may lack the adaptability required for dynamic scenarios. Dynamic allocation, on the other hand, introduces flexibility and adaptability by allowing memory to be allocated and deallocated at runtime. However, this flexibility comes with added complexity and responsibilities for the programmer, including the proper management of memory to avoid issues such as memory leaks and fragmentation. The choice between static and dynamic allocation depends on the specific needs of the application, and modern programming practices often involve a judicious combination of both approaches to strike a balance between efficiency and flexibility.

Memory allocation's impact on program execution.

Memory allocation plays a pivotal role in the execution of computer programs, exerting a profound impact on their efficiency, performance, and overall behavior. The manner in which a program acquires, utilizes, and releases memory resources influences not only its runtime characteristics but also its responsiveness to varying workloads and the efficiency of resource utilization. At the core of this impact is the dichotomy between static and dynamic memory allocation, each presenting a distinct set of advantages and challenges that reverberate throughout the program's lifecycle.

Static memory allocation, often employed in languages like C and C++, involves reserving memory during the compilation phase, with the size and structure of memory blocks predetermined and fixed. This predictability offers a streamlined and efficient memory model, where the program's memory needs are known in advance, enabling direct access to allocated memory locations without the need for runtime adjustments. However, the impact of static allocation is most evident in its limitations, as it constrains adaptability and responsiveness to changing runtime conditions. The fixed nature of static allocation can lead to inefficiencies, especially when dealing with variable-sized data structures or dynamic memory requirements. While it excels in scenarios with stable memory footprints, static allocation falls short in environments where flexibility and adaptability are paramount.

Dynamic memory allocation, in contrast, introduces a level of flexibility and adaptability crucial for handling varying memory requirements during program execution. Commonly used in languages like C and C++ with mechanisms such as pointers and the heap, dynamic allocation allows memory to be reserved and released at runtime. This flexibility is particularly advantageous when dealing with scenarios where memory needs are uncertain, dynamic data structures are prevalent, or variable-sized datasets are encountered. The ability to allocate and deallocate memory dynamically during execution empowers programmers to respond dynamically to changing conditions, facilitating more versatile and adaptive applications. However, the impact of dynamic allocation is not without its challenges, as it introduces complexities associated with proper memory management, the prevention of memory leaks, and the mitigation of fragmentation.

The impact of memory allocation on program execution extends beyond the choice between static and dynamic strategies. It delves into the intricacies of memory management algorithms, each influencing the efficiency of memory utilization and, consequently, the overall performance of the program. Algorithms such as first-fit, best-fit, and worst-fit, employed in dynamic memory allocation, determine how available memory is allocated to processes or data structures. First-fit, which assigns the first available block of memory that meets the size requirements, strikes a balance between simplicity and efficiency but can lead to fragmentation. Best-fit aims to minimize fragmentation by selecting the smallest available block that satisfies the requirements, potentially leaving behind larger unused blocks. Worst-fit allocates the largest available block, intending to leave smaller free blocks for future use, but it may result in inefficient memory usage. The impact of these allocation strategies is intertwined with the broader goals of optimizing memory usage, minimizing fragmentation, and ensuring a balance between speed and efficiency.

The concept of fragmentation itself underscores the profound impact of memory allocation on program execution. Fragmentation, be it external or internal, can significantly affect the availability and efficient utilization of memory. External fragmentation occurs when free memory is scattered throughout the address space, making it challenging to allocate contiguous blocks of memory. This fragmentation can result in inefficient memory usage and a reduced ability to allocate large, contiguous memory blocks. Internal fragmentation, on the other hand, transpires when allocated memory is larger than needed, leading to inefficient use of the reserved space. The impact of fragmentation extends beyond mere inefficiency; it can influence the overall responsiveness of a program, especially when it relies on rapid and sequential memory access.

Memory allocation's impact on program execution is further accentuated in the realm of virtual memory, a concept that extends the apparent size of available memory beyond the physical constraints of RAM. Virtual memory allows programs to address more memory than physically available by utilizing secondary storage, such as hard drives or SSDs, as an extension of RAM. This capability is particularly beneficial in handling large datasets and complex applications, enhancing the program's ability to manage resources efficiently. However, the impact of virtual memory introduces considerations related to page faults, excessive swapping, and the need for efficient page replacement algorithms. Balancing the advantages of virtual memory in expanding addressable space with the potential drawbacks requires careful consideration in program design.

The hierarchical structure of memory in computer systems further influences the impact of memory allocation on program execution. From fast but limited registers within the processor to larger but slower RAM and the even slower secondary storage devices, the efficiency of memory usage directly affects the speed and responsiveness of a program. Effective memory allocation strategies optimize the use of different levels of memory hierarchy, ensuring that frequently accessed data resides in faster memory tiers, minimizing latency and improving overall performance. The impact of memory allocation is especially pronounced in resource-intensive tasks and applications that demand rapid data access, such as video editing, gaming, scientific simulations, and real-time processing.

Security considerations also intertwine with the impact of memory allocation on program execution. Memory-related vulnerabilities, such as buffer overflows, pose significant threats to program integrity and can be exploited for unauthorized access or control. Modern programming languages and operating systems incorporate security mechanisms within the memory allocation process to mitigate these risks. Address space layout randomization (ASLR), for instance, randomizes the memory addresses of key system components, making it more challenging for attackers to predict or manipulate their locations. The impact of these security measures is not only in preventing unauthorized access but also in ensuring the stability and reliability of program execution.

Moreover, the impact of memory allocation extends to multiuser environments where multiple programs or users share the same system resources. Memory must be allocated equitably to prevent one user or application from monopolizing available resources. Memory allocation algorithms and policies in these environments play a crucial role in distributing resources fairly, ensuring a balanced and responsive computing environment. Techniques such as time-sharing and fair queuing are employed to manage memory resources based on priorities, facilitating a shared environment without compromising performance or responsiveness.

The impact of 64-bit computing architectures on memory allocation further shapes program execution. With 64-bit processors, systems can address larger amounts of memory, providing the foundation for handling increasingly complex and memory-intensive applications. The transition to 64-bit architectures addresses the limitations of 32-bit systems, allowing programs to access and manipulate larger datasets more efficiently. The impact is especially evident in applications that demand extensive memory addressing capabilities, such as high-performance computing, scientific simulations, and large-scale data analytics.

In conclusion, the impact of memory allocation on program execution is profound and multifaceted. The choice between static and dynamic allocation, the intricacies of memory management algorithms, the challenges of fragmentation, the utilization of virtual memory, the hierarchical structure of memory, security considerations, and the evolution of computing architectures collectively shape how programs utilize and interact with memory. The efficiency, responsiveness, and overall performance of a program are intricately linked to the decisions made in memory allocation, underscoring its critical role in the broader landscape of computer systems and software development. As technology continues to advance and the demands on computing resources grow, the impact of memory allocation remains a central consideration in designing robust, efficient, and secure software systems.

Unveiling the concept of virtual memory.

Virtual memory is a pivotal concept in computer systems that revolutionizes the way programs manage and access memory resources. At its core, virtual memory provides an illusion of a larger, contiguous address space than physically available in the Random Access Memory (RAM). This innovation addresses the challenge of limited physical memory by extending the apparent size of the available memory through the intelligent use of secondary storage, such as hard disk drives or solid-state drives. Virtual memory introduces a layer of abstraction that decouples a program's logical memory from the physical RAM, enabling more extensive and flexible memory management. This concept represents a fundamental evolution in the realm of memory architectures, shaping the efficiency, scalability, and overall performance of modern computer systems.

The foundation of virtual memory lies in the division of the address space into logical and physical addresses. Logical addresses, generated by programs during execution, form the virtual address space. In contrast, physical addresses correspond to the actual locations in the physical RAM. The operating system, acting as the arbiter between the program and the hardware, orchestrates the translation between logical and physical addresses. This translation is facilitated through a data structure known as the page table, which maintains a mapping between the logical and physical addresses.

Each entry in the page table corresponds to a page—a fixed-size block of memory—allowing the system to efficiently manage the transfer of data between RAM and secondary storage.

The concept of pages is integral to the operation of virtual memory. When a program is executed, only the portions of its code and data that are actively in use need to reside in the physical RAM. The remaining parts of the program, stored in secondary storage, can be swapped in and out of RAM dynamically based on demand. This on-the-fly movement of data between RAM and secondary storage is known as paging and is a cornerstone of virtual memory management. Paging ensures that the limited physical memory is optimally utilized, allowing programs to address more memory than the actual RAM capacity.

Virtual memory provides several benefits, and one of its primary advantages lies in overcoming the limitations of physical memory size. In scenarios where a program's memory requirements exceed the available RAM, virtual memory enables the system to execute programs that would otherwise be too large to fit entirely in physical memory. This is particularly crucial for handling resource-intensive applications, large datasets, and complex computations. By utilizing secondary storage as an extension of RAM, virtual memory allows programs to access and manipulate vast amounts of data without the need for excessive physical memory.

Furthermore, virtual memory facilitates the illusion of a contiguous address space, simplifying the programming model. Programs can operate under the assumption that they have access to a large and continuous block of memory, even if the physical RAM is fragmented or limited. This abstraction enhances the portability of software, as programs can be developed without intricate knowledge of the specific hardware architecture or the physical memory constraints of a particular system. It also allows for the dynamic allocation and deallocation of memory during program execution, contributing to a more flexible and adaptive memory management environment.

The efficiency of virtual memory is deeply entwined with the concept of demand paging. In a demand-paged system, pages of a program are loaded into RAM only when they are explicitly requested during execution. This approach minimizes the initial memory footprint, allowing programs to start quickly and use resources more efficiently. When a program accesses a portion of memory that is not currently in physical memory, a page fault occurs. The operating system responds by swapping the required page from secondary storage to RAM, ensuring that the needed data is available for the program to continue execution seamlessly. This demand-driven approach enhances the responsiveness of the system by prioritizing the allocation of physical memory based on actual usage.

Despite its advantages, virtual memory is not without challenges. One significant consideration is the potential performance impact associated with page faults and the movement of data between RAM and secondary storage. Excessive paging, where the system frequently swaps pages in and out, can introduce latency and degrade overall performance. The choice of page replacement algorithms becomes crucial in mitigating these performance concerns. Algorithms like Least Recently Used (LRU), Clock, and Least Frequently Used (LFU) are employed to determine which pages to evict from RAM when space is needed. The effectiveness of these algorithms influences the system's ability to maintain optimal performance while managing the demands of multiple concurrently executing programs.

Another consideration in the implementation of virtual memory is the potential for thrashing. Thrashing occurs when the system spends a significant portion of its time swapping pages in and out of RAM, leading to excessive disk activity and a substantial decline in overall performance. This phenomenon is often a result of inadequate physical memory to support the concurrent demands of running programs. Effective memory management and careful consideration of system resources are crucial to prevent thrashing and maintain system responsiveness.

Security considerations are also integral to the understanding of virtual memory. The illusion of a vast, contiguous address space created by virtual memory introduces security challenges, particularly in the realm of address space layout randomization (ASLR). ASLR is a security technique that randomizes the memory addresses of key system components and program elements to thwart potential attackers. While ASLR enhances security by making it challenging for attackers to predict the locations of critical structures in memory, it relies on the consistent behavior of virtual memory across different system instances. This delicate balance between security and the consistent abstraction provided by virtual memory underscores the complex interplay of considerations in modern computing environments.

The impact of virtual memory extends beyond individual programs to the efficient utilization of system resources in a multitasking environment. In a multi-user or multi-process system, where multiple programs or users share the same hardware resources, virtual memory allows each program to operate as if it has its dedicated and contiguous address space. The operating system, through the coordination of page tables and memory management units, ensures the isolation and protection of each program's memory space. This enables concurrent execution of diverse applications without mutual interference, contributing to a stable and secure computing environment.

The hierarchical organization of memory in computer systems also influences the impact of virtual memory on overall system performance. Registers, cache memory, RAM, and secondary storage devices collectively form a hierarchical structure with varying access times. Virtual memory optimally utilizes this hierarchy, allowing frequently accessed pages to reside in faster memory tiers while relegating less frequently accessed pages to slower storage. This tiered approach ensures that programs can quickly access critical data while still being able to manipulate large datasets that exceed the capacity of the physical RAM.

In conclusion, virtual memory is a foundational concept that transforms the landscape of memory management in computer systems. By creating an illusion of a larger and contiguous address space, virtual memory addresses the constraints of physical memory size, enabling programs to handle larger datasets and more complex computations. The dynamic nature of demand paging optimizes memory usage, allowing systems to respond to changing demands efficiently. Despite the challenges associated with page faults, thrashing, and security considerations, virtual memory remains a cornerstone of modern computing environments, supporting the execution of diverse applications in a multitasking, multi-user, and resource-constrained landscape. The ongoing evolution of virtual memory techniques and their integration with advancements in hardware architectures continue to shape the efficiency, scalability, and adaptability of computer systems, underscoring the enduring significance of this concept in contemporary computing.

Chapter 2: Dynamic Memory Allocation

Defining dynamic memory allocation.

Dynamic memory allocation is a foundational concept in computer science that refers to the process of reserving and managing memory during a program's execution dynamically. In contrast to static memory allocation, where memory is allocated at compile time and remains fixed throughout a program's run, dynamic memory allocation enables programs to adaptively allocate and deallocate memory at runtime based on evolving requirements. This flexibility is particularly essential when the size and structure of data structures or the memory needs of a program are not known in advance. Dynamic memory allocation empowers programmers to efficiently use memory resources, catering to scenarios where the demand for memory changes dynamically, such as when dealing with variable-sized data structures, user input, or tasks with unpredictable memory requirements.

At the heart of dynamic memory allocation is the heap, a region of memory separate from the program's stack. Unlike the stack, which manages local variables and function call information with automatic allocation and deallocation, the heap provides a pool of memory for dynamic memory operations. The heap allows programs to allocate memory as needed and release it when it is no longer required, providing a more flexible and adaptive memory management mechanism. This adaptability is achieved through the use of pointers, variables that store memory addresses, facilitating dynamic memory operations by pointing to the locations of allocated memory blocks.

In languages like C and C++, dynamic memory allocation is commonly accomplished through functions such as `malloc()`, `calloc()`, `realloc()`, and `free()`. The `malloc()` function allocates a specified amount of memory on the heap, and `free()` deallocates previously allocated memory, releasing it back to the heap for future use. The `calloc()` function not only allocates memory but also initializes it to zero, and `realloc()` allows for the resizing of an already allocated memory block. These functions, collectively, provide programmers with the tools to manage memory dynamically, responding to the changing needs of a program during its execution.

Dynamic memory allocation introduces several advantages. One of its primary benefits is the ability to allocate memory based on the actual size requirements of a program. This contrasts with static allocation, where memory sizes are predetermined, potentially leading to inefficient use of memory when the actual requirements differ. Dynamic memory allocation ensures that memory is allocated only when needed, preventing unnecessary consumption of resources and allowing for more efficient use of available memory.

Moreover, dynamic memory allocation supports the creation of variable-sized data structures. In scenarios where the size of a data structure cannot be predetermined or may change during program execution, dynamic memory allocation becomes indispensable. Data structures like linked lists, trees, and dynamic arrays can dynamically grow or shrink based on runtime conditions, adapting to the data manipulation needs of the program. This flexibility is crucial in applications dealing with evolving datasets or scenarios where the size of data structures is determined by user input or external factors.

However, the advantages of dynamic memory allocation come with certain responsibilities. One of the key challenges is proper memory management to prevent issues like memory leaks. A memory leak occurs when allocated memory is not properly deallocated or released after it is no longer needed. This can lead to a gradual depletion of available memory resources, potentially causing the program or system to become unstable or unresponsive over time. Programmers must carefully manage the lifecycle of dynamically allocated memory, ensuring that every allocation is matched with an appropriate deallocation to maintain optimal resource utilization.

Another challenge associated with dynamic memory allocation is the potential for fragmentation. Fragmentation occurs when free memory is scattered throughout the address space, making it challenging to allocate contiguous blocks of memory. There are two main types of fragmentation: external fragmentation and internal fragmentation. External fragmentation arises when free memory is distributed in small, non-contiguous chunks, hindering the allocation of large, contiguous memory blocks. Internal fragmentation, on the other hand, occurs when the allocated memory is larger than necessary, resulting in inefficient use of the reserved space. Managing fragmentation is a critical aspect of dynamic memory allocation, and various memory management strategies and algorithms are employed to address these challenges.

Several memory allocation algorithms influence the efficiency and performance of dynamic memory allocation. One common approach is the use of linked lists to manage free memory blocks on the heap. Each block of free memory is associated with a data structure containing information about its size and location. When a program requests memory, the allocator traverses the linked list to find a suitable free block. While this approach helps mitigate external fragmentation, it introduces overhead due to the storage requirements of the linked list nodes.

To address internal fragmentation, memory allocators may employ strategies such as memory pooling or slab allocation. Memory pooling involves preallocating fixed-size memory blocks and grouping them into pools. These pools are then allocated to specific tasks or data types, reducing internal fragmentation by ensuring that allocated memory closely matches the required size. Slab allocation is a technique where memory is divided into slabs, each containing blocks of a specific size. This approach is particularly effective in managing objects of varying sizes within the same pool, minimizing both internal and external fragmentation.

Dynamic memory allocation plays a crucial role in the efficient management of resources in multi-user or multi-process environments. In such scenarios, multiple programs or users share the same system resources, including the heap. Memory allocation algorithms and policies must be designed to address the dynamic nature of resource demands, ensuring fair and equitable distribution of memory resources among concurrently executing programs. Techniques such as time-sharing and fair queuing aim to allocate memory based on priorities, fostering a balanced and responsive computing environment.

Furthermore, the transition to 64-bit computing architectures has influenced dynamic memory allocation. With 64-bit processors, systems can potentially address exabytes of memory, significantly expanding the addressable memory space. This advancement addresses the limitations of 32-bit architectures, which have a theoretical maximum addressable space of 4 gigabytes. The larger addressable space in 64-bit systems provides more room for memory-intensive applications, enabling them to handle and process vast datasets more efficiently.

In conclusion, dynamic memory allocation is a fundamental concept that empowers programs to adaptively manage memory resources during their execution. It provides flexibility and adaptability, enabling the creation of variable-sized data structures and efficient resource utilization. The use of pointers, along with functions like `**malloc()**` and `**free()**`, facilitates dynamic memory operations, allowing programs to allocate and deallocate memory as needed. However, the advantages of dynamic memory allocation come with responsibilities, including the proper management of memory to avoid issues like memory leaks and fragmentation. The challenges associated with fragmentation and the impact of dynamic memory allocation in multi-user environments underscore its significance in the broader landscape of computer systems and software development. As computing environments continue to evolve, the efficient management of memory resources through dynamic memory allocation remains a critical aspect of building robust, adaptable, and high-performance software systems.

Importance in managing varying memory requirements.

The importance of managing varying memory requirements in computing is a fundamental aspect that underpins the efficiency, adaptability, and overall performance of software systems. In the dynamic landscape of computing environments, where applications serve diverse purposes and encounter fluctuating workloads, the ability to effectively handle varying memory needs is paramount. This importance manifests in various dimensions, encompassing aspects of resource utilization, responsiveness, and the ability to accommodate diverse data structures and applications with unpredictable memory footprints.

At the core of this significance lies the dynamic nature of modern computing workloads. Unlike static environments where memory requirements remain constant and predictable, contemporary applications often operate in dynamic and ever-changing scenarios. For example, web servers experience variable loads based on user traffic, databases handle fluctuating query complexities, and scientific simulations adapt to evolving computational demands. In such contexts, the rigidity of fixed memory allocations can result in inefficiencies, either leading to underutilization when memory allocations are excessive or causing out-of-memory errors when demands exceed predefined limits. Effectively managing varying memory requirements allows systems to gracefully adapt to these dynamic conditions, optimizing resource utilization and ensuring consistent performance.

One key facet of the importance in managing varying memory requirements is the ability to cater to applications with unpredictable memory footprints. Many modern programs, particularly those dealing with large datasets, complex algorithms, or user-generated content, exhibit dynamic memory needs that are hard to foresee during the design phase. Consider a video editing application processing media files of varying sizes or a data analytics tool analyzing datasets with unpredictable dimensions. In these scenarios, the capacity to dynamically allocate and deallocate memory in response to the immediate needs of the program is indispensable. A system equipped to manage varying memory requirements facilitates the development of versatile applications capable of handling diverse data types and sizes, accommodating the inherent variability of real-world computing tasks.

The flexibility to adapt to varying memory requirements becomes especially critical in the realm of dynamic data structures. Data structures like linked lists, trees, and dynamic arrays may need to grow or shrink during program execution based on user interactions, input data, or algorithmic processing. Dynamic memory management empowers programmers to create applications that efficiently scale with changing data structures, avoiding unnecessary preallocations or limitations on data size. This adaptability is particularly evident in scenarios where user interactions, such as those in interactive applications or video games, lead to dynamic changes in data structure sizes. By dynamically managing memory, systems can seamlessly adjust to the evolving needs of these applications, ensuring a responsive and user-friendly experience.

Moreover, the importance of managing varying memory requirements extends to scenarios where memory-intensive tasks are commonplace. Scientific simulations, numerical computations, artificial intelligence algorithms, and simulations in fields such as physics or engineering often involve large datasets and complex calculations that demand significant memory resources. The ability to dynamically allocate additional memory when needed allows these applications to tackle intricate problems without being constrained by fixed memory limits. In scientific research, for instance, simulations that model complex phenomena may require substantial memory for efficient data representation and processing. A system capable of managing varying memory requirements ensures that such computational endeavors can leverage the available resources optimally, pushing the boundaries of scientific discovery and technological innovation.

Beyond application-level considerations, the importance of managing varying memory requirements is accentuated in multi-user and multi-process environments. In shared computing environments, multiple programs or users concurrently access and utilize system resources, including memory. Each program may have distinct memory requirements based on its specific tasks, and the ability to dynamically allocate and deallocate memory ensures equitable distribution of resources. Time-sharing systems, where multiple users share the same computing resources, rely on dynamic memory management to prevent one user or application from monopolizing the available memory. This fair allocation fosters a responsive and balanced computing environment, where diverse applications coexist harmoniously without compromising performance or responsiveness.

The advent of cloud computing further amplifies the importance of managing varying memory requirements. Cloud environments are characterized by dynamic workloads, scalability, and resource elasticity. Applications hosted in the cloud may experience fluctuations in user demand, requiring the system to dynamically scale resources, including memory, in response to changing requirements. Effective memory management becomes integral to achieving optimal performance, cost-efficiency, and scalability in cloud-based architectures. Cloud service providers leverage dynamic memory allocation strategies to optimize resource utilization, ensuring that applications hosted in the cloud can seamlessly adapt to varying workloads while minimizing operational costs.

The significance of managing varying memory requirements is intertwined with the broader concept of resource optimization. In computing, resources are finite, and effective resource utilization is a key determinant of system efficiency. Memory, being a critical resource, directly influences the performance and responsiveness of applications. Dynamic memory management allows systems to adapt to the ebb and flow of computational demands, avoiding resource wastage and ensuring that memory is allocated judiciously. In scenarios where memory needs fluctuate, the ability to allocate additional memory on-the-fly or release unused memory back to the system enhances overall resource efficiency, contributing to a more sustainable and high-performing computing environment.

Furthermore, managing varying memory requirements is essential in the context of embedded systems and real-time applications. Embedded systems, commonly found in devices such as smartphones, IoT devices, and automotive control systems, often operate in resource-constrained environments. Real-time applications, including those in medical devices, industrial control systems, and communication systems, require predictable and timely responses. In these contexts, the dynamic nature of memory requirements necessitates efficient and deterministic memory management. The ability to allocate and deallocate memory dynamically allows embedded systems and real-time applications to adapt to changing conditions, handle diverse tasks, and meet stringent performance requirements.

Security considerations also underscore the importance of managing varying memory requirements. Inadequate memory management can lead to vulnerabilities such as buffer overflows, where a program writes beyond the boundaries of allocated memory. This type of vulnerability can be exploited by malicious actors to execute arbitrary code, compromise system integrity, or gain unauthorized access. Effective dynamic memory management, including bounds checking and proper deallocation of memory, mitigates the risk of such security threats. Security mechanisms incorporated into modern programming languages and operating systems contribute to the robustness of dynamic memory management, enhancing the overall security posture of software systems.

In conclusion, the importance of managing varying memory requirements in computing is multifaceted and foundational to the efficient operation of software systems. The dynamic nature of modern computing workloads, the diverse memory needs of applications, and the evolving landscape of computing environments underscore the significance of adaptive memory management. From accommodating unpredictable data structures and varying application workloads to ensuring equitable resource distribution in multi-user environments and optimizing resource utilization in the cloud, the ability to manage varying memory requirements is pivotal. As technology advances, the challenges associated with dynamic memory management continue to evolve, and innovative solutions in memory allocation, real-time systems, and security mechanisms will play a crucial role in shaping the future of computing environments.

Comparison with static memory allocation.

The comparison between dynamic and static memory allocation forms a critical discourse in the landscape of computer science, shaping the design, efficiency, and adaptability of software systems. At its core, the distinction between these two memory allocation strategies lies in their approach to reserving and managing memory during a program's lifecycle. Static memory allocation, a traditional paradigm, involves the reservation of memory at compile time with fixed sizes determined during the program's development. Dynamic memory allocation, on the other hand, provides a more flexible and adaptive model, allowing memory to be allocated and deallocated during runtime based on the program's evolving needs.

Static memory allocation, prevalent in languages like C and C++, adheres to a predictable and rigid approach. During the compilation phase, memory is allocated for variables, arrays, and data structures based on explicit declarations in the source code. The sizes and structures of these memory allocations are predetermined, resulting in a fixed memory layout that remains constant throughout the program's execution. While static allocation offers simplicity and efficiency by eliminating the need for runtime management, its inflexibility becomes evident in scenarios where memory requirements are dynamic, variable-sized data structures are prevalent, or the program encounters unpredictable workloads.

The efficiency of static memory allocation is most pronounced in scenarios characterized by stability and predictability. Applications with well-defined and constant memory needs, such as small utility programs or embedded systems with fixed specifications, benefit from the straightforwardness of static allocation. Memory addresses are known in advance, facilitating direct and efficient access to allocated memory locations without the overhead of runtime adjustments. Moreover, static allocation minimizes runtime overhead associated with dynamic memory management, resulting in faster and deterministic memory access. However, the trade-off is apparent as this efficiency comes at the cost of reduced adaptability and responsiveness, limiting the program's ability to handle dynamic or unpredictable scenarios.

In contrast, dynamic memory allocation introduces a level of flexibility and adaptability that addresses the shortcomings of static allocation. Commonly used in languages like C and C++ through mechanisms like pointers and the heap, dynamic allocation allows memory to be reserved and released at runtime. This adaptability is particularly advantageous when dealing with scenarios where memory needs are uncertain, variable-sized data structures are prevalent, or dynamic memory requirements arise during program execution. Dynamic memory allocation empowers programmers to respond dynamically to changing conditions, facilitating more versatile and adaptive applications. However, this flexibility is not without its challenges, as it introduces complexities associated with proper memory management, the prevention of memory leaks, and the mitigation of fragmentation.

The impact of static and dynamic memory allocation on program efficiency extends beyond the initial decision-making phase into the realm of memory management algorithms. In static allocation, memory layout is predetermined during compilation, resulting in a straightforward memory structure. The predictability of memory layout simplifies access patterns and optimizations but comes at the expense of adaptability. Static allocation excels in scenarios where memory access patterns are well-defined and constant, leading to efficient program execution. However, the rigid nature of static allocation hampers its suitability for applications with dynamic memory needs or those requiring the allocation of variable-sized data structures.

Dynamic memory allocation, conversely, relies on memory management algorithms to handle the allocation and deallocation of memory during runtime. Algorithms such as first-fit, best-fit, and worst-fit determine how available memory is allocated to processes or data structures. First-fit allocates the first available block of memory that meets the size requirements, striking a balance between simplicity and efficiency but potentially leading to fragmentation. Best-fit aims to minimize fragmentation by selecting the smallest available block that satisfies the requirements, potentially leaving behind larger unused blocks. Worst-fit allocates the largest available block, intending to leave smaller free blocks for future use but may result in inefficient memory usage. The impact of these allocation strategies is intertwined with the broader goals of optimizing memory usage, minimizing fragmentation, and ensuring a balance between speed and efficiency.

Fragmentation is a crucial aspect that differentiates static and dynamic memory allocation. In static allocation, the memory layout is fixed, and there is no concern about fragmentation during program execution. The memory is allocated contiguously, ensuring that there are no gaps between allocated memory blocks. This simplicity comes at the cost of adaptability, as any changes in memory requirements or the introduction of new data structures may lead to inefficient use of memory. Moreover, static allocation is susceptible to the risk of wasted memory space when dealing with variable-sized data structures, potentially resulting in underutilization.

Dynamic memory allocation, on the other hand, grapples with the challenge of fragmentation. The dynamic nature of allocation and deallocation can lead to two main types of fragmentation: external and internal. External fragmentation occurs when free memory is scattered throughout the address space, making it challenging to allocate contiguous blocks of memory. This fragmentation can result in inefficient memory usage and a reduced ability to allocate large, contiguous memory blocks. Internal fragmentation transpires when allocated memory is larger than needed, leading to inefficient use of the reserved space. The management of fragmentation becomes a critical consideration in dynamic memory allocation, influencing the choice of allocation algorithms and strategies employed to maintain a balance between efficient use of resources and responsiveness to varying workloads.

Security considerations also come into play when comparing static and dynamic memory allocation. The fixed nature of memory layout in static allocation may offer a level of predictability that can be leveraged for security measures. However, this predictability can be exploited by attackers who may gain insights into the memory structure, potentially leading to security vulnerabilities. Dynamic memory allocation, with its ability to change memory layouts during runtime, introduces challenges in terms of security. Memory-related vulnerabilities, such as buffer overflows, pose significant threats to program integrity and can be exploited for unauthorized access or control. Modern programming languages and operating systems incorporate security mechanisms within the dynamic memory allocation process to mitigate these risks. Address space layout randomization (ASLR), for instance, randomizes the memory addresses of key system components, making it more challenging for attackers to predict or manipulate their locations. The impact of these security measures is not only in preventing unauthorized access but also in ensuring the stability and reliability of program execution.

The connection between memory allocation strategies and the hierarchical structure of memory in computer systems further shapes the comparison between static and dynamic allocation. In a typical computer system, memory exists in a hierarchy, ranging from fast but limited registers within the processor to larger but slower RAM and the even slower secondary storage devices. Static memory allocation, with its fixed memory layout, can be optimized to take advantage of this hierarchy, ensuring that frequently accessed data resides in faster memory tiers. This optimization minimizes latency and improves overall performance, especially in resource-intensive tasks that demand rapid data access. Dynamic memory allocation, while providing flexibility, introduces challenges in optimizing memory usage across this hierarchy. The dynamic movement of data between different levels of the memory hierarchy during runtime may lead to suboptimal access patterns, impacting the overall speed and responsiveness of the program.

The impact of static and dynamic memory allocation is also evident in their connection to the overall speed and performance of a system. In applications where performance is a critical consideration, the efficiency of memory access patterns becomes paramount. Static memory allocation, with its fixed and predictable memory layout, enables compilers and hardware to optimize memory access, resulting in faster and more deterministic execution. This predictability is advantageous in scenarios where the overhead of dynamic memory management may be deemed unacceptable. However, the rigidity of static allocation becomes a limiting factor in scenarios where adaptability and responsiveness to changing workloads are crucial. Dynamic memory allocation, while introducing additional complexities, allows for more versatile and adaptive applications that can dynamically adjust their memory usage based on runtime conditions. The trade-off between speed and adaptability forms a key aspect of the decision-making process when choosing between static and dynamic memory allocation strategies.

In conclusion, the comparison between static and dynamic memory allocation is nuanced and multifaceted, involving considerations of efficiency, adaptability, security, and overall system performance. Static memory allocation, with its predictability and simplicity, excels in scenarios where memory needs are constant and well-defined. The fixed memory layout enables efficient access patterns, minimizes runtime overhead, and offers a level of predictability that can be leveraged for security measures. However, the inflexibility of static allocation becomes a limitation in dynamic environments where memory requirements fluctuate, and variable-sized data structures are prevalent. Dynamic memory allocation addresses these limitations by providing adaptability and flexibility. The ability to allocate and deallocate memory during runtime caters to changing workloads, supports variable-sized data structures, and enables more responsive and versatile applications. The trade-offs involve the complexities of memory management, the challenge of fragmentation, and potential security considerations. The decision between static and dynamic memory allocation depends on the specific requirements of the application, the nature of the workload, and the trade-offs deemed acceptable for the goals of the system or software being developed. As computing environments continue to evolve, the interplay between these memory allocation strategies will shape the landscape of software development, influencing the design principles and performance characteristics of the systems we build.

In-depth exploration of allocation strategies.

The exploration of memory allocation strategies represents a nuanced journey into the heart of computer systems, where the effective management of memory resources is pivotal for system efficiency and overall performance. Memory allocation, a fundamental aspect of operating systems and programming languages, involves determining how to assign portions of memory to different processes or data structures. The efficiency of these strategies significantly impacts the responsiveness, resource utilization, and overall stability of software systems. This exploration delves into various memory allocation strategies, encompassing both static and dynamic approaches, shedding light on the intricacies of how memory is allocated, accessed, and reclaimed during program execution.

Static memory allocation, a traditional approach, involves reserving memory at compile time based on predetermined sizes specified in the source code. Memory layout is fixed, and the addresses of variables or data structures are determined during the compilation phase. This simplicity offers advantages in terms of speed and determinism, as memory addresses are known in advance, facilitating direct access. However, the rigid nature of static allocation becomes evident in its inability to adapt to dynamic workloads or varying memory requirements. Memory sizes are fixed, leading to potential inefficiencies when dealing with dynamic data structures or applications with unpredictable memory needs.

Dynamic memory allocation, in contrast, provides a more adaptive model where memory is reserved and released at runtime. This approach, commonly employed in languages like C and C++ through mechanisms like pointers and the heap, caters to scenarios where memory needs fluctuate or variable-sized data structures are prevalent. The flexibility of dynamic allocation empowers programmers to allocate memory as needed and release it when it is no longer required, offering adaptability to changing conditions. However, the advantages of dynamic allocation come with responsibilities, including proper memory management to avoid issues such as memory leaks or fragmentation.

Fragmentation, a critical consideration in memory allocation, refers to the presence of unused memory that is not part of any allocated block. Two main types of fragmentation exist: external and internal. External fragmentation occurs when free memory is scattered throughout the address space, making it challenging to allocate contiguous blocks of memory. This form of fragmentation can lead to inefficient memory usage and a reduced ability to allocate large, contiguous memory blocks. Internal fragmentation, on the other hand, transpires when allocated memory is larger than needed, resulting in inefficient use of the reserved space. Both types of fragmentation introduce challenges in optimizing memory usage and necessitate the development of allocation strategies that balance efficiency and responsiveness.

One classical strategy for memory allocation is the fixed or static partitioning scheme. In this approach, memory is divided into fixed-size partitions, each dedicated to a specific process. This method simplifies allocation, as each process is allocated a predefined portion of memory, and fragmentation is minimized. However, fixed partitioning is inflexible and may lead to inefficient use of memory when processes have varying memory requirements. Additionally, it limits the number of concurrently running processes, impacting the overall multitasking capability of the system.

An evolution of fixed partitioning is the variable or dynamic partitioning scheme, where memory is divided into variable-sized partitions to accommodate processes with different memory requirements. This approach addresses some of the limitations of fixed partitioning by allowing for more efficient use of memory. However, dynamic partitioning introduces challenges related to external fragmentation, as free memory blocks of varying sizes may become scattered, hindering the allocation of contiguous memory for large processes. Various algorithms, such as first-fit, best-fit, and worst-fit, are employed to determine how available memory is allocated to processes, each with its trade-offs in terms of efficiency and fragmentation.

The first-fit algorithm allocates the first available block of memory that meets the size requirements of a process. While simple and quick, this approach may lead to fragmentation, as larger free blocks may be left unused. The best-fit algorithm aims to minimize fragmentation by selecting the smallest available block that satisfies the size requirements. However, this strategy may result in more fragmented free space, making it challenging to find suitable blocks for larger processes. The worst-fit algorithm allocates the largest available block, intending to leave smaller unused blocks for future use. Although this approach minimizes fragmentation, it may lead to inefficient use of memory and can be slower due to the search for large enough blocks.

Buddy memory allocation, another strategy, addresses fragmentation concerns by dividing memory into fixed-size blocks, often powers of two. When a process requests memory, the system allocates the smallest available block that is larger than the requested size. If no suitable block is found, the system splits a larger block into two smaller ones until an appropriate size is reached. Buddy allocation minimizes external fragmentation by grouping free blocks of similar sizes together, simplifying the search for suitable memory blocks. However, it may introduce internal fragmentation if allocated blocks are significantly larger than required.

The concept of paging introduces a more granular approach to memory allocation, dividing physical memory and processes into fixed-size pages. Similarly, virtual memory, a foundational concept in modern operating systems, provides an abstraction layer that decouples a program's logical memory from physical memory. The operating system, through the use of a page table, translates logical addresses generated by the program into physical addresses, facilitating dynamic loading and unloading of pages in and out of physical memory. Paging minimizes external fragmentation and allows for efficient use of physical memory by only loading the necessary pages, but it introduces challenges related to page faults and the overhead of managing the page table.

Segmentation, an alternative to paging, divides a program's logical address space into segments representing different areas of functionality, such as code, data, and stack. Each segment can grow or shrink dynamically based on the program's requirements. While segmentation provides flexibility in managing different aspects of a program, it may lead to fragmentation within segments and requires complex memory management mechanisms.

In the context of dynamic memory allocation, the malloc(), free(), calloc(), and realloc() functions in languages like C and C++ play a crucial role. These functions allow programmers to request memory from the heap during runtime and release it when no longer needed. The malloc() function allocates a specified amount of memory, while free() deallocates previously allocated memory, preventing memory leaks. The calloc() function not only allocates memory but also initializes it to zero, and realloc() allows for the resizing of an already allocated memory block. The careful use of these functions is essential to ensuring proper memory management in dynamic allocation scenarios.

The connection between memory allocation and system performance is intricate and multifaceted. Efficient memory allocation directly impacts the speed and responsiveness of programs. In systems with fixed memory allocations, the deterministic nature of memory access patterns allows for optimizations that enhance performance. However, this predictability comes at the cost of adaptability. In contrast, dynamic memory allocation, while introducing additional complexities, enables systems to adapt to changing workloads, allocate memory as needed, and release unused memory. The trade-off involves potential overhead and challenges related to fragmentation, impacting overall system performance.

The impact of memory allocation strategies extends beyond single-user systems to the domain of multi-user or multi-process environments. In shared computing environments, where multiple processes or users concurrently access and utilize system resources, effective memory allocation is crucial for maintaining a balanced and responsive system. Time-sharing systems, a common paradigm in such environments, allocate CPU time and memory resources among multiple users or processes. Memory allocation strategies in these scenarios must ensure fair distribution, preventing one user or process from monopolizing the available memory and impacting overall system responsiveness.

In cloud computing environments, where resources are dynamically allocated based on demand, memory allocation strategies play a pivotal role in achieving optimal performance and cost efficiency. Cloud systems leverage dynamic memory allocation to scale resources, including memory, in response to changing workloads. Efficient memory utilization in the cloud is essential for minimizing operational costs and ensuring that applications can seamlessly adapt to varying demands. Memory allocation strategies become integral components of cloud service providers' resource management systems, contributing to the scalability and reliability of cloud-based applications.

The evolution of computing architectures, including the transition to 64-bit systems, introduces new considerations in memory allocation. With 64-bit processors, systems can address larger memory spaces, potentially impacting the efficiency of memory allocation strategies. While the larger addressable space provides more room for memory-intensive applications, it also necessitates careful consideration of how memory is managed and allocated. Efficient memory allocation in 64-bit systems becomes essential for harnessing the full potential of the expanded address space and delivering optimal performance in memory-intensive tasks.

Security considerations are paramount in the exploration of memory allocation strategies. Inadequate memory management can lead to vulnerabilities, such as buffer overflows, where a program writes beyond the boundaries of allocated memory. These vulnerabilities can be exploited by malicious actors to execute arbitrary code, compromise system integrity, or gain unauthorized access. Modern programming languages and operating systems incorporate security mechanisms within memory allocation processes to mitigate these risks. Techniques such as address space layout randomization (ASLR) randomize the memory addresses of key system components, making it more challenging for attackers to predict or manipulate their locations. The integration of security measures within memory allocation strategies contributes to the overall robustness and resilience of software systems.

In conclusion, the exploration of memory allocation strategies is a multifaceted journey encompassing static and dynamic approaches, fragmentation concerns, and the intricate interplay between memory and system performance. Static allocation provides simplicity and speed in predictable environments but lacks adaptability in dynamic scenarios. Dynamic allocation, with its flexibility, empowers systems to adapt to changing workloads but introduces challenges related to fragmentation and proper memory management. Various strategies, from fixed and dynamic partitioning to paging, segmentation, and dynamic memory allocation functions, cater to diverse requirements in different computing environments. The impact of memory allocation strategies extends beyond single-user systems to multi-user environments, cloud computing, and considerations in evolving computing architectures. Efficient memory allocation is essential for achieving optimal system performance, scalability, and security, making it a foundational aspect of software design and system architecture. As computing continues to advance, the exploration and refinement of memory allocation strategies remain pivotal for building robust, efficient, and secure software systems.

Pros and cons of first fit, best fit, and worst fit.

The evaluation of memory allocation strategies, such as First Fit, Best Fit, and Worst Fit, involves a nuanced examination of their respective advantages and drawbacks. These strategies play a critical role in determining how available memory is allocated to processes in dynamic partitioning schemes, and their impact extends to aspects of system efficiency, fragmentation management, and overall responsiveness. Understanding the pros and cons of each strategy is essential for making informed decisions in the design and implementation of memory allocation systems.

First Fit, a straightforward allocation strategy, allocates the first available block of memory that is large enough to accommodate a process. One notable advantage of First Fit is its simplicity and speed. The algorithm traverses the list of free memory blocks sequentially and allocates the first block that meets the size requirements, minimizing search time. This simplicity is particularly advantageous in scenarios where quick allocation is prioritized over optimal memory utilization. However, the simplicity of First Fit comes with trade-offs. One significant drawback is the potential for fragmentation, both external and internal. Allocating the first available block may leave behind smaller free blocks that are not immediately usable for larger processes, contributing to external fragmentation. Additionally, internal fragmentation may occur when the allocated block is larger than necessary, leading to inefficient use of memory.

Best Fit, an allocation strategy that selects the smallest available block that satisfies the size requirements of a process, aims to minimize fragmentation. One notable advantage of Best Fit is its potential to reduce external fragmentation by selecting the smallest suitable block, thereby leaving behind larger contiguous free blocks for future allocations. This characteristic makes Best Fit appealing in scenarios where efficient use of memory and the mitigation of fragmentation are critical considerations. However, the benefits of Best Fit come at the cost of increased complexity and potentially slower allocation times. The algorithm needs to search through the entire list of free memory blocks to find the smallest one that meets the size requirements. This search process introduces overhead and may impact overall system performance. Additionally, while Best Fit can be effective in minimizing external fragmentation, it may lead to more fragmented free space, making it challenging to find suitable blocks for larger processes.

Worst Fit, an allocation strategy that allocates the largest available block, aims to minimize fragmentation by leaving behind smaller free blocks for future allocations. The primary advantage of Worst Fit is its potential to reduce external fragmentation, as larger free blocks are preserved for subsequent allocations. This characteristic is beneficial in scenarios where the efficient allocation of large memory blocks is a priority. However, the benefits of Worst Fit are accompanied by challenges. One notable drawback is the potential for inefficient memory utilization. Allocating the largest available block may result in internal fragmentation when the allocated block is larger than necessary for the process. Additionally, the search for the largest available block introduces overhead and may lead to slower allocation times compared to simpler algorithms like First Fit. Worst Fit's trade-offs highlight the delicate balance between mitigating fragmentation and optimizing memory usage.

Comparing First Fit, Best Fit, and Worst Fit underscores the diverse considerations that influence the choice of a memory allocation strategy. First Fit, with its simplicity and speed, is well-suited for scenarios where quick allocation is prioritized, and fragmentation concerns are secondary. Best Fit, by aiming to minimize fragmentation, is suitable in environments where memory efficiency is crucial, even at the cost of increased complexity and potential performance impact. Worst Fit, with its focus on preserving larger free blocks, finds application in scenarios prioritizing the allocation of large memory chunks while accepting potential inefficiencies in memory usage.

The impact of these allocation strategies extends beyond individual process allocations to the broader context of system performance, especially in multi-process environments or shared computing systems. In a multi-user setting, where multiple processes concurrently access and utilize system resources, the choice of a memory allocation strategy becomes a critical determinant of system responsiveness and fairness. First Fit's simplicity may make it suitable for environments where the overhead of allocation strategies needs to be minimized, and rapid allocation is essential. Best Fit's emphasis on fragmentation reduction becomes valuable in shared environments where efficient use of memory is a priority, even if it entails a moderate increase in allocation complexity. Worst Fit, while potentially slower, can be effective in scenarios where preserving larger free blocks is crucial for accommodating subsequent allocations in a multi-process context.

Moreover, the impact of these allocation strategies is intertwined with the dynamic nature of memory requirements in modern computing environments. As workloads fluctuate, applications demand varying amounts of memory, and data structures evolve, the adaptability of memory allocation strategies becomes a key consideration. The inherent trade-offs of First Fit, Best Fit, and Worst Fit highlight the need for a nuanced approach that aligns with the specific requirements and characteristics of the computing environment.

In the realm of security, the choice of a memory allocation strategy can also have implications. While these strategies primarily focus on optimizing memory usage and mitigating fragmentation, their impact on security cannot be overlooked. Inadequate memory management, including issues such as buffer overflows or vulnerabilities arising from fragmentation, can be exploited by malicious actors to compromise system integrity. Security mechanisms, including those addressing memory-related vulnerabilities, are integral components of modern programming languages and operating systems. The interplay between memory allocation strategies and security considerations emphasizes the importance of a holistic approach to system design that encompasses both performance optimization and robust security measures.

In conclusion, the evaluation of memory allocation strategies involves a comprehensive examination of the pros and cons associated with First Fit, Best Fit, and Worst Fit. Each strategy carries its own set of trade-offs, influencing factors such as simplicity, speed, fragmentation mitigation, and memory efficiency. The choice of an allocation strategy depends on the specific requirements and priorities of the computing environment, considering factors such as system responsiveness, multi-process fairness, and security considerations. As computing environments continue to evolve, the exploration and refinement of memory allocation strategies remain crucial for achieving an optimal balance between efficiency, adaptability, and security in software systems.

Choosing the optimal strategy for specific scenarios.

Selecting the optimal memory allocation strategy for specific scenarios is a nuanced decision that depends on a myriad of factors, including the nature of the computing environment, application characteristics, and overarching system goals. Each memory allocation strategy—First Fit, Best Fit, and Worst Fit—comes with its own set of advantages and drawbacks, making the choice a delicate balance between conflicting considerations. The decision-making process involves a careful assessment of the unique requirements, constraints, and priorities of the given scenario, ultimately aiming to strike a harmonious equilibrium between efficiency, adaptability, and overall system performance.

In scenarios where simplicity and rapid allocation are paramount, First Fit emerges as a viable choice. Its straightforward approach involves allocating the first available block of memory that satisfies the size requirements of a process. This simplicity translates to faster allocation times, making it suitable for environments where minimizing overhead is crucial. For example, in embedded systems or real-time applications with stringent response time requirements, First Fit may be preferred due to its expeditious allocation process. However, the trade-off inherent in First Fit is the potential for fragmentation, both external and internal. The sequential allocation of memory may leave behind smaller unused blocks, contributing to fragmentation and potentially impacting overall memory efficiency.

On the other end of the spectrum, scenarios emphasizing efficient memory usage and fragmentation reduction may lean towards Best Fit. This strategy selects the smallest available block that satisfies the size requirements of a process, aiming to minimize wasted memory and external fragmentation. Best Fit finds applicability in environments where memory resources are at a premium, and optimizing memory utilization is a critical consideration. Cloud computing platforms, where cost efficiency and resource optimization are paramount, may benefit from Best Fit to ensure efficient use of virtualized memory resources. However, the increased complexity and potentially slower allocation times associated with Best Fit need to be carefully weighed against the benefits of reduced fragmentation, especially in scenarios where rapid allocation is a secondary concern.

In scenarios where preserving larger free blocks for subsequent allocations takes precedence, Worst Fit may be a strategic choice. This strategy allocates the largest available block to a process, with the intention of minimizing external fragmentation and accommodating larger memory requests in the future. Use cases for Worst Fit can be found in systems where the allocation of sizable memory chunks is a common requirement, such as scientific simulations or simulations in physics and engineering. However, the potential for inefficient memory utilization due to internal fragmentation and the slower allocation times associated with searching for the largest available block necessitate a careful evaluation of the specific needs and trade-offs of the scenario.

Multi-process or multi-user environments introduce additional considerations into the decision-making process. In shared computing environments, where multiple processes or users concurrently access and utilize system resources, fairness and overall system responsiveness become key factors. First Fit's simplicity may make it suitable for scenarios where a balance between responsiveness and ease of implementation is crucial. Its quick allocation times and minimal overhead can contribute to a more responsive system in environments where the allocation of memory resources is not the primary bottleneck. However, the potential for fragmentation may lead to suboptimal memory usage over time, impacting overall system efficiency.

Best Fit, with its emphasis on minimizing fragmentation and efficient memory use, becomes valuable in shared environments where resource optimization is a priority. Time-sharing systems, where multiple users share the same computing resources, may benefit from Best Fit's ability to allocate memory in a manner that reduces wasted space and external fragmentation. The slightly increased allocation complexity and potential for slower allocation times may be deemed acceptable trade-offs in environments where memory efficiency and fair resource distribution take precedence.

Worst Fit, with its focus on preserving larger free blocks, may find application in scenarios where accommodating subsequent allocations of substantial memory chunks is critical. In environments where processes may have varying and unpredictable memory requirements, such as dynamic simulations or data-intensive processing tasks, Worst Fit's strategy of maintaining larger available blocks can be advantageous. However, the potential for internal fragmentation and the associated trade-offs in memory usage efficiency and allocation times need to be carefully considered in the context of the specific workload and system priorities.

The nature of the applications running in a given scenario also plays a pivotal role in determining the optimal memory allocation strategy. Applications with consistent and predictable memory requirements, such as embedded systems or dedicated utility programs, may find First Fit to be a suitable choice due to its simplicity and quick allocation times. In contrast, applications with dynamic and varying memory needs, such as data analytics tools or cloud-based services, may benefit from the adaptability of Best Fit, which strives to minimize fragmentation and optimize memory usage in the face of changing workloads.

Similarly, Worst Fit may be advantageous in applications with sporadic but substantial memory demands, where the preservation of larger free blocks can facilitate the efficient allocation of resources when needed. Real-time systems, where deterministic response times are crucial, may necessitate careful consideration of the allocation strategy. The inherent trade-offs between simplicity, fragmentation reduction, and adaptability become pronounced in these contexts, requiring a nuanced evaluation of the specific requirements and priorities of the application.

Cloud computing environments, characterized by dynamic workloads, scalability, and resource elasticity, introduce a unique set of considerations in the choice of memory allocation strategy. The ability to dynamically scale resources in response to changing demands is a defining feature of cloud computing. Best Fit, with its focus on fragmentation reduction and efficient memory usage, aligns well with the optimization goals of cloud environments. The dynamic nature of cloud workloads, where applications may experience fluctuations in user demand, benefits from the adaptability of Best Fit to efficiently allocate and deallocate memory resources as needed.

However, the decision in cloud computing is not a one-size-fits-all scenario. The choice of memory allocation strategy depends on the specific characteristics of the applications hosted in the cloud, the variability of workloads, and the overarching goals of the cloud infrastructure. Worst Fit, with its focus on preserving larger free blocks, may also find application in cloud environments where accommodating occasional substantial memory requests is a common requirement. The trade-offs between allocation speed, fragmentation reduction, and adaptability become integral considerations in the dynamic and diverse landscape of cloud computing.

The evolution of computing architectures, such as the transition to 64-bit systems, introduces additional considerations in the selection of memory allocation strategies. With 64-bit processors, systems can address larger memory spaces, providing an expanded canvas for memory-intensive applications. In this context, the efficiency of memory allocation becomes crucial for harnessing the full potential of the increased address space. The adaptability of Best Fit may be particularly relevant in scenarios where large-scale memory usage optimization is essential, leveraging the additional addressable space to allocate and deallocate memory dynamically.

Security considerations, an ever-present aspect of modern computing, further influence the choice of memory allocation strategy. Inadequate memory management can lead to vulnerabilities such as buffer overflows, which may be exploited by malicious actors. While the primary focus of memory allocation strategies is on optimizing memory usage and mitigating fragmentation, their impact on security cannot be ignored. The predictability introduced by certain allocation strategies, such as First Fit, may be leveraged by attackers to exploit vulnerabilities. Security mechanisms, including address space layout randomization (ASLR) and other techniques, contribute to the overall robustness and resilience of systems, ensuring that memory-related vulnerabilities are mitigated irrespective of the chosen allocation strategy.

In conclusion, selecting the optimal memory allocation strategy for specific scenarios is a complex decision-making process that involves a careful weighing of trade-offs and considerations. The characteristics of the computing environment, the nature of applications, multi-process or multi-user dynamics, and overarching system goals all play pivotal roles in shaping this decision. Each memory allocation strategy—First Fit, Best Fit, and Worst Fit—offers unique advantages and drawbacks, making them suitable for different scenarios. The choice involves a nuanced evaluation of factors such as simplicity, allocation speed, fragmentation reduction, memory efficiency, adaptability to dynamic workloads, and security considerations. As computing environments continue to evolve, the optimal selection of memory allocation strategies remains integral to achieving an optimal balance between system performance, adaptability, and security in diverse and dynamic scenarios.

Understanding fragmentation challenges.

Fragmentation poses multifaceted challenges across various domains, encompassing technology, ecosystems, societies, and beyond. In the realm of technology, particularly within the field of computing, fragmentation emerges as a significant hurdle. Operating systems, software applications, and hardware components often undergo divergent paths, leading to a splintered landscape where interoperability becomes a daunting task. This technological fragmentation not only complicates seamless integration but also demands additional resources for developers who must navigate a maze of different standards, protocols, and platforms. The ensuing inefficiencies impede progress, hinder innovation, and result in suboptimal user experiences.

Within ecosystems, fragmentation can manifest in ecological niches, where isolated populations of species develop unique traits, sometimes leading to speciation. While biodiversity is generally considered beneficial, fragmentation can threaten the stability of ecosystems by disrupting the natural flow of energy and resources. This disruption can have cascading effects, impacting the intricate web of relationships between species and compromising the resilience of ecosystems in the face of environmental changes.

In societal contexts, fragmentation manifests in the form of social divisions and disparities. Cultural, economic, and political fragmentation can sow the seeds of discord, hampering social cohesion and fostering a sense of isolation among different groups. This division can lead to polarization, where individuals and communities retreat into their respective echo chambers, amplifying existing prejudices and inhibiting the exchange of diverse perspectives. Such societal fragmentation can have profound implications for governance, as it becomes challenging to establish common ground and implement inclusive policies that address the needs of a heterogeneous population.

Moreover, the digital age has ushered in a new dimension of fragmentation—information fragmentation. The proliferation of online platforms, each catering to specific interests or ideologies, has contributed to the segmentation of information consumption. This phenomenon gives rise to echo chambers, where individuals are exposed primarily to information that aligns with their preexisting beliefs, reinforcing cognitive biases and hindering a comprehensive understanding of complex issues. Information fragmentation thus poses a threat to the foundation of an informed and engaged citizenry, vital for the functioning of democratic societies.

Economic fragmentation is another facet of this multifaceted challenge. In the globalized world, economic systems are interconnected, but disparities in wealth distribution, trade policies, and resource allocation create fragmentation in economic opportunities. This economic disjunction can lead to unequal access to resources, hindering the development of marginalized communities and exacerbating social inequalities. The resulting economic fragmentation not only stymies sustainable development but also undermines the potential for global collaboration to address pressing issues such as climate change and public health crises.

In the realm of healthcare, fragmentation poses substantial obstacles to the delivery of effective and coordinated medical services. Healthcare systems often suffer from disjointed information systems, making it difficult for healthcare providers to access comprehensive patient data. This lack of interoperability can compromise patient care, leading to suboptimal outcomes and increased healthcare costs. Additionally, fragmented healthcare policies and disparities in access to medical resources can contribute to unequal health outcomes, further exacerbating social and economic inequalities.

Environmental fragmentation, particularly in the context of urban planning and land use, is a critical concern. Urbanization and infrastructure development can lead to the fragmentation of natural habitats, disrupting ecosystems and threatening biodiversity. Fragmented landscapes can impede the movement of wildlife, reducing genetic diversity and increasing the vulnerability of species to environmental changes. This ecological fragmentation not only jeopardizes the delicate balance of ecosystems but also poses long-term risks to the sustainability of our planet.

Addressing the challenges posed by fragmentation requires a holistic and interdisciplinary approach. In the technological realm, efforts to standardize protocols, promote open-source collaboration, and encourage cross-platform compatibility can mitigate the adverse effects of technological fragmentation. Similarly, in ecosystems, conservation strategies that focus on creating connected corridors to facilitate the movement of species can help counteract the negative impacts of habitat fragmentation.

Societal challenges stemming from fragmentation necessitate concerted efforts to bridge divides, promote inclusivity, and foster a sense of shared identity. Initiatives that prioritize dialogue, cultural exchange, and education can contribute to breaking down social barriers and building bridges between diverse communities. Tackling information fragmentation requires promoting media literacy, encouraging diverse media sources, and developing platforms that facilitate exposure to a variety of perspectives.

Economic disparities and fragmentation can be addressed through inclusive economic policies, social safety nets, and initiatives that empower marginalized communities. Global cooperation and fair trade practices are essential to mitigating economic fragmentation on a global scale. In healthcare, the adoption of interoperable health information systems, standardized protocols, and equitable healthcare policies can enhance the continuity and quality of patient care.

Environmental challenges arising from fragmentation demand sustainable urban planning, conservation efforts, and policies that prioritize the preservation of natural habitats. Balancing human development with ecological preservation is crucial to minimizing the negative impacts of environmental fragmentation.

In conclusion, fragmentation presents a pervasive and interconnected challenge across technological, ecological, societal, economic, healthcare, and environmental domains. Recognizing the intricate web of relationships between these different facets of fragmentation is imperative for devising effective solutions. By fostering collaboration, promoting inclusivity, and prioritizing sustainability, societies can strive towards overcoming the challenges posed by fragmentation and building a more interconnected and resilient world.

Techniques to minimize fragmentation.

Minimizing fragmentation across diverse domains necessitates a multifaceted approach that addresses technological, ecological, societal, economic, healthcare, and environmental challenges. In the technological sphere, standardization emerges as a paramount technique to mitigate fragmentation. Establishing common protocols, formats, and interoperability standards can streamline communication and collaboration among different systems, software applications, and hardware components. Open-source development models, which promote transparency and collaborative innovation, also play a pivotal role in reducing technological fragmentation by fostering a shared foundation for development.

Furthermore, in the ecosystem domain, conservation strategies aimed at maintaining connectivity between habitats represent a crucial technique to counteract fragmentation. Creating wildlife corridors, protected areas, and sustainable land-use planning can facilitate the movement of species, preserving genetic diversity and restoring ecological balance. Emphasizing the importance of preserving natural habitats and biodiversity in urban planning and infrastructure development is essential for mitigating environmental fragmentation.

On a societal level, techniques to minimize fragmentation involve fostering inclusivity, dialogue, and understanding among diverse communities. Educational initiatives that promote cultural exchange, diversity appreciation, and mutual respect can help bridge societal divides. Platforms and forums that encourage open discourse, where individuals with varying perspectives can engage in constructive dialogue, contribute to breaking down echo chambers and combating social fragmentation.

In the economic realm, addressing disparities requires the implementation of inclusive policies and social safety nets. Efforts to promote fair trade practices, international cooperation, and equitable resource allocation can mitigate economic fragmentation on a global scale. Empowering marginalized communities through targeted economic development initiatives and access to education and opportunities is crucial for creating a more balanced and integrated economic landscape.

In healthcare, minimizing fragmentation involves the adoption of interoperable health information systems and standardized protocols. Creating a unified and comprehensive approach to patient data management ensures that healthcare providers can access relevant information efficiently, leading to improved patient care. Additionally, implementing equitable healthcare policies that prioritize accessibility and affordability can contribute to reducing disparities and fragmentation within healthcare systems.

Tackling information fragmentation requires concerted efforts to enhance media literacy and promote diverse media sources. Initiatives that encourage critical thinking, fact-checking, and exposure to a variety of perspectives can help individuals navigate the information landscape more effectively. Developing platforms that facilitate the dissemination of accurate and diverse information while discouraging the spread of misinformation is crucial for combating information fragmentation.

Environmental techniques to minimize fragmentation involve sustainable land-use planning, conservation efforts, and policies that prioritize ecological preservation. Balancing human development with the protection of natural habitats requires strategic approaches to minimize the impact of urbanization on ecosystems. Implementing measures to restore fragmented landscapes, such as reforestation and habitat restoration projects, contributes to the overall resilience and sustainability of the environment.

In conclusion, minimizing fragmentation requires a comprehensive and coordinated effort across various domains. Standardization, conservation strategies, inclusivity, and equitable policies are essential techniques that can be applied to address fragmentation in technology, ecosystems, societies, economies, healthcare, and the environment. By embracing these techniques, societies can work towards creating a more interconnected and harmonious world, fostering collaboration and resilience in the face of complex challenges.

Compaction and its role in handling fragmentation.

Compaction plays a pivotal role in addressing fragmentation, a pervasive challenge across diverse domains such as technology, databases, file systems, and memory management. In the context of databases, compaction refers to the process of reorganizing and optimizing stored data to reduce fragmentation and enhance efficiency. Database systems often encounter fragmentation due to frequent inserts, updates, and deletes, leading to scattered and non-contiguous data. Compaction helps consolidate and organize data, mitigating the inefficiencies caused by fragmented storage structures. By rearranging data blocks and reclaiming unused space, compaction improves data access performance, reduces storage overhead, and facilitates more effective resource utilization within databases.

In the realm of file systems, compaction is a strategy employed to consolidate fragmented files on storage devices. As files are created, modified, and deleted, free space becomes scattered across the storage medium, resulting in fragmented file allocations. Compaction involves rearranging file fragments and freeing up contiguous space, minimizing seek times and enhancing overall file system performance. This process is particularly beneficial for storage devices with limited sequential access capabilities, such as hard disk drives (HDDs). Efficient compaction strategies contribute to faster file retrieval and improved system responsiveness, promoting a more streamlined and reliable file storage environment.

Memory management systems also leverage compaction techniques to address fragmentation challenges. In this context, fragmentation can occur as a result of memory allocations and deallocations, leading to fragmented free memory blocks. Compaction involves rearranging the allocated and free memory regions to create larger contiguous blocks. This helps alleviate external fragmentation, where free memory is dispersed throughout the address space. By compacting memory, the system can provide more contiguous blocks for new allocations, reducing the likelihood of allocation failures and improving overall memory utilization efficiency.

In the context of programming languages and compilers, compaction may refer to optimizing code to minimize memory footprint and enhance execution efficiency. Compilers often employ techniques like code folding, dead code elimination, and loop unrolling to compact the generated machine code, reducing the program's memory requirements and improving runtime performance. This form of compaction is essential for resource-constrained environments, such as embedded systems or mobile devices, where efficient memory utilization is critical.

In the broader domain of technology, compaction is crucial for managing data in storage devices. Solid-state drives (SSDs), for instance, benefit from compaction strategies to optimize wear leveling and extend the lifespan of the storage medium. Compaction in this context involves redistributing data evenly across the storage cells, preventing uneven wear on specific blocks and ensuring a more uniform utilization of the SSD's available capacity.

Beyond technology, compaction also plays a role in ecological and urban planning. Ecological compaction involves designing urban spaces to minimize fragmentation of natural habitats, creating interconnected green corridors and wildlife-friendly landscapes. This approach helps preserve biodiversity by facilitating the movement of species across urban areas, counteracting the negative impacts of habitat fragmentation caused by urbanization.

In conclusion, compaction serves as a versatile and indispensable tool across various domains to handle fragmentation effectively. Whether applied in databases, file systems, memory management, programming languages, or urban planning, compaction techniques contribute to optimizing resource utilization, improving performance, and mitigating the challenges posed by fragmented structures. As technology continues to evolve and interdisciplinary applications of compaction techniques emerge, their role in addressing fragmentation becomes increasingly central to achieving efficiency and sustainability in diverse systems and environments.

Identifying causes and consequences of memory leaks.

Memory leaks represent a persistent and challenging issue in software development, where the identification of causes and consequences is crucial for maintaining robust and efficient applications. One of the primary causes of memory leaks lies in improper memory management practices within a program. When developers allocate memory dynamically for data structures or objects but fail to release or deallocate it when it is no longer needed, memory leaks occur. This oversight can result from coding errors, such as forgetting to free allocated memory or losing references to objects, preventing the automatic garbage collection mechanisms from reclaiming unused memory. Inadequate error handling and lack of thorough testing can exacerbate the likelihood of such issues going unnoticed during development.

Consequences of memory leaks extend beyond the immediate impact on system resources. One notable consequence is the gradual degradation of application performance over time. As a program continues to run, unreleased memory accumulates, leading to increased memory consumption. This can result in heightened demand on system resources, causing slowdowns, responsiveness issues, and even system crashes. In long-running processes, such as server applications or services, the cumulative effect of memory leaks can lead to a gradual deterioration of system stability, negatively impacting user experience and overall system reliability.

Another significant consequence of memory leaks is the potential for increased operational costs. The continuous allocation of memory without proper deallocation can strain hardware resources, leading to the need for more extensive and powerful hardware to support the growing memory demands. This, in turn, escalates infrastructure costs, as organizations may need to invest in additional server capacity or memory resources to accommodate the escalating memory usage. Additionally, the time and effort required to identify and rectify memory leaks during the development and maintenance phases contribute to increased labor costs, making effective memory management a critical consideration for both economic and operational reasons.

Security vulnerabilities represent another serious consequence of memory leaks. When sensitive information, such as passwords or cryptographic keys, is stored in memory but not properly released, it becomes susceptible to unauthorized access. Memory leaks can inadvertently expose critical data to attackers who exploit the vulnerabilities to gain unauthorized access or compromise the integrity of the application. Thus, addressing memory leaks is not only crucial for system performance but also for safeguarding sensitive information and maintaining the security of applications, particularly in contexts where data privacy and confidentiality are paramount.

Furthermore, memory leaks can have implications for scalability, especially in applications designed to handle multiple concurrent users or processes. As memory leaks accumulate over time, the scalability of an application becomes compromised. The increased memory consumption may limit the number of simultaneous users an application can support, hindering its ability to scale efficiently. This limitation can have far-reaching consequences for businesses and organizations that rely on scalable applications, impacting their ability to handle growing workloads and adapt to changing user demands.

In the context of embedded systems and resource-constrained environments, memory leaks pose a unique set of challenges. These systems often operate with limited memory resources, and unchecked memory leaks can quickly deplete the available memory, leading to system instability or failure. In scenarios where devices have restricted memory capacity, such as Internet of Things (IoT) devices or embedded controllers, memory leaks become even more critical to address, as they can directly impact the functionality and reliability of the entire system.

Identifying the causes of memory leaks involves thorough debugging and profiling techniques. Memory profiling tools help developers analyze the memory usage patterns of an application, pinpointing areas where memory is allocated but not released. Techniques such as static code analysis and runtime analysis can aid in detecting memory leaks early in the development process. Additionally, the use of memory debugging tools and runtime monitoring can provide valuable insights into memory allocation and deallocation behavior during the execution of the program.

Once identified, addressing memory leaks requires a systematic approach to memory management. Adopting best practices, such as proper resource deallocation, reference counting, and effective garbage collection, is essential for preventing memory leaks in the first place. Regular code reviews, testing, and continuous integration practices can help catch memory leaks during the development life-cycle, reducing the likelihood of these issues making their way into production environments.

In conclusion, understanding the causes and consequences of memory leaks is integral to building resilient and efficient software systems. Causes often stem from inadequate memory management practices, coding errors, and insufficient testing, while consequences manifest in degraded performance, increased operational costs, se-curity vulnerabilities, scalability limitations, and challenges in re-source-constrained environments. Addressing memory leaks re-quires a proactive and systematic approach that encompasses debug-ging, profiling, and adopting best practices in memory management throughout the software development lifecycle. As software appli-cations continue to grow in complexity and scale, the importance of mitigating memory leaks becomes increasingly critical for ensur-ing the reliability, security, and performance of modern software sys-tems.

Chapter 3: Memory Paging and Segmentation

Defining memory paging and its purpose.

Memory paging is a fundamental concept in computer systems that involves the division of physical memory into fixed-size blocks called pages. These pages serve as a mechanism for managing the transfer of data between the primary storage (RAM) and secondary storage (typically, a hard disk or solid-state drive). The primary purpose of memory paging is to facilitate efficient memory management by allowing the operating system to selectively load and unload pages of data into and from physical memory, based on the current requirements of running processes.

The concept of memory paging is closely tied to the notion of virtual memory, a technique employed by operating systems to provide the illusion of a larger address space than the physical memory available. In a virtual memory system, each process is allocated its own address space, referred to as virtual address space. This address space is divided into fixed-size units known as pages, which correspond to the pages in physical memory. The operating system, through a component called the Memory Management Unit (MMU), is responsible for mapping the virtual addresses used by processes to the corresponding physical addresses in the underlying physical memory.

When a process is initiated, not all of its pages need to be loaded into physical memory immediately. Instead, the operating system can use memory paging to selectively bring in only the pages that are actively being accessed or modified. This process is known as demand paging, and it plays a crucial role in optimizing memory utilization. By loading only the necessary pages into RAM, demand paging minimizes the wasteful use of resources and allows for more efficient management of available memory.

One of the key advantages of memory paging is its ability to overcome the limitations imposed by physical memory constraints. In scenarios where the total memory required by all running processes exceeds the available physical memory, the operating system can use paging to swap pages in and out of secondary storage as needed. This technique is known as page swapping or page fault handling. When a process attempts to access a page that is not currently in physical memory, a page fault occurs. The operating system responds by bringing the required page into memory from secondary storage, possibly swapping out a less frequently used page to make room. This dynamic swapping of pages allows the system to effectively utilize secondary storage as an extension of physical memory, mitigating the impact of limited RAM on overall system performance.

Memory paging also plays a crucial role in supporting the sharing of code and data among multiple processes. In a multitasking environment, where multiple processes run concurrently, there is often a need for efficiency in memory utilization. Rather than duplicating the same code or data in multiple locations in physical memory, the operating system can use memory paging to allow multiple processes to share common pages. This is achieved through a technique called shared memory, where multiple processes are granted access to the same physical pages in RAM, reducing redundancy and conserving valuable memory resources.

Furthermore, memory paging contributes to the concept of Copy-On-Write (COW), a strategy that enhances efficiency in managing memory resources. When a process forks (creates a copy of itself), the child process initially shares the same memory pages as the parent process. However, with the COW mechanism, the operating system only duplicates the pages that are modified by either the parent or the child process. Until a modification occurs, both processes continue to share the same physical pages. This approach minimizes the immediate memory overhead associated with process creation and supports resource-efficient forking in modern operating systems.

In addition to its role in addressing memory constraints and optimizing memory utilization, memory paging provides benefits in terms of memory protection and security. By assigning different access permissions to pages (such as read-only, read-write, or execute-only), the operating system can implement memory protection mechanisms. Unauthorized attempts to modify or execute certain pages result in memory protection faults, allowing the operating system to enforce security policies and prevent unintended interference between processes.

While memory paging offers numerous advantages, it is not without its challenges. The most notable challenge is the potential for increased I/O (input/output) operations due to page swapping between primary and secondary storage. Excessive paging, commonly referred to as thrashing, occurs when the system spends a significant amount of time transferring pages between RAM and disk, leading to a degradation in overall performance. To mitigate thrashing, modern operating systems employ various algorithms, such as the Least Recently Used (LRU) algorithm, to make intelligent decisions about which pages to keep in physical memory and which to swap out.

In conclusion, memory paging is a foundational concept in computer systems that enables efficient memory management, supports virtual memory, and addresses the challenges posed by limited physical memory. Its purpose extends to optimizing memory utilization, overcoming memory constraints, facilitating demand paging and page swapping, supporting shared memory and Copy-On-Write mechanisms, and enhancing memory protection and security. While memory paging introduces complexities, especially in scenarios of thrashing, its careful implementation and integration within modern operating systems contribute significantly to the stability, performance, and scalability of computer systems in a wide range of computing environments.

The role of page tables in mapping memory.

Page tables play a fundamental role in the intricate process of mapping memory in computer systems, forming a crucial component of the virtual memory management subsystem. The concept of page tables is essential for efficiently translating virtual addresses used by processes into corresponding physical addresses in the underlying physical memory (RAM). This translation is imperative in a virtual memory system, where the address space perceived by a process, known as the virtual address space, often exceeds the available physical memory. The page table acts as a vital intermediary, facilitating this translation and enabling the seamless interaction between the logical address space and the physical memory space.

At its core, a page table is a data structure maintained by the operating system to keep track of the mapping between virtual pages and physical frames. In a virtual memory system, both the virtual address space and physical memory are divided into fixed-size units called pages and frames, respectively. The page table stores the mapping information, indicating which virtual pages correspond to which physical frames. The size of each page and frame is typically determined by the hardware architecture and the operating system.

The process of mapping a virtual address to a physical address begins with the generation of a virtual address by a process. The virtual address is composed of two components: a page number and an offset within that page. The page number serves as an index into the page table, allowing the operating system to retrieve the corresponding entry. Each entry in the page table contains the frame number in physical memory to which the virtual page is mapped. The offset within the page remains unchanged during the translation, signifying the location within the chosen physical frame.

One of the key advantages of using page tables is the ability to provide each process with its own isolated virtual address space. This isolation is crucial for maintaining security and preventing processes from interfering with each other's memory. Each process operates within its dedicated virtual address space, blissfully unaware of the underlying physical memory layout. The page table ensures that the mapping between virtual and physical addresses remains unique to each process, safeguarding the integrity and privacy of their respective memory spaces.

Page tables also contribute significantly to the concept of demand paging, a strategy aimed at optimizing memory usage by loading into physical memory only the pages that are actively being used. When a process attempts to access a virtual page that is not currently in physical memory, a page fault occurs. The page table, in conjunction with the operating system's memory manager, handles this situation by loading the required page from secondary storage (such as a hard disk) into an available physical frame. The page table is then updated to reflect the new mapping, allowing the process to continue execution seamlessly.

In multiprogramming environments where multiple processes share the same physical memory, the page table plays a critical role in facilitating the illusion of independent and expansive address spaces for each process. Through the use of a Memory Management Unit (MMU), the page table ensures that virtual addresses generated by different processes are correctly translated to their corresponding physical addresses. This enables the concurrent execution of multiple processes without the need for each process to be aware of the others' memory layouts, fostering a more efficient and secure computing environment.

Page tables are not without their challenges, particularly in terms of efficiency and memory overhead. As the size of the virtual address space and the number of processes increase, the page table grows in size. Large page tables can consume a considerable amount of memory, impacting the overall efficiency of the system. To address this issue, hierarchical page table structures are often employed. In a hierarchical page table, the page table entries themselves form a tree-like structure, allowing for more efficient use of memory and faster lookups. This hierarchical organization enables the system to locate the relevant page table entry more quickly, mitigating the impact of large address spaces on performance.

Translation Lookaside Buffers (TLBs) are another crucial element that works in conjunction with page tables to optimize memory access times. TLBs store recently used virtual-to-physical address mappings, allowing the system to bypass the time-consuming process of searching the page table for frequently accessed pages. TLBs provide a high-speed cache for these mappings, significantly improving the efficiency of the virtual-to-physical address translation process.

In conclusion, page tables are instrumental in the complex task of mapping memory in computer systems, acting as a bridge between the logical, virtual address space perceived by processes and the physical memory space. They facilitate the translation of virtual addresses to corresponding physical addresses, enabling the efficient utilization of virtual memory and supporting essential concepts such as demand paging and multiprogramming. Despite challenges related to memory overhead, innovative solutions like hierarchical page table structures and TLBs contribute to the overall optimization and performance of the memory management subsystem. As a cornerstone of virtual memory systems, page tables play a pivotal role in ensuring the seamless, secure, and efficient operation of modern computer systems.

Benefits and challenges of memory paging.

Memory paging, a fundamental aspect of virtual memory management in computer systems, brings forth a myriad of benefits and challenges that significantly impact the efficiency, scalability, and overall performance of modern computing environments. One of the primary advantages of memory paging lies in its ability to provide the illusion of a larger address space than the physical memory available. This is achieved by dividing the virtual address space into fixed-size units called pages, which are then mapped to corresponding physical frames in the underlying physical memory. As a result, processes can operate within expansive virtual address spaces, even if the physical memory is limited. This abstraction allows for the concurrent execution of multiple processes, contributing to the versatility and multitasking capabilities of modern operating systems.

A key benefit of memory paging is its role in demand paging, a strategy that optimizes memory usage by loading into physical memory only the pages that are actively being used. When a process attempts to access a virtual page not currently in physical memory, a page fault occurs. The operating system, in collaboration with the page table and memory manager, can dynamically load the required page from secondary storage into available physical frames. This on-demand loading minimizes the wasteful use of memory resources, ensuring that only the necessary data is resident in physical memory at any given time. Consequently, demand paging contributes to the efficient utilization of memory, allowing for the execution of processes that might otherwise be constrained by physical memory limitations.

Furthermore, memory paging facilitates the concept of shared memory, enabling multiple processes to share common pages in physical memory. This shared memory mechanism supports efficient communication and data exchange between processes, eliminating the need for redundant copies of the same data. Processes can coordinate and collaborate by accessing shared data structures stored in shared memory pages, leading to enhanced efficiency in resource utilization and streamlined inter-process communication.

Memory paging also plays a pivotal role in the Copy-On-Write (COW) mechanism, particularly when processes fork (create copies of themselves). Initially, the child process shares the same physical pages with the parent process. Only when either the parent or the child process modifies a shared page does the operating system duplicate the page, ensuring that each process has its own writable copy. This COW strategy minimizes the immediate memory overhead associated with process creation, contributing to the efficiency and speed of forking operations in modern operating systems.

In terms of security, memory paging supports the implementation of memory protection mechanisms. By assigning different access permissions (such as read-only, read-write, or execute-only) to pages, the operating system can control the level of access processes have to specific regions of memory. Unauthorized attempts to modify or execute certain pages result in memory protection faults, allowing the operating system to enforce security policies and prevent unintended interference between processes. This granular control over memory access enhances the overall security and integrity of the computing environment.

Despite these benefits, memory paging is not without its challenges. One of the primary challenges is the potential for increased Input/Output (I/O) operations due to page swapping between primary and secondary storage. Excessive paging, commonly referred to as thrashing, occurs when the system spends a significant amount of time transferring pages between Random Access Memory (RAM) and disk. Thrashing can severely degrade system performance, leading to sluggish responsiveness and decreased throughput. To address thrashing, modern operating systems employ various algorithms, such as the Least Recently Used (LRU) algorithm, to make intelligent decisions about which pages to keep in physical memory and which to swap out.

Another challenge associated with memory paging is the memory overhead introduced by large page tables. As the size of the virtual address space and the number of processes increase, the page table grows in size. Large page tables can consume a considerable amount of memory, impacting the overall efficiency of the system. To mitigate this issue, hierarchical page table structures are often employed. In a hierarchical page table, the page table entries themselves form a tree-like structure, allowing for more efficient use of memory and faster lookups. This hierarchical organization enables the system to locate the relevant page table entry more quickly, mitigating the impact of large address spaces on performance.

Additionally, the use of Translation Lookaside Buffers (TLBs) in conjunction with page tables introduces complexities and trade-offs. TLBs serve as high-speed caches for recently used virtual-to-physical address mappings, significantly improving the efficiency of address translation. However, TLBs have a limited capacity, and misses occur when the required mapping is not found in the TLB. TLB misses lead to additional overhead as the system must consult the page table to find the correct mapping. Efficient TLB management and replacement policies are essential to mitigate the impact of TLB misses on system performance.

In conclusion, memory paging brings forth a range of benefits and challenges that shape the landscape of virtual memory management in computer systems. The advantages include the provision of expansive virtual address spaces, support for demand paging, shared memory mechanisms, and the Copy-On-Write strategy, contributing to the versatility and efficiency of modern operating systems. However, challenges such as thrashing, memory overhead associated with large page tables, and complexities introduced by TLBs require careful consideration and effective mitigation strategies. Balancing the benefits and challenges of memory paging is essential for achieving optimal system performance, scalability, and resource utilization in diverse computing environments.

Understanding memory segmentation principles.

Memory segmentation, a memory management technique, plays a significant role in organizing and structuring the memory space of a computer system. Unlike the more common memory management method, paging, segmentation divides the address space into variable-sized segments, each serving a specific purpose or containing a specific type of data. This approach allows for a more flexible and intuitive organization of memory, catering to the diverse requirements of modern computing systems.

At its core, memory segmentation involves dividing the logical address space into segments, where each segment represents a distinct region with a unique identifier and a defined purpose. These segments can be of varying sizes, accommodating the specific needs of different parts of a program or data structures. For example, a program may have separate segments for code, data, and stack, each with its own size and characteristics.

One fundamental concept within memory segmentation is the use of segment registers to keep track of the starting address of each segment. These registers store the base address of the segment, allowing the system to determine the location of a specific segment within the overall address space. Additionally, a limit register is often employed to specify the size of each segment, defining the range of valid addresses within that segment. The combination of the segment base and limit registers facilitates the translation of logical addresses to physical addresses, ensuring that memory references stay within the bounds of the allocated segments.

The segmentation process involves the generation of logical addresses by a program, where each address is composed of two components: a segment identifier and an offset within that segment. The segment identifier serves as an index into a segment table or descriptor table, where the corresponding segment base and limit information is stored. The offset within the segment signifies the specific location within the chosen segment. By combining the base address of the segment with the offset, the system can calculate the physical address in the underlying physical memory.

One of the key advantages of memory segmentation is its support for a modular and hierarchical organization of code and data. In a program, different segments can represent distinct modules or functions, allowing for a more modular and maintainable code structure. Similarly, data structures can be organized into separate segments, enhancing clarity and facilitating more straightforward memory management. This modular organization aligns well with the principles of software engineering, where the separation of concerns and the modularization of code contribute to better code readability, reusability, and maintainability.

Furthermore, segmentation facilitates the implementation of protection mechanisms and access control. Each segment can be assigned specific access rights, such as read-only, read-write, or execute-only. These access rights are enforced by the system, preventing unauthorized access or modification of segments by processes or users. Protection mechanisms contribute to the security and reliability of the system, ensuring the integrity of code and data and preventing unintended interference between different segments.

Despite its benefits, memory segmentation is not without its challenges. One significant limitation is the potential for fragmentation, both external and internal. External fragmentation occurs when free memory is scattered throughout the address space, making it challenging to allocate contiguous segments. Internal fragmentation, on the other hand, arises when a segment is allocated more memory than it needs, leading to wasted space within the segment. These forms of fragmentation can impact system performance, as they may require more extensive memory management and compaction efforts to maintain efficient memory utilization.

To address fragmentation concerns, some systems implement segmentation with paging, combining the benefits of both techniques. This hybrid approach, known as segmented paging, divides the logical address space into segments and further subdivides each segment into fixed-sized pages. This allows for the flexibility of segmentation while mitigating external fragmentation through the use of paging. The combination of segmentation and paging is particularly advantageous in systems with varying memory requirements for different types of data and code.

Another challenge associated with memory segmentation is the complexity introduced in the translation process. Unlike paging, where fixed-size pages simplify the translation of addresses, segmentation requires additional calculations involving segment base and limit values. These calculations add overhead to the address translation process, potentially impacting system performance. Efficient algorithms and hardware support, such as segment registers and segment tables, are crucial for minimizing this overhead and ensuring a swift and accurate translation process.

In conclusion, memory segmentation is a versatile memory management technique that offers flexibility, modularity, and protection mechanisms in organizing the address space of a computer system. Its support for modular code and data organization aligns well with the principles of software engineering, promoting maintainability and readability. However, challenges such as fragmentation and increased complexity in address translation need to be carefully addressed. Hybrid approaches, such as segmented paging, showcase the adaptability of memory management techniques to diverse computing requirements. As computing systems continue to evolve, the principles of memory segmentation remain relevant, contributing to the efficient and secure organization of memory in modern computer architectures.

Advantages and disadvantages of segmentation.

Memory segmentation, as a memory management technique, presents a set of advantages and disadvantages that significantly influence the design and performance of computer systems. Understanding these aspects is crucial for architects, developers, and system administrators seeking to optimize the use of memory resources while addressing the challenges inherent to segmentation.

One notable advantage of memory segmentation lies in its ability to support a modular and hierarchical organization of code and data within a program. By dividing the logical address space into variable-sized segments, each serving a distinct purpose or containing a specific type of data, segmentation enables a more flexible and intuitive organization of memory. This modularity aligns well with software engineering principles, allowing developers to compartmentalize different aspects of a program, such as code, data, and stack, into separate segments. This modular organization enhances code readability, maintainability, and reusability by isolating different functionalities and components, contributing to more scalable and manageable software systems.

Furthermore, segmentation facilitates the implementation of protection mechanisms and access control. Each segment can be assigned specific access rights, such as read-only, read-write, or execute-only. These access rights are enforced by the system, preventing unauthorized access or modification of segments by processes or users. This granular control over memory access contributes to the security and reliability of the system, ensuring the integrity of code and data and preventing unintended interference between different segments. Protection mechanisms are particularly crucial in multi-user environments, where processes with different privilege levels share the same physical memory.

Another advantage of memory segmentation is its support for demand paging. Demand paging is a strategy that optimizes memory usage by loading into physical memory only the pages that are actively being used. Segmentation facilitates demand paging by allowing the loading and unloading of entire segments, which can include both code and data, based on the requirements of the executing processes. This dynamic loading minimizes the wasteful use of memory resources, ensuring that only the necessary data is resident in physical memory at any given time. Consequently, demand paging contributes to the efficient utilization of memory, allowing for the execution of processes that might otherwise be constrained by physical memory limitations.

However, memory segmentation comes with its share of disadvantages, with fragmentation being a prominent concern. Fragmentation can manifest in two forms: external fragmentation and internal fragmentation. External fragmentation occurs when free memory is scattered throughout the address space, making it challenging to allocate contiguous segments. Internal fragmentation arises when a segment is allocated more memory than it needs, leading to wasted space within the segment. These forms of fragmentation can impact system performance, as they may require more extensive memory management and compaction efforts to maintain efficient memory utilization. The challenge is particularly pronounced in scenarios where processes have varying memory requirements, leading to a fragmented memory layout.

To address the issue of fragmentation, some systems employ a combination of segmentation and paging, known as segmented paging. Segmented paging subdivides each segment into fixed-sized pages, introducing the benefits of both segmentation and paging while mitigating external fragmentation. This hybrid approach combines the flexibility of segmentation with the efficient memory utilization and address translation simplicity offered by paging. Segmented paging is particularly advantageous in systems with diverse memory requirements for different types of data and code.

Another disadvantage of memory segmentation is the increased complexity introduced in the translation process. Unlike paging, where fixed-size pages simplify the translation of addresses, segmentation requires additional calculations involving segment base and limit values. These calculations add overhead to the address translation process, potentially impacting system performance. Efficient algorithms and hardware support, such as segment registers and segment tables, are crucial for minimizing this overhead and ensuring a swift and accurate translation process. The complexity of address translation in segmented memory management systems can pose challenges for system designers aiming to balance performance and simplicity.

Moreover, segmentation can complicate the implementation of shared memory and inter-process communication. While segmentation allows for the isolation of code and data within a process, sharing data between processes or allowing processes to communicate may require additional mechanisms. Coordinating the sharing of segments across multiple processes introduces synchronization challenges and necessitates careful consideration of data consistency and access control. Shared memory mechanisms in segmented systems demand robust coordination to prevent conflicts and ensure the reliable exchange of information between processes.

In conclusion, memory segmentation offers advantages in terms of modularity, protection mechanisms, and support for demand paging. Its ability to organize code and data into separate segments aligns well with software engineering principles, contributing to the development of scalable and maintainable software systems. However, segmentation comes with challenges, including fragmentation concerns and increased complexity in the address translation process. The disadvantages underscore the importance of thoughtful system design and optimization strategies, such as the adoption of hybrid approaches like segmented paging, to address the limitations and enhance the overall efficiency of memory management in diverse computing environments.

Combining paging and segmentation for optimized memory use.

Combining paging and segmentation represents a sophisticated approach to memory management that aims to harness the benefits of both techniques while mitigating their individual limitations. In this integrated model, known as segmented paging, the virtual address space is organized into variable-sized segments, each serving a specific purpose or containing a specific type of data. Within each segment, fixed-sized pages are employed to enhance address translation simplicity, facilitate demand paging, and address the challenges associated with fragmentation. The synergistic integration of these two memory management paradigms aims to optimize memory utilization, enhance system performance, and provide a versatile framework for accommodating the diverse requirements of modern computing environments.

One of the primary advantages of the segmented paging model is its ability to offer the flexibility and modularity of segmentation while leveraging the simplicity and efficiency of paging. Segmentation allows the logical address space to be divided into segments, each with its unique characteristics and purpose. This modular organization aligns well with software engineering principles, enabling developers to compartmentalize different aspects of a program, such as code, data, and stack, into separate segments. Meanwhile, the use of fixed-sized pages within each segment simplifies the translation of virtual addresses to physical addresses, providing a level of uniformity that facilitates efficient memory management and hardware support.

Segmented paging effectively addresses the challenges posed by fragmentation, a concern inherent in both segmentation and paging. External fragmentation, caused by scattered free memory throughout the address space, is mitigated by the fixed-sized pages within each segment. By using pages, the system can allocate contiguous blocks of memory within segments, reducing the likelihood of external fragmentation. Additionally, the use of paging helps alleviate internal fragmentation, a concern within segments where allocated memory may exceed the actual needs of a process. Fixed-sized pages ensure that only the necessary amount of memory is allocated, minimizing wasted space and promoting efficient memory utilization.

The integration of segmentation and paging also contributes to the support of demand paging, a strategy that optimizes memory usage by loading into physical memory only the pages that are actively being used. Demand paging is facilitated by the modularity of segments, allowing for the loading and unloading of entire segments based on the requirements of executing processes. This dynamic loading minimizes the wasteful use of memory resources, ensuring that only the necessary data is resident in physical memory at any given time. Consequently, demand paging contributes to the efficient utilization of memory, allowing for the execution of processes that might otherwise be constrained by physical memory limitations.

Efficient address translation is a critical aspect of any memory management system, and the segmented paging model is designed to strike a balance between simplicity and performance. In this approach, the translation of logical addresses to physical addresses involves two steps: first translating the virtual address to a linear address using the segment table, and then mapping the linear address to a physical address using the page table. The segment table provides the base address and limit of each segment, while the page table specifies the frame number within the segment where a particular page resides. This dual-layered translation process retains the advantages of segmentation while incorporating the benefits of paging, offering an effective compromise that ensures address translation efficiency without sacrificing the flexibility of segmentation.

Furthermore, the combination of segmentation and paging enhances the system's ability to support shared memory and inter-process communication. Segmentation allows for the isolation of code and data within a process, while paging within segments enables controlled sharing of memory between multiple processes. Shared memory mechanisms in segmented paging systems demand robust coordination to prevent conflicts and ensure the reliable exchange of information between processes. This versatility in supporting both isolation and controlled sharing of memory is particularly advantageous in multi-process and multi-user environments, where collaboration and communication are essential aspects of system functionality.

While the segmented paging model addresses many challenges associated with segmentation and paging individually, it is not without its complexities. Managing multiple layers of translation requires careful consideration of system architecture, and the potential for increased hardware complexity may impact overall system design. Additionally, ensuring synchronization and consistency in shared memory scenarios demands thorough coordination mechanisms to prevent conflicts and data corruption. Balancing the benefits and complexities of the segmented paging model requires a thoughtful and tailored approach that considers the specific requirements of the computing environment.

In conclusion, the integration of segmentation and paging in the segmented paging model offers a sophisticated solution for optimized memory use in modern computer systems. By combining the flexibility and modularity of segmentation with the simplicity and efficiency of paging, this approach addresses challenges related to fragmentation, enhances support for demand paging, and facilitates efficient address translation. The model also accommodates the diverse needs of software engineering, providing a versatile framework for organizing code and data while supporting shared memory and inter-process communication. While introducing some complexity, the segmented paging model stands as a testament to the adaptability and innovation within memory management strategies, contributing to the efficiency and performance of computing systems in a wide range of applications.

Contrasting paging and segmentation approaches.

Paging and segmentation are two distinct memory management approaches, each with its own set of characteristics, advantages, and limitations. Contrasting these approaches provides insights into their fundamental differences and the trade-offs associated with their use in organizing and managing the memory space of a computer system.

Paging, a memory management technique, divides the logical address space and physical memory into fixed-sized units known as pages and frames, respectively. The primary advantage of paging lies in its simplicity and uniformity. The fixed-size pages simplify the translation of virtual addresses to physical addresses, as the offset within a page remains constant. This simplicity streamlines the address translation process and facilitates the implementation of efficient hardware support, such as Translation Lookaside Buffers (TLBs). However, the fixed-size nature of pages introduces challenges related to internal fragmentation, as the allocated memory within a page may exceed the actual requirements of a process, leading to wasted space. Despite this limitation, paging is widely adopted in various computing environments due to its ease of implementation and consistent memory access patterns.

In contrast, segmentation divides the logical address space into variable-sized segments, each serving a distinct purpose or containing specific types of data. This approach offers a more flexible and intuitive organization of memory, aligning well with the modular nature of software design. Segmentation allows different parts of a program, such as code, data, and stack, to be isolated into separate segments, promoting code readability, maintainability, and reusability. However, the flexibility of segmentation introduces complexities in the address translation process. The varying sizes of segments require additional calculations involving segment base and limit values, contributing to overhead in translation. Additionally, segmentation is susceptible to fragmentation issues, both external and internal, which can impact system performance and memory utilization efficiency.

When examining the advantages and disadvantages of these approaches, it becomes evident that paging and segmentation address different aspects of memory management, and their suitability depends on the specific requirements of a computing environment. Paging excels in providing a straightforward and uniform structure, simplifying address translation and hardware implementation. Its fixed-size pages contribute to efficient memory utilization when processes exhibit similar memory access patterns. However, the rigid nature of paging may lead to increased internal fragmentation when memory allocations do not align perfectly with page boundaries.

On the other hand, segmentation excels in providing a modular and hierarchical organization of code and data, aligning well with software engineering principles. This approach supports the isolation of different functionalities within a program, enhancing code modularity and maintainability. Segmentation is particularly advantageous in scenarios where processes have varying memory requirements for different types of data and code. However, the flexibility of segmentation introduces challenges in address translation efficiency and fragmentation, both of which may impact system performance.

An approach that combines the strengths of both paging and segmentation is known as segmented paging. In segmented paging, the logical address space is organized into variable-sized segments, each subdivided into fixed-sized pages. This hybrid model aims to leverage the benefits of segmentation's modularity while mitigating external fragmentation through the use of fixed-sized pages. The integration of these two techniques results in a versatile memory management strategy that balances simplicity and flexibility. Segmented paging can provide support for demand paging, optimize address translation efficiency, and address fragmentation concerns, offering a well-rounded solution for diverse computing environments.

In terms of address translation, paging relies on a single translation step, where the virtual page number is translated directly to the physical frame number using a page table. This simplicity contributes to the efficiency of the translation process. In contrast, segmentation involves a two-step translation process. The virtual address is first translated to a linear address using a segment table, and then the linear address is mapped to a physical address using a page table. This dual-layered translation process introduces additional complexity, potentially impacting system performance. However, the hierarchical structure of segmentation allows for more fine-grained control over memory access permissions, contributing to enhanced security in multi-user environments.

When considering the impact on fragmentation, both approaches exhibit distinct challenges. Paging is susceptible to external fragmentation, where free memory is scattered throughout the address space, making it challenging to allocate contiguous pages. While internal fragmentation can occur within pages, the fixed-size nature of pages helps control this issue. Segmentation, on the other hand, is vulnerable to both external and internal fragmentation. External fragmentation arises due to varying segment sizes, leading to scattered free memory blocks. Internal fragmentation occurs within segments when allocated memory exceeds the actual requirements of a process, leading to wasted space. The variable size of segments exacerbates fragmentation concerns.

The concept of shared memory and inter-process communication is approached differently in paging and segmentation. Paging, by design, supports shared memory through the allocation of identical page frames to different processes. Processes can communicate and share data through shared pages. However, segmentation can complicate the sharing of data between processes. While segmentation allows for the isolation of code and data within a process, sharing data between processes or allowing processes to communicate may require additional coordination mechanisms. The modular organization of code and data in segments can enhance isolation but may introduce complexities in controlled sharing.

In conclusion, paging and segmentation represent contrasting approaches to memory management, each with its distinct strengths and weaknesses. Paging excels in simplicity, uniformity, and ease of hardware implementation, making it suitable for scenarios with consistent memory access patterns. However, it is prone to internal fragmentation and may not adapt well to varying memory requirements. Segmentation, on the other hand, provides flexibility, modularity, and support for diverse memory access patterns. Yet, it introduces complexities in address translation and is susceptible to fragmentation issues. The hybrid approach of segmented paging aims to strike a balance by combining the modularity of segmentation with the simplicity and efficiency of paging, offering a versatile solution that can be tailored to meet the specific demands of modern computing environments. Ultimately, the choice between paging and segmentation, or their integration in segmented paging, depends on the specific requirements and priorities of a given system or application.

Situational suitability for each method.

The suitability of memory management methods, specifically paging and segmentation, is inherently tied to the characteristics and requirements of the computing environment. Each method has its strengths and weaknesses, making them more or less suitable for different situations based on factors such as system architecture, application design, and memory access patterns.

Paging, with its fixed-size page structure, is particularly well-suited for scenarios where simplicity, hardware efficiency, and uniform memory access patterns are critical. Systems with consistent memory requirements across processes can benefit from the straightforward translation process and ease of hardware implementation associated with paging. Moreover, paging is inherently resistant to external fragmentation, as each page is of a consistent size, facilitating the allocation of contiguous memory blocks. This makes paging a suitable choice for applications where predictability and ease of implementation are paramount.

In situations where a modular and hierarchical organization of code and data is a priority, segmentation emerges as a more suitable approach. Software engineering principles often call for the isolation of different functionalities within a program, and segmentation allows for this modular structuring by dividing the logical address space into variable-sized segments. This flexibility aligns well with the diverse memory requirements of different parts of a program. Systems that prioritize code readability, maintainability, and reusability may find segmentation to be a better fit, as it enables developers to compartmentalize code and data into separate segments based on their functionality.

However, the suitability of segmentation is contingent on the ability to effectively manage the associated challenges. Systems with varying memory access patterns or diverse process requirements can benefit from segmentation's adaptability. Yet, the potential for external and internal fragmentation in segmentation demands careful consideration. The varying sizes of segments can lead to scattered free memory blocks, posing challenges in efficient memory allocation. Therefore, in scenarios where fragmentation is a critical concern, such as environments with frequent process creation and termination, additional measures may be required to address these issues.

The combination of paging and segmentation in the segmented paging model aims to harness the benefits of both approaches while mitigating their individual limitations. This hybrid method is particularly well-suited for computing environments that demand a balance between the simplicity of paging and the flexibility of segmentation. In segmented paging, the logical address space is organized into variable-sized segments, each further subdivided into fixed-sized pages. This model caters to systems with diverse memory access patterns and varying memory requirements for different types of data and code. By addressing fragmentation concerns through the use of fixed-sized pages within segments, segmented paging offers a versatile solution that can adapt to the complexities of modern computing environments.

The situational suitability of each memory management method is further influenced by the specific goals of the system. For example, systems prioritizing security and access control may find segmentation advantageous due to its ability to assign specific access rights to individual segments. This granular control over memory access permissions contributes to the overall security of the system, preventing unauthorized access or modification of segments by processes or users. Segmentation's support for protection mechanisms aligns well with multi-user environments where different processes may have distinct privilege levels.

On the other hand, systems emphasizing demand paging and efficient memory utilization may lean towards paging. The fixed-size pages in paging facilitate demand paging strategies, where only the actively used pages are loaded into physical memory. This dynamic loading minimizes wasteful memory consumption and contributes to the efficient utilization of resources. In scenarios where the focus is on optimizing memory usage and responsiveness, paging may be the preferred choice.

The nature of the applications running on a system also plays a crucial role in determining the most suitable memory management method. Applications with predictable and uniform memory access patterns, such as scientific simulations or embedded systems, may benefit from the simplicity and hardware efficiency of paging. Conversely, applications with complex memory access requirements, such as databases or multimedia processing, may find segmentation's modularity more accommodating.

In real-time systems, where responsiveness and predictability are paramount, the choice between paging and segmentation may hinge on the ability to meet strict timing constraints. Paging's uniformity and simplicity contribute to faster address translation times, making it well-suited for real-time applications with stringent performance requirements. However, the additional complexities introduced by segmentation may impact translation times, necessitating careful consideration of the trade-offs in such time-sensitive scenarios.

In distributed computing environments, where multiple interconnected systems collaborate to perform tasks, the choice between paging and segmentation may depend on the communication and data-sharing requirements. Paging's support for shared memory through identical page frames can simplify data exchange between processes in a distributed system. However, segmentation's modular organization can enhance isolation, preventing unintended interference between different components of a distributed application.

As technology advances and computing environments evolve, the situational suitability of memory management methods continues to adapt. Hybrid approaches and innovative solutions that combine the strengths of different methods may emerge to address the ever-changing demands of modern computing. Ultimately, the choice between paging, segmentation, or a hybrid model like segmented paging depends on a thorough understanding of the system's characteristics, goals, and the trade-offs inherent in each memory management approach.

Hybrid models for advanced memory organization.

Hybrid models for advanced memory organization represent innovative approaches that combine elements of different memory management techniques to harness their collective benefits while mitigating individual limitations. These models aim to address the complexities and diverse requirements of modern computing environments, offering a balance between efficiency, flexibility, and adaptability. One prominent example of a hybrid model is segmented paging, which integrates aspects of both segmentation and paging to create a versatile framework for memory organization.

Segmented paging builds upon the strengths of segmentation, a memory management technique that divides the logical address space into variable-sized segments, each with a unique purpose or type of data. This modularity aligns well with software engineering principles, facilitating a hierarchical and organized structure for code and data within a program. However, segmentation introduces complexities in the address translation process and is susceptible to fragmentation, both external and internal. To address these challenges, segmented paging combines segmentation with the fixed-size page structure of paging, creating a hybrid model that strives to optimize memory use.

In segmented paging, the logical address space is organized into variable-sized segments, each further subdivided into fixed-sized pages. This hybrid organization aims to leverage the flexibility of segmentation while mitigating external fragmentation through the uniformity introduced by paging. Each segment retains its unique characteristics, allowing for the isolation of different functionalities within a program. Simultaneously, the use of fixed-sized pages within segments helps overcome the challenges associated with varying segment sizes, making memory allocation more predictable and efficient.

One of the key advantages of segmented paging is its ability to support demand paging effectively. Demand paging is a strategy that optimizes memory usage by loading into physical memory only the pages that are actively being used. Segmented paging allows for the loading and unloading of entire segments based on the requirements of executing processes. This dynamic loading minimizes the wasteful use of memory resources, ensuring that only the necessary data is resident in physical memory at any given time. Consequently, demand paging contributes to the efficient utilization of memory, allowing for the execution of processes that might otherwise be constrained by physical memory limitations.

The address translation process in segmented paging involves two steps: translating the virtual address to a linear address using the segment table, and then mapping the linear address to a physical address using the page table. While this two-step translation process introduces some complexity, it retains the advantages of segmentation's modularity while incorporating the efficiency and simplicity of paging. Segment tables store the base address and limit of each segment, facilitating the determination of the linear address within a segment. The page table, in turn, specifies the frame number within the segment where a particular page resides, aiding in the final translation to the physical address. This dual-layered approach to translation aims to strike a balance between simplicity and performance.

One of the primary challenges addressed by segmented paging is external fragmentation. External fragmentation occurs when free memory is scattered throughout the address space, making it challenging to allocate contiguous memory blocks. The fixed-size pages within each segment contribute to overcoming this challenge by allowing for the allocation of contiguous memory within segments. While external fragmentation is a concern in pure segmentation models, the integration of paging principles helps mitigate this issue, ensuring more efficient use of memory in environments where processes have varying memory requirements.

Moreover, the integration of segmentation and paging in segmented paging provides an effective solution for the security and protection of memory. Each segment in segmented paging can be assigned specific access rights, such as read-only, read-write, or execute-only. These access rights are enforced by the system, preventing unauthorized access or modification of segments by processes or users. The granular control over memory access permissions enhances the overall security and integrity of the computing environment, making segmented paging suitable for multi-user systems where different processes may have distinct privilege levels.

Despite its advantages, segmented paging is not without its complexities. The dual-layered address translation process, involving both segment and page tables, introduces overhead compared to simpler memory management models. Efficient algorithms and hardware support, such as segment registers and TLBs, are crucial to minimize this overhead and ensure a swift and accurate translation process. The trade-offs inherent in segmented paging emphasize the importance of careful consideration and optimization based on the specific requirements and priorities of the computing environment.

In addition to segmented paging, other hybrid models may emerge as computing systems continue to evolve. These models may integrate elements of other memory management techniques, such as paging with techniques from hierarchical memory systems or combinations of paging and advanced caching mechanisms. The design of hybrid models depends on the goals of the system, the characteristics of the applications running on it, and the evolving demands of the computing landscape.

In conclusion, hybrid models for advanced memory organization, exemplified by segmented paging, showcase the adaptability and innovation within memory management strategies. By combining the strengths of different techniques, these models aim to provide a versatile and efficient framework for addressing the diverse requirements of modern computing environments. The integration of segmentation and paging in segmented paging balances the modularity of segmentation with the simplicity and efficiency of paging, offering a well-rounded solution for memory organization. As technology continues to progress, hybrid models are likely to play a crucial role in optimizing memory use, performance, and adaptability in a wide range of computing applications.

Introduction to page replacement strategies.

Page replacement strategies are fundamental components of virtual memory management in computer systems, playing a crucial role in optimizing the utilization of physical memory resources. Virtual memory is an abstraction that enables the execution of processes as if they have access to a larger address space than the physical memory actually available. As processes execute, they generate a stream of virtual addresses, and the mapping of these addresses to physical memory locations is managed by the operating system. In scenarios where the physical memory is insufficient to accommodate all the processes concurrently, page replacement strategies come into play to determine which pages should be retained in physical memory and which should be swapped out to secondary storage.

The need for page replacement arises from the limited capacity of physical memory compared to the expansive virtual address spaces of running processes. When a process accesses a page that is not currently present in physical memory, a page fault occurs. Page replacement strategies are responsible for deciding which page to evict from memory to make room for the required page. Various algorithms have been devised to address this challenge, each with its own set of principles and trade-offs, aiming to optimize performance metrics such as page fault rate, response time, and overall system efficiency.

One of the most basic page replacement strategies is the Optimal algorithm, which, as the name implies, makes decisions based on future knowledge of page accesses. The Optimal algorithm selects the page that will not be used for the longest duration into the future. While theoretically providing the lowest possible page fault rate, the Optimal algorithm is impractical in real-world scenarios due to its reliance on foreknowledge, which is unattainable in a dynamic and unpredictable computing environment.

In contrast to the Optimal algorithm, practical page replacement strategies operate based on historical or observed patterns of page accesses. The First-In-First-Out (FIFO) algorithm is one such strategy, which evicts the oldest page in memory when a page fault occurs. FIFO maintains a queue of pages in the order they were brought into memory, and the page at the front of the queue is the one selected for replacement. While conceptually simple, FIFO suffers from the "Belady's Anomaly," where increasing the number of frames in memory may lead to an increase in page faults rather than a decrease.

Another widely used page replacement strategy is the Least Recently Used (LRU) algorithm, which selects the page that has not been used for the longest time. LRU maintains a record of the order in which pages were accessed and prioritizes the eviction of the least recently used page. Implementing a precise LRU algorithm, however, requires maintaining an access history for every page, which can be computationally expensive. Approximations, such as the clock algorithm or counter-based approaches, are often employed to strike a balance between accuracy and efficiency.

The Clock algorithm, also known as the Second-Chance algorithm, maintains a circular list of pages and a "hand" pointing to the next page to be considered for replacement. When a page fault occurs, the algorithm examines the page at the hand position. If the page has been referenced since the last examination, its reference bit is cleared, and the hand moves to the next page. This process repeats until an unreferenced page is found for replacement. The Clock algorithm combines simplicity with effectiveness, offering a compromise between accuracy and computational overhead.

Counter-based approaches assign a counter to each page and increment the counter on each access. When a page fault occurs, the algorithm selects the page with the lowest counter value for replacement. This approach provides a straightforward means of estimating recency of use, with lower counter values indicating less recent usage. However, the implementation of counters for every page introduces additional storage requirements and computational overhead.

The Least Frequently Used (LFU) algorithm takes a different approach by selecting the page with the lowest access frequency. LFU maintains a counter for each page that is incremented on every access. When a page fault occurs, the algorithm selects the page with the lowest counter value. LFU aims to evict pages that are used infrequently, making it suitable for scenarios where certain pages are accessed sporadically. However, LFU may struggle in dynamic environments where access patterns change over time.

In contrast, the Most Recently Used (MRU) algorithm selects the page that has been accessed most recently. MRU prioritizes the eviction of the most recently used page in the hope that less recently used pages will still be relevant. While MRU seems intuitive, it may not always align with the principle of retaining pages likely to be used soon, and its effectiveness depends on the specific characteristics of the workload.

The Working Set algorithm introduces the concept of the working set, which represents the set of pages a process is actively using. Pages outside the working set are considered for replacement. The working set is defined by a window of recent references, and pages are selected for replacement if they fall outside this window. The

Working Set algorithm aims to capture the temporal locality of reference, ensuring that frequently used pages remain in memory. However, determining an optimal window size and adapting to changing working set sizes present challenges in real-world implementations.

Adaptive replacement strategies, such as the Least Recently Used and Most Recently Used (LRU-MRU) algorithm, dynamically adjust their behavior based on observed access patterns. LRU-MRU maintains two lists, one for recently used pages (MRU) and another for less recently used pages (LRU). When a page fault occurs, the algorithm selects the least recently used page from the LRU list for replacement unless it has been accessed more recently than any page in the MRU list. This adaptive approach allows the algorithm to adapt to changing access patterns and improve overall efficiency.

The concept of page replacement strategies extends beyond single-level algorithms, as some systems implement multi-level page replacement strategies. Hierarchical or multi-level page replacement involves selecting a candidate page for replacement from a subset of pages based on specific criteria. This subset can be determined by factors such as process priorities, memory classes, or access patterns. Multi-level page replacement aims to provide a more nuanced and context-aware approach to selecting pages for replacement, enhancing the adaptability of memory management strategies in complex computing environments.

In conclusion, page replacement strategies play a pivotal role in optimizing the utilization of physical memory in computer systems. The selection of an appropriate strategy depends on factors such as access patterns, computational overhead, and system goals. From basic algorithms like FIFO to more sophisticated approaches like LRU and adaptive strategies, the landscape of page replacement is diverse and continually evolving. The quest for efficient and adaptive page replacement strategies remains a central focus in the realm of virtual memory management, as modern computing environments demand increasingly sophisticated approaches to memory organization and optimization.

Chapter 4: Cache Memory Optimization

Definition and purpose of cache memory.
Cache memory is a critical component of modern computer systems, serving as a high-speed intermediary between the central processing unit (CPU) and the main memory (RAM). Its fundamental purpose is to bridge the significant speed disparity between the CPU and RAM, thereby enhancing overall system performance. The term "cache" is derived from the French word for "hidden," reflecting the notion that cache memory operates behind the scenes, transparently managing data to facilitate faster access for the CPU. As the CPU executes instructions and processes data, cache memory stores frequently accessed or recently used information, aiming to reduce the latency associated with fetching data from the comparatively slower main memory.

The primary motivation for incorporating cache memory into computer architecture lies in the principle of temporal and spatial locality of reference observed in typical program execution. Temporal locality suggests that recently accessed data is likely to be accessed again in the near future, while spatial locality indicates that data located near a recently accessed piece of information is also likely to be accessed soon. Cache memory exploits these locality principles to store a subset of the most relevant data, minimizing the need for the CPU to repeatedly access the main memory. By storing a copy of frequently used data closer to the CPU, cache memory significantly reduces the time it takes for the processor to retrieve information, thereby enhancing overall system efficiency.

Cache memory operates based on the hierarchical organization of memory in a computer system. The hierarchy typically includes multiple levels of memory, with registers being the fastest but smallest, followed by cache memory, and then main memory. Registers are directly accessible by the CPU but are limited in capacity. Cache memory, situated between registers and main memory, strikes a balance by offering larger storage than registers while maintaining faster access times than main memory. This hierarchical organization ensures that data is progressively moved closer to the CPU based on its frequency of access, with the goal of minimizing latency and optimizing data retrieval.

Cache memory is often categorized into multiple levels, denoted as L1, L2, and sometimes L3 caches. L1 cache is the smallest but fastest, residing directly on the CPU chip. It is typically divided into separate instruction and data caches to allow simultaneous access to both types of information. L2 cache, which is larger but slightly slower, is shared among the CPU cores within a processor. Some systems also incorporate an L3 cache, which is shared among multiple CPU cores or processors, further expanding the capacity of cached data.

The cache management process involves determining which data should be stored in the cache and how it should be organized. Cache management strategies include techniques such as direct-mapped, set associative, and fully associative mapping, each influencing how data is stored and retrieved from the cache. Direct-mapped caching assigns each block of main memory to a specific location in the cache, simplifying the addressing but potentially leading to conflicts. Set-associative caching groups multiple cache locations into sets, reducing conflicts and allowing flexibility in block placement. Fully associative caching, on the other hand, permits any block of main memory to be placed in any cache location, eliminating conflicts but introducing increased complexity.

Cache management also involves addressing the challenge of maintaining coherency between the cache and main memory. When a change is made to a piece of data in the cache, it must be reflected in the corresponding location in main memory to ensure consistency. Cache coherency protocols, such as MESI (Modified, Exclusive, Shared, Invalid) or MOESI (Modified, Owned, Exclusive, Shared, Invalid), help manage the state of cache lines and coordinate data updates between the cache and main memory.

The efficiency of cache memory is often evaluated using metrics such as hit rate, miss rate, and hit time. A cache hit occurs when the requested data is found in the cache, resulting in faster access times, while a cache miss occurs when the requested data is not in the cache, necessitating retrieval from the slower main memory. The hit rate is the ratio of cache hits to total memory accesses, providing an indication of cache effectiveness. The miss rate is the complement of the hit rate and represents the proportion of accesses resulting in cache misses. Hit time refers to the time taken to access data from the cache, while miss penalty is the additional time required to fetch data from the main memory in the event of a cache miss.

Cache memory's significance extends beyond mere performance enhancement; it also plays a crucial role in power efficiency. The energy consumption of accessing data in the cache is considerably lower than accessing data from the main memory. As a result, cache memory contributes to reducing the overall power consumption of a computer system, making it a pivotal component in modern computing architectures that prioritize energy efficiency and sustainability.

In conclusion, cache memory is a vital element in computer architecture designed to overcome the speed disparity between the CPU and main memory. By storing frequently accessed or recently used data closer to the processor, cache memory minimizes latency, optimizes data retrieval, and significantly enhances system performance. The hierarchical organization of memory, with multiple cache levels, allows for a balance between speed and capacity. Cache management strategies, addressing issues such as mapping and coherency, play a crucial role in determining the effectiveness of cache memory. With its impact on hit rates, miss rates, and overall system efficiency, cache memory stands as a cornerstone in modern computing, contributing not only to performance gains but also to power efficiency in the pursuit of more sustainable computing practices.

Types of cache memory and their functions.

Cache memory, a vital component of modern computer architectures, comes in various types, each serving distinct functions within the memory hierarchy. These types, typically classified as L1, L2, and L3 caches, are designed to optimize data access patterns, reduce latency, and enhance overall system performance. L1 cache, the smallest and fastest level, is often divided into separate instruction and data caches. The instruction cache stores frequently executed machine code instructions, while the data cache holds recently accessed data. This separation allows simultaneous access to instruction and data, minimizing instruction wait times and improving instruction throughput. L1 cache is usually located on the CPU chip, providing immediate access to data for the processor cores.

Moving to the next level, L2 cache is larger than L1 and is often shared among the CPU cores within a processor. It functions as a secondary layer of cache, capturing data that may not fit in the L1 cache or has a longer temporal locality. L2 cache further optimizes data access by providing a larger pool of cached information to serve the CPU cores efficiently. Its shared nature enables different cores to benefit from the same pool of cached data, promoting resource sharing and reducing redundancy.

In systems with multiple processors or multicore CPUs, an additional level of cache, known as L3 cache, may be present. L3 cache is shared among multiple CPU cores or processors, enhancing the overall system's capacity to store and retrieve frequently accessed data. Its shared nature allows for improved data sharing and coordination between cores, contributing to better overall system performance. L3 cache operates at a slightly higher latency compared to L1 and L2 caches but provides a substantial increase in capacity.

The functions of these cache levels are intricately tied to the principles of temporal and spatial locality of reference observed in program execution. Temporal locality suggests that recently accessed data is likely to be accessed again in the near future, while spatial locality indicates that data located near a recently accessed piece of information is also likely to be accessed soon. L1 cache, being the closest to the CPU cores, is particularly adept at capturing and serving frequently used instructions and data, exploiting the high likelihood of repeated accesses within a short time frame.

L2 and L3 caches extend the concept of temporal locality by accommodating larger sets of data that exhibit slightly lower frequencies of access. They capture a broader range of information, catering to the diverse data access patterns exhibited by various processes and applications running on a computer system. The hierarchical organization of these cache levels aligns with the increasing size and latency, ensuring a balance between speed and capacity to meet the dynamic needs of modern computing workloads.

Cache memory types also differ in their access times and storage capacities. L1 cache, being the fastest but smallest, offers minimal latency and quick access to frequently used instructions and data. L2 cache, with a slightly higher latency, provides a larger storage capacity to accommodate a broader range of data. L3 cache, while slower than L1 and L2, serves as a shared resource among multiple cores or processors, further expanding the system's capacity to store and retrieve data efficiently. The overall architecture of these cache types aims to strike a balance between minimizing access times and maximizing storage capacity.

Cache management strategies play a pivotal role in determining how each cache type operates. These strategies include mapping techniques, such as direct-mapped, set-associative, and fully associative mapping, which influence how data is stored and retrieved from the cache. Direct-mapped caching assigns each block of main memory to a specific location in the cache, simplifying the addressing but potentially leading to conflicts. Set-associative caching groups multiple cache locations into sets, reducing conflicts and allowing flexibility in block placement. Fully associative caching permits any block of main memory to be placed in any cache location, eliminating conflicts but introducing increased complexity.

The functions of cache memory extend beyond mere performance enhancement; they also play a crucial role in power efficiency. The energy consumption of accessing data in the cache is considerably lower than accessing data from the main memory. As a result, cache memory contributes to reducing the overall power consumption of a computer system, making it a pivotal component in modern computing architectures that prioritize energy efficiency and sustainability.

In conclusion, cache memory types, including L1, L2, and L3 caches, are integral to the hierarchical organization of modern computer architectures. Each cache level serves specific functions, optimizing data access patterns, minimizing latency, and enhancing overall system performance. The principles of temporal and spatial locality of reference guide the design of these cache types, ensuring that frequently accessed data is stored closer to the CPU cores. Cache management strategies, such as mapping techniques, further influence how data is stored and retrieved from the cache. The functions of cache memory, spanning from the fastest and smallest L1 cache to the shared and larger L3 cache, contribute not only to performance gains but also to power efficiency, making them crucial components in the pursuit of more efficient and sustainable computing practices.

Cache hierarchy and levels of caching.

The cache hierarchy is a fundamental aspect of modern computer architectures, designed to bridge the speed gap between the fast central processing unit (CPU) and the slower main memory. This hierarchical structure comprises multiple levels of cache, denoted as L1, L2, and sometimes L3, each with specific functions and characteristics. L1 cache, the first level in the hierarchy, is located directly on the CPU chip, making it the closest and fastest cache level. It is further divided into separate instruction and data caches to allow concurrent access to both types of information. L1 cache is characterized by its small size, typically ranging from 16 to 128 kilobytes, but its proximity to the CPU ensures quick access to frequently used instructions and data.

Moving to the second level of the cache hierarchy, L2 cache provides a larger but slightly slower pool of cached data. L2 cache is often shared among the CPU cores within a processor, fostering resource sharing and reducing redundancy. Its increased size, ranging from hundreds of kilobytes to several megabytes, allows it to capture a broader range of data that may not fit in the smaller L1 cache. L2 cache plays a crucial role in optimizing data access patterns, serving as a secondary layer of cache that caters to the temporal and spatial locality of reference observed in program execution.

In systems with multiple processors or multicore CPUs, an additional level of cache, known as L3 cache, may be present. L3 cache is shared among multiple CPU cores or processors, contributing to the overall system's capacity to store and retrieve frequently accessed data. It acts as a shared resource, facilitating improved data sharing and coordination between cores. While L3 cache introduces slightly higher latency compared to L1 and L2 caches, its larger capacity, often measured in megabytes, provides a substantial increase in the system's ability to cache data and minimize the need for accessing the slower main memory.

The cache hierarchy is built on the principles of temporal and spatial locality of reference, which suggest that recently accessed data is likely to be accessed again in the near future, and data located near a recently accessed piece of information is also likely to be accessed soon. L1 cache, being the closest to the CPU cores, excels at capturing and serving frequently used instructions and data, exploiting the high likelihood of repeated accesses within a short time frame. L2 and L3 caches extend this concept by accommodating larger sets of data that exhibit slightly lower frequencies of access, catering to the diverse data access patterns exhibited by various processes and applications running on a computer system.

The hierarchical organization of the cache levels ensures a balance between speed and capacity, addressing the dynamic needs of modern computing workloads. The progression from L1 to L3 cache involves a trade-off between access time and storage capacity. L1 cache, being the fastest but smallest, offers minimal latency and quick access to frequently used instructions and data. L2 cache, with a slightly higher latency, provides a larger storage capacity to accommodate a broader range of data. L3 cache, while slower than L1 and L2, serves as a shared resource among multiple cores or processors, further expanding the system's capacity to store and retrieve data efficiently.

Cache management strategies, integral to the cache hierarchy, play a pivotal role in determining how each cache level operates. These strategies include mapping techniques, such as direct-mapped, set-associative, and fully associative mapping, which influence how data is stored and retrieved from the cache. Direct-mapped caching assigns each block of main memory to a specific location in the cache, simplifying the addressing but potentially leading to conflicts. Set-associative caching groups multiple cache locations into sets, reducing conflicts and allowing flexibility in block placement. Fully associative caching permits any block of main memory to be placed in any cache location, eliminating conflicts but introducing increased complexity.

Cache management also involves addressing the challenge of maintaining coherency between the cache and main memory. When a change is made to a piece of data in the cache, it must be reflected in the corresponding location in main memory to ensure consistency. Cache coherency protocols, such as MESI (Modified, Exclusive, Shared, Invalid) or MOESI (Modified, Owned, Exclusive, Shared, Invalid), help manage the state of cache lines and coordinate data updates between the cache and main memory.

The efficiency of the cache hierarchy is often evaluated using metrics such as hit rate, miss rate, and hit time. A cache hit occurs when the requested data is found in the cache, resulting in faster access times, while a cache miss occurs when the requested data is not in the cache, necessitating retrieval from the slower main memory. The hit rate is the ratio of cache hits to total memory accesses, providing an indication of cache effectiveness. The miss rate is the complement of the hit rate and represents the proportion of accesses resulting in cache misses. Hit time refers to the time taken to access data from the cache, while miss penalty is the additional time required to fetch data from the main memory in the event of a cache miss.

The functions of the cache hierarchy extend beyond mere performance enhancement; they also play a crucial role in power efficiency. The energy consumption of accessing data in the cache is considerably lower than accessing data from the main memory. As a result, the cache hierarchy contributes to reducing the overall power consumption of a computer system, making it a pivotal component in modern computing architectures that prioritize energy efficiency and sustainability.

In conclusion, the cache hierarchy, consisting of L1, L2, and L3 caches, represents a crucial aspect of modern computer architectures. Each cache level serves specific functions within the memory hierarchy, optimizing data access patterns, minimizing latency, and enhancing overall system performance. The hierarchical organization of these cache levels, guided by the principles of temporal and spatial locality of reference, ensures a balance between speed and capacity to meet the dynamic needs of modern computing workloads. Cache management strategies, addressing issues such as mapping and coherency, play a crucial role in determining the effectiveness of the cache hierarchy. With its impact on hit rates, miss rates, and overall system efficiency, the cache hierarchy stands as a cornerstone in modern computing, contributing not only to performance gains but also to power efficiency in the pursuit of more efficient and sustainable computing practices.

Explaining the concepts of spatial and temporal locality.

Spatial and temporal locality are fundamental concepts in computer science and memory management, providing insights into the patterns of data access and utilization within a computing system. These principles guide the design of memory hierarchies and caching strategies, aiming to optimize the efficiency of data retrieval and overall system performance.

Temporal locality refers to the tendency of a computer program to access the same memory locations repeatedly within a short time frame. This concept is grounded in the observation that, in typical program execution, the same data or instructions are often accessed multiple times in close succession. As a result, maintaining a record of recently accessed data allows for more efficient retrieval, as the likelihood of the same data being accessed again in the near future is high. Temporal locality is exploited by cache memory systems, where recently accessed data is stored in a fast and accessible cache, reducing the need to repeatedly access slower main memory. Caching mechanisms, influenced by temporal locality, contribute significantly to minimizing latency and optimizing the performance of modern computer systems.

On the other hand, spatial locality refers to the tendency of a computer program to access memory locations that are in close proximity to each other. This principle is based on the observation that, once a particular memory location is accessed, nearby locations are also likely to be accessed soon. Spatial locality is manifested in various ways, such as sequential access patterns, where data is accessed in a contiguous manner, or through the use of arrays and data structures where adjacent elements are accessed sequentially. The concept of spatial locality is crucial for memory systems, especially when considering the transfer of data between different levels of the memory hierarchy. Caches, which store blocks of data rather than individual elements, benefit from spatial locality as fetching a block into the cache increases the likelihood of accessing other elements within the same block.

Understanding temporal and spatial locality is essential for designing memory management systems that efficiently cater to the dynamic needs of computer programs. These principles are intricately linked and often coexist in typical workloads. For instance, a loop in a program that iterates over an array demonstrates both temporal and spatial locality. The loop accesses the same array elements repeatedly (temporal locality) and accesses adjacent elements in sequence (spatial locality).

The hierarchical organization of memory systems, including levels of cache and main memory, is influenced by these locality principles. Cache memory, organized into multiple levels such as L1, L2, and sometimes L3, capitalizes on temporal locality by storing recently accessed data closer to the CPU. The hierarchy allows for progressively larger but slower memory layers, aligning with the trade-off between access time and storage capacity. As a result, the cache hierarchy caters to both temporal and spatial locality, optimizing the retrieval of frequently used data and minimizing the latency associated with accessing main memory.

Caching strategies leverage temporal and spatial locality to enhance the hit rates, which measure the proportion of memory accesses satisfied by the cache. A high hit rate indicates that a significant portion of data accesses are successfully serviced by the cache, reducing the need to fetch data from slower levels of the memory hierarchy. Cache management techniques, such as the replacement policies in case of a cache miss, also take into account these locality principles. Replacement policies aim to retain data in the cache that is likely to be accessed again soon, aligning with temporal locality, and consider the grouping of data into blocks to leverage spatial locality.

In the context of virtual memory systems, which involve the use of both main memory and secondary storage, the concepts of temporal and spatial locality remain crucial. Paging and segmentation mechanisms, which manage the mapping of virtual addresses to physical addresses, benefit from these locality principles. Demand paging, a strategy where pages are loaded into physical memory only when accessed, exploits temporal locality by minimizing the wasteful use of memory resources. Similarly, memory segmentation, which divides the logical address space into segments, aligns with the modularity inherent in spatial locality.

While temporal and spatial locality are powerful guiding principles, it's important to recognize that not all workloads exhibit these characteristics to the same degree. Certain applications and algorithms may demonstrate stronger or weaker locality, influencing the effectiveness of caching and memory management strategies. Adaptive approaches, including dynamic caching policies that adjust to changing access patterns, seek to optimize memory systems across a range of workloads by dynamically adapting to the prevailing locality characteristics.

In conclusion, the concepts of temporal and spatial locality are foundational to the design and optimization of memory systems in computer architecture. These principles guide the organization of memory hierarchies, caching strategies, and memory management mechanisms. By understanding and leveraging the tendencies of computer programs to access data repeatedly and in proximity, memory systems aim to minimize latency, optimize hit rates, and enhance overall system performance. The ongoing evolution of computing workloads and applications requires continued consideration of these locality principles to design memory systems that effectively meet the demands of modern computing.

How these concepts influence caching efficiency.

The concepts of temporal and spatial locality exert a profound influence on the efficiency of caching systems, shaping the design and operation of memory hierarchies in modern computer architectures. Temporal locality, rooted in the idea that recently accessed data is likely to be accessed again in the near future, plays a pivotal role in enhancing caching efficiency. Caches exploit temporal locality by storing recently accessed data in a fast and accessible memory layer, typically closer to the central processing unit (CPU) than the slower main memory. This approach minimizes the need to repeatedly fetch the same data from the main memory, significantly reducing latency and optimizing the overall performance of the system. The caching of frequently used instructions and data aligns with the temporal patterns exhibited by many computer programs, ensuring that the most relevant information is readily available for swift retrieval by the CPU.

Spatial locality, the tendency of a computer program to access memory locations in close proximity to each other, is another critical factor shaping caching efficiency. This concept recognizes that, once a particular memory location is accessed, nearby locations are also likely to be accessed soon. Caches leverage spatial locality by storing data in blocks or lines rather than individual elements. When a particular memory block is accessed, the cache brings the entire block into its storage. This strategy aligns with the spatial patterns observed in various access scenarios, such as sequential data access or the use of arrays and data structures where adjacent elements are accessed sequentially. By capturing and retaining spatially proximate data in the cache, spatial locality contributes to more efficient memory utilization and retrieval.

The hierarchical organization of cache memory levels, including L1, L2, and sometimes L3 caches, is designed to harness the benefits of both temporal and spatial locality. L1 cache, the smallest and fastest cache level, caters to the immediate needs of the CPU, storing recently accessed instructions and data. The proximity of L1 cache to the CPU ensures that the most frequently used information is readily available, exploiting temporal locality to the fullest extent. L2 cache, which is larger but slightly slower, extends the caching strategy to capture a broader range of data that may not fit within the confines of L1 cache. The shared nature of L2 cache among CPU cores promotes resource sharing and further optimizes data access patterns. In systems with multiple processors or multicore CPUs, an additional level of cache, L3 cache, acts as a shared resource among cores or processors, enhancing the overall system's capacity to store and retrieve frequently accessed data.

Caching efficiency is deeply intertwined with cache management strategies, which are influenced by temporal and spatial locality principles. Mapping techniques, such as direct-mapped, set-associative, and fully associative mapping, play a crucial role in determining how data is stored and retrieved from the cache. Direct-mapped caching assigns each block of main memory to a specific location in the cache, simplifying the addressing but potentially leading to conflicts. The simplicity of direct-mapped caching aligns well with certain types of spatial locality, where sequential or patterned accesses can be efficiently captured. Set-associative caching groups multiple cache locations into sets, reducing conflicts and allowing flexibility in block placement. This approach accommodates a balance between spatial locality and the need for efficient data retrieval, providing more flexibility than direct-mapped caching. Fully associative caching, permitting any block of main memory to be placed in any cache location, eliminates conflicts but introduces increased complexity. Fully associative caching is particularly adept at capturing both temporal and spatial locality effectively but may incur higher computational overhead.

Cache replacement policies, another key aspect of cache management, further reflect the influence of temporal locality on caching efficiency. Policies such as Least Recently Used (LRU), which evicts the least recently accessed data when space is needed in the cache, align with the principle that recently accessed data is more likely to be accessed again soon. LRU is designed to retain data that exhibits strong temporal locality, contributing to a high hit rate by prioritizing the caching of frequently accessed information. Other replacement policies, such as First-In-First-Out (FIFO) or Random, provide alternatives with varying trade-offs between simplicity and effectiveness in capturing temporal locality.

Spatial locality, influencing the grouping of data into cache blocks or lines, affects the granularity of data stored in the cache. The decision to bring an entire block into the cache when a single element is accessed capitalizes on spatial locality, anticipating that adjacent elements within the same block are likely to be accessed soon. This strategy enhances cache efficiency by reducing the need to fetch individual elements separately, especially when spatially proximate data is accessed in sequence.

Cache coherency mechanisms also play a role in maintaining efficiency in the presence of temporal and spatial locality. When a change is made to a piece of data in the cache, ensuring coherency with the corresponding location in main memory is essential. Cache coherency protocols, such as MESI (Modified, Exclusive, Shared, Invalid) or MOESI (Modified, Owned, Exclusive, Shared, Invalid), help manage the state of cache lines and coordinate data updates between the cache and main memory. These protocols consider the access patterns influenced by temporal locality, ensuring that recently modified or shared data is appropriately synchronized to maintain a consistent view across the memory hierarchy.

The efficiency of caching systems is frequently evaluated using metrics such as hit rate, miss rate, hit time, and miss penalty. A high hit rate, indicating a significant proportion of memory accesses being satisfied by the cache, reflects efficient caching strategies that capitalize on both temporal and spatial locality. The miss rate, representing the proportion of accesses resulting in cache misses, provides insights into the effectiveness of caching in capturing frequently accessed information. Hit time, the time taken to access data from the cache, is minimized when temporal and spatial locality principles are effectively leveraged. Miss penalty, the additional time required to fetch data from the main memory in the event of a cache miss, is mitigated by robust caching strategies that anticipate and prioritize the retrieval of relevant data.

In conclusion, the concepts of temporal and spatial locality profoundly shape the efficiency of caching systems in modern computer architectures. Temporal locality, grounded in the repetition of data access patterns, is harnessed by caching mechanisms to store recently accessed information closer to the CPU, minimizing latency. Spatial locality, derived from the tendency to access nearby memory locations, influences the grouping of data into cache blocks and informs cache management strategies. The hierarchical organization of cache levels, cache mapping techniques, replacement policies, and coherency mechanisms are all designed with these locality principles in mind. By effectively capitalizing on temporal and spatial locality, caching systems optimize memory utilization, enhance retrieval efficiency, and contribute to the overall performance of modern computing systems.

Strategies to leverage locality for optimization.

Strategies to leverage locality for optimization are fundamental in designing efficient computer systems, focusing on the principles of temporal and spatial locality to enhance data access patterns and minimize latency. Temporal locality, which suggests that recently accessed data is likely to be accessed again in the near future, can be leveraged through various optimization strategies. One key approach is caching, where frequently accessed data is stored in a fast and accessible cache, reducing the need to repeatedly fetch the same information from slower main memory. Cache hierarchies, including levels such as L1, L2, and L3 caches, are strategically organized to capture and exploit temporal locality, with smaller and faster caches closer to the central processing unit (CPU) to ensure quick access to the most relevant data. Adaptive caching policies, guided by temporal locality, dynamically adjust to changing access patterns, optimizing the hit rates and overall efficiency of the cache system.

Spatial locality, indicating that data located near a recently accessed piece of information is likely to be accessed soon, presents additional opportunities for optimization. One prevalent strategy is block or line caching, where an entire block of memory is brought into the cache upon accessing a single element. This approach aligns with spatial locality, anticipating that adjacent elements within the same block will be accessed in close succession. The granularity of data stored in the cache influences spatial locality optimization, as larger blocks capture more spatially proximate data. Additionally, memory hierarchies, such as those involving paging and segmentation in virtual memory systems, can benefit from spatial locality by managing the placement of memory blocks or segments based on their spatial proximity.

Cache management techniques play a crucial role in optimizing locality for performance gains. Mapping strategies, including direct-mapped, set-associative, and fully associative mapping, determine how data is stored and retrieved from the cache. Direct-mapped caching assigns each block of main memory to a specific location in the cache, simplifying the addressing but potentially leading to conflicts. This strategy is particularly effective in scenarios where access patterns exhibit a high degree of spatial or temporal locality, as conflicts are minimized. Set-associative caching groups multiple cache locations into sets, offering a balance between simplicity and flexibility, which is valuable in capturing varying degrees of locality in different workloads. Fully associative caching permits any block of main memory to be placed in any cache location, eliminating conflicts but introducing increased complexity. The choice of mapping strategy is influenced by the specific characteristics of the application and the degree of locality exhibited in its data access patterns.

Cache replacement policies are another aspect of cache management that contributes to optimizing locality. Policies such as Least Recently Used (LRU), which evicts the least recently accessed data when space is needed in the cache, align with the principle that recently accessed data is likely to be accessed again soon. LRU is designed to retain data that exhibits strong temporal locality, contributing to a high hit rate by prioritizing the caching of frequently accessed information. Other replacement policies, such as First-In-First-Out (FIFO) or Random, provide alternatives with varying trade-offs between simplicity and effectiveness in capturing temporal locality. The selection of an appropriate replacement policy depends on the specific characteristics of the application and the degree to which temporal locality influences its data access patterns.

In virtual memory systems, strategies such as demand paging leverage temporal locality for optimization. Demand paging involves loading pages into physical memory only when they are accessed, based on the expectation that recently accessed pages are likely to be accessed again in the near future. This approach minimizes the wasteful use of memory resources, aligning with the efficient utilization of spatial and temporal locality. Similarly, memory segmentation, which divides the logical address space into segments, caters to the modularity inherent in spatial locality. Segments that are spatially proximate in the logical address space are likely to be accessed together, contributing to the optimization of data retrieval.

Adaptive strategies that dynamically adjust to changing access patterns are crucial for optimizing locality in the face of evolving workloads. Dynamic caching policies, responsive to variations in temporal and spatial locality, ensure that the cache system remains effective across a range of scenarios. These adaptive policies may involve adjusting the cache size, altering mapping strategies, or modifying replacement policies based on real-time analysis of data access patterns. By dynamically responding to the prevailing locality characteristics, these strategies contribute to sustained optimization and improved overall system performance.

Coherency mechanisms in caching systems also play a role in ensuring optimization by maintaining consistency between the cache and main memory. Cache coherency protocols, such as MESI (Modified, Exclusive, Shared, Invalid) or MOESI (Modified, Owned, Exclusive, Shared, Invalid), help manage the state of cache lines and coordinate data updates between the cache and main memory. These protocols are designed to accommodate the dynamic nature of data access patterns influenced by temporal and spatial locality. They ensure that modifications to cached data are appropriately reflected in main memory, preventing inconsistencies that could arise due to the interleaved access of multiple cache copies.

Efforts to optimize locality extend beyond caching to include the design of algorithms and data structures that align with these principles. Locality-aware algorithms, which organize data and computations to exploit temporal and spatial patterns, contribute to enhanced cache and memory efficiency. Data structures, such as arrays and contiguous memory allocations, are designed to facilitate spatial locality, ensuring that adjacent elements are stored close to each other. Locality-aware algorithmic optimizations, coupled with efficient data structures, create synergies that amplify the benefits of caching strategies and memory hierarchies.

In conclusion, strategies to leverage locality for optimization are central to the design and performance of computer systems. Temporal and spatial locality principles guide caching strategies, cache management techniques, and virtual memory systems to efficiently capture and exploit repetitive and proximate data access patterns. Adaptive policies, dynamic adjustments, and coherency mechanisms contribute to the flexibility required to optimize locality across diverse workloads. Locality-aware algorithms and data structures further enhance the effectiveness of optimization efforts, creating a holistic approach that maximizes the benefits of spatial and temporal locality in the pursuit of efficient and high-performance computing systems.

Direct-mapped, set-associative, and fully associative mapping.

The mapping of memory addresses to cache locations is a crucial aspect of cache management, and three common strategies are employed: direct-mapped, set-associative, and fully associative mapping. Direct-mapped caching is a straightforward approach where each block of main memory is mapped to a specific location in the cache. This method simplifies the addressing process as each block has a unique location in the cache. However, the simplicity comes at the cost of potential conflicts, where multiple blocks may be mapped to the same cache location, leading to what is known as a "collision." These collisions can result in cache misses when accessing conflicting memory blocks, impacting efficiency. Despite this drawback, direct-mapped caching offers simplicity and is often effective in scenarios where memory access patterns exhibit a high degree of spatial or temporal locality.

Set-associative mapping seeks to strike a balance between the simplicity of direct-mapped caching and the flexibility of fully associative mapping. In set-associative mapping, the cache is divided into a number of sets, each containing multiple cache locations. The mapping of a memory block to a particular set is determined by the use of specific bits from the memory address. Within each set, the block can be placed in any of the cache locations. This strategy aims to reduce conflicts compared to direct-mapped caching by allowing for a degree of flexibility within each set. The level of associativity refers to the number of cache locations within each set. For example, a 2-way set-associative cache has two locations per set. As associativity increases, the potential for conflicts decreases, improving the cache's ability to capture spatial and temporal locality. Set-associative mapping is widely used in modern cache designs, offering a good compromise between simplicity and flexibility.

Fully associative mapping represents the most flexible mapping strategy, allowing any memory block to be placed in any cache location. In this approach, the entire cache acts as a single set. While this eliminates conflicts altogether, it introduces increased complexity in terms of address matching, as each block can potentially be placed in any location within the cache. To address this, fully associative caches often employ techniques such as content-addressable memory (CAM) to quickly determine the presence of a block in the cache. Fully associative mapping is effective in capturing both spatial and temporal locality with a high degree of flexibility. However, the complexity of the mapping process and the associated hardware requirements make fully associative caches less common than direct-mapped or set-associative caches.

The choice between these mapping strategies involves trade-offs in terms of hardware complexity, access speed, and the ability to capture locality effectively. Direct-mapped caches are simple and easy to implement but may suffer from conflicts. Set-associative caches offer a balance between simplicity and flexibility, suitable for a wide range of applications. Fully associative caches provide maximum flexibility but require more sophisticated hardware and may have higher access times. The decision often depends on the specific requirements of the system, the characteristics of the workload, and the desired trade-offs between hardware complexity and caching efficiency.

Advantages and disadvantages of each mapping technique.

Direct-mapped caching, set-associative caching, and fully associative caching are three distinct mapping techniques used in designing cache systems, each with its own set of advantages and disadvantages. Direct-mapped caching, being the simplest of the three, offers advantages in terms of implementation simplicity and reduced hardware complexity. With each memory block mapped to a specific location in the cache, direct-mapped caching is easy to manage and requires minimal hardware resources for address matching. However, this simplicity comes at a cost. Direct-mapped caches are more susceptible to conflicts, as multiple memory blocks may be mapped to the same cache location, leading to what is known as a "collision." These collisions can result in higher cache miss rates, limiting the effectiveness of the cache in capturing spatial and temporal locality. The primary advantage of direct-mapped caching lies in its simplicity, but this simplicity is accompanied by potential efficiency drawbacks, particularly in scenarios with challenging access patterns.

Set-associative mapping aims to address some of the limitations of direct-mapped caching by introducing a level of flexibility. The cache is divided into multiple sets, each containing multiple cache locations. This allows for a degree of freedom in placing memory blocks within each set, reducing the likelihood of conflicts compared to direct-mapped caching. One of the key advantages of set-associative mapping is its ability to strike a balance between simplicity and flexibility. The associativity level, determining the number of cache locations within each set, can be adjusted to suit the specific requirements of the system. This adaptability makes set-associative caches well-suited for a variety of applications. The increased flexibility reduces conflicts, leading to lower cache miss rates and improved overall performance. However, set-associative caches are not without their drawbacks. The hardware complexity is higher than that of direct-mapped caches, as the mapping logic must handle the additional complexity introduced by multiple sets. Additionally, the benefits in terms of reduced conflicts may diminish as associativity levels increase, potentially impacting the cost-effectiveness of highly associative designs.

Fully associative mapping represents the most flexible approach, allowing any memory block to be placed in any cache location. This strategy effectively eliminates conflicts, providing the highest degree of flexibility in capturing spatial and temporal locality. The primary advantage of fully associative mapping is its ability to adapt to a wide range of access patterns, making it highly effective in scenarios where spatial and temporal locality are challenging to predict. Fully associative caches excel in capturing complex patterns present in diverse workloads. However, this flexibility comes at the cost of increased hardware complexity. The mapping logic must be capable of quickly identifying the presence of a memory block anywhere in the cache, typically requiring the use of content-addressable memory (CAM) or similar techniques. This added complexity results in higher access times and greater hardware costs compared to direct-mapped or set-associative caches. Fully associative caches are also more prone to power consumption due to the increased hardware requirements. While offering unparalleled flexibility, fully associative mapping may be considered overkill for certain applications where simpler mapping strategies provide sufficient performance.

In summary, the choice between direct-mapped, set-associative, and fully associative mapping techniques involves a delicate balance between simplicity and flexibility, hardware complexity, and the ability to capture locality effectively. Direct-mapped caching is advantageous in its simplicity and ease of implementation but may suffer from higher conflict rates and suboptimal performance in certain scenarios. Set-associative mapping strikes a balance, offering flexibility with varying levels of associativity to adapt to different workloads. While effective in reducing conflicts, set-associative caches incur higher hardware complexity. Fully associative mapping provides the utmost flexibility in capturing complex access patterns but at the expense of increased hardware complexity, higher access times, and potentially higher power consumption. The optimal choice depends on the specific requirements of the system, the characteristics of the workload, and the desired trade-offs between simplicity and caching efficiency.

Choosing the right mapping method for specific scenarios.

Selecting the appropriate mapping method for a cache system is a critical decision that depends on the characteristics of the workload, the specific requirements of the system, and the desired trade-offs between simplicity and caching efficiency. The choice between direct-mapped, set-associative, and fully associative mapping techniques involves considerations of hardware complexity, access speed, and the cache's ability to capture spatial and temporal locality effectively. In scenarios where simplicity is a top priority, and the access patterns of the workload exhibit a high degree of regularity and predictability, direct-mapped caching may be a suitable choice. The straightforward implementation of direct-mapped caches requires minimal hardware resources for address matching, making it an attractive option for applications with relatively simple and repetitive memory access patterns. However, it is crucial to acknowledge that direct-mapped caches may struggle in scenarios with more complex access patterns, where conflicts lead to higher cache miss rates, potentially impacting performance.

Set-associative mapping emerges as a versatile choice, offering a balance between simplicity and flexibility. By dividing the cache into multiple sets, each containing multiple cache locations, set-associative caches reduce the likelihood of conflicts compared to direct-mapped caches. The associativity level, determining the number of cache locations within each set, can be adjusted to match the requirements of the workload. For applications with moderately complex access patterns and a need for adaptability, set-associative mapping provides an effective compromise. The flexibility introduced by set-associative caches enables them to capture a broader range of spatial and temporal locality, making them suitable for a diverse array of workloads. However, it is important to recognize that the benefits of set-associative mapping come with increased hardware complexity, which can impact implementation costs and potentially lead to higher power consumption.

Fully associative mapping is a powerful choice when the workload exhibits highly unpredictable and complex access patterns, making it challenging to anticipate where data will be accessed in the cache. Fully associative caches offer the highest degree of flexibility by allowing any memory block to be placed in any cache location, eliminating conflicts. This makes fully associative mapping ideal for scenarios with irregular or dynamic access patterns, where spatial and temporal locality are challenging to predict. However, the advantages of fully associative mapping come at a cost. The complexity of the mapping logic, often involving content-addressable memory (CAM) or similar techniques, leads to higher access times and increased hardware requirements. Fully associative caches may be considered overkill for applications with simpler access patterns, where the additional complexity and potential performance gains may not justify the associated costs.

In scenarios where the workload exhibits a mix of regular and irregular access patterns, a hybrid approach combining different mapping techniques may be advantageous. For example, a system may feature a combination of direct-mapped and set-associative caches, with different levels of associativity for different cache levels. This hybrid model allows for targeted optimization based on the specific characteristics of different portions of the workload. By tailoring the cache hierarchy to the workload's diverse requirements, the system can achieve a balance between simplicity and efficiency. This approach requires careful analysis of the workload's characteristics and often involves dynamic adaptation based on runtime conditions.

Moreover, advancements in hardware design and caching algorithms continue to influence the choice of mapping methods. Novel techniques, such as way prediction, aim to dynamically adjust the associativity level of set-associative caches based on runtime behavior, providing a degree of adaptability without the need for a fully associative structure. Similarly, intelligent prefetching algorithms and sophisticated replacement policies contribute to enhancing the efficiency of different mapping methods in various scenarios.

Considerations for choosing the right mapping method extend beyond the cache structure itself to encompass the broader memory hierarchy, including levels of cache and the interaction with main memory. In multicore systems or those with multiple processors, the choice of mapping method may be influenced by the need for coherence between caches. Cache coherency protocols, which ensure that modifications to cached data are reflected in main memory, may impact the effectiveness of certain mapping techniques.

In conclusion, selecting the right mapping method for specific scenarios involves a nuanced evaluation of the workload's access patterns, the desired trade-offs between simplicity and efficiency, and considerations of hardware complexity. Direct-mapped caching, set-associative mapping, and fully associative mapping each offer unique advantages and disadvantages, catering to different requirements. The decision may involve a careful balance, potentially incorporating hybrid models or leveraging advancements in hardware design to adapt to the dynamic nature of modern workloads. The ongoing evolution of computing applications and architectures further emphasizes the need for a thoughtful and context-specific approach to choosing the optimal mapping method for cache systems in diverse scenarios.

Overview of cache replacement policies.

Cache replacement policies are fundamental aspects of cache management, influencing the efficiency and performance of memory hierarchies in computer systems. These policies determine how cache entries are selected for eviction when new data needs to be loaded into a cache line that is already occupied. The choice of a cache replacement policy has a profound impact on the cache hit rate, which measures the proportion of memory accesses satisfied by the cache, and consequently, on the overall system performance.

One of the simplest cache replacement policies is the First-In-First-Out (FIFO) policy. In a FIFO cache, the oldest cache entry is evicted when new data needs to be loaded. This policy is based on the principle that the first data to be brought into the cache should be the first to be replaced. While FIFO is easy to implement and requires minimal overhead, it may not always reflect the access patterns of the workload. Workloads with dynamic or irregular access patterns may not benefit optimally from a rigid FIFO policy, as the oldest data may not necessarily be the least likely to be accessed in the near future.

Another widely used cache replacement policy is Least Recently Used (LRU), which evicts the least recently accessed cache entry when a new one needs to be loaded. LRU is based on the principle of temporal locality, assuming that recently accessed data is more likely to be accessed again soon. LRU keeps track of the access history of each cache entry and selects the one that has not been accessed for the longest time. While LRU is more adaptive to varying access patterns compared to FIFO, its implementation can be complex and resource-intensive. Maintaining accurate access time information for each cache entry requires additional storage and computational overhead.

Random replacement is a simplistic cache replacement policy where a randomly selected cache entry is evicted when new data needs to be loaded. Despite its lack of sophistication, the random replacement policy has certain advantages. It is easy to implement and can provide a degree of unpredictability that may be beneficial in certain scenarios. However, random replacement lacks the intelligence to consider the actual access patterns of the workload, making it less efficient in capturing temporal and spatial locality. The inherent randomness may lead to suboptimal cache performance in workloads with specific access characteristics.

The Not Recently Used (NRU) policy is a compromise between simplicity and adaptability. NRU categorizes cache entries based on recent access information and prioritizes the eviction of entries that have not been recently accessed. This policy typically divides cache entries into categories such as "recently used" and "not recently used," with eviction preference given to the latter. NRU attempts to capture temporal locality by considering recent access information while maintaining a level of simplicity in implementation. However, the effectiveness of NRU may be limited, especially in scenarios where fine-grained access history information is crucial for making eviction decisions.

The Clock algorithm, an approximation of LRU, offers a compromise between complexity and efficiency. In the Clock algorithm, a circular list of cache entries is maintained, and a "clock hand" points to the next entry to be examined. When a cache replacement is needed, the clock hand advances, and the entry it points to is examined.

If the entry has been accessed since the last examination, it is given a "second chance" and remains in the cache. If not, it is considered for eviction. The Clock algorithm provides a balance between capturing temporal locality and minimizing implementation complexity. However, it may not be as precise as more sophisticated LRU-based policies in certain scenarios.

Additionally, variations of LRU, such as the Approximate LRU (ALRU) and Pseudo-LRU policies, aim to strike a balance between accuracy and implementation simplicity. These policies use approximations or heuristics to estimate the least recently used entry without maintaining a complete access history. While these approximations reduce computational overhead, they may sacrifice some accuracy in eviction decisions.

Recently, machine learning-based approaches have gained attention in cache replacement policies. Reinforcement learning and predictive modeling techniques are employed to dynamically adapt the cache replacement strategy based on real-time access patterns. These approaches aim to learn and predict the likelihood of future cache accesses, optimizing replacement decisions for diverse workloads. Machine learning-based policies have the potential to adapt to evolving workloads and provide effective cache management in complex scenarios, but their implementation requires careful consideration of training, prediction accuracy, and computational overhead.

The efficiency of cache replacement policies is often evaluated using metrics such as hit rate, miss rate, hit time, and miss penalty. A high hit rate indicates that a significant portion of memory accesses are satisfied by the cache, reflecting effective replacement decisions. Miss rate represents the proportion of accesses resulting in cache misses, providing insights into the ability of the replacement policy to capture the actual access patterns. Hit time, the time taken to access data from the cache, is influenced by the replacement policy's ability to retain frequently accessed data. Miss penalty, the additional time required to fetch data from the main memory in the event of a cache miss, reflects the efficiency of replacement decisions in minimizing the impact of cache misses.

In conclusion, cache replacement policies play a crucial role in optimizing the performance of memory hierarchies in computer systems. The choice of a replacement policy involves trade-offs between simplicity and adaptability, computational overhead, and the ability to capture temporal and spatial locality. Each policy, from simple FIFO and random replacement to more complex LRU-based strategies and machine learning approaches, offers a unique balance of advantages and disadvantages. The selection of an appropriate replacement policy depends on the specific characteristics of the workload, the system's requirements, and the desired trade-offs for optimizing cache efficiency. Ongoing research continues to explore innovative approaches, including machine learning-based policies, to further enhance the adaptability and effectiveness of cache replacement strategies in the ever-evolving landscape of computing workloads.

Chapter 5: Memory Protection and Security

Significance of protecting memory from unauthorized access. The significance of protecting memory from unauthorized access is paramount in the realm of computing, spanning various domains from personal computing devices to large-scale data centers. The memory of a computer system holds a wealth of sensitive information, including personal data, financial records, passwords, and proprietary business information. Unauthorized access to this information can lead to severe consequences, ranging from privacy breaches and identity theft to financial losses and compromises of intellectual property.

One fundamental aspect of memory protection is safeguarding user data and system files stored in volatile and non-volatile memory. In modern computer systems, volatile memory, such as Random Access Memory (RAM), holds actively used data and program code during the system's operation. Unauthorized access to RAM could potentially expose critical information currently in use by the operating system or applications. Similarly, non-volatile memory, which includes storage devices like hard drives and solid-state drives, retains data even when the system is powered off. Protecting non-volatile memory is crucial to prevent unauthorized users from extracting sensitive information stored persistently, whether it be personal documents or system configurations.

Beyond the realm of personal computing, memory protection becomes even more critical in server environments and cloud computing infrastructures. Servers often host multiple users or applications simultaneously, and memory protection mechanisms are essential to ensure the isolation and security of each user's data and processes. Unauthorized access to the memory space of one user or application could lead to the compromise of data belonging to other users, potentially resulting in data breaches and the violation of privacy regulations.

In a networked environment, where data is transmitted between systems, securing memory becomes a vital component of overall cybersecurity. Data in transit, whether within a local network or over the internet, can be intercepted by malicious actors if proper memory protection mechanisms are not in place. Encryption of data in memory is a key strategy to mitigate the risks associated with unauthorized access during transmission. By encrypting data, even if an unauthorized entity gains access to the memory, the information remains indecipherable without the appropriate decryption keys.

Memory protection is also integral to the integrity and security of software execution. Malicious actors often attempt to exploit vulnerabilities in software to gain unauthorized access or control over a system. Techniques such as buffer overflow attacks involve overwriting memory regions to inject malicious code into a program's execution flow. Memory protection mechanisms, including Address Space Layout Randomization (ASLR) and Data Execution Prevention (DEP), mitigate the risk of such attacks by randomizing memory addresses and preventing the execution of code in certain memory regions.

In the context of operating systems, memory protection is a foundational security feature. Operating systems use memory protection mechanisms to create isolated memory spaces for each running application or process. This isolation prevents one application from accessing the memory space of another, contributing to system stability, reliability, and security. Memory protection is achieved through features like virtual memory, which allows each application to operate in its own virtual address space. Virtual memory mapping, backed by physical memory management, ensures that applications do not inadvertently overwrite each other's data or execute unauthorized code.

Moreover, the significance of protecting memory extends to the defense against sophisticated cyber threats, such as privilege escalation attacks. In a multi-user environment, users are assigned different levels of privileges or permissions to access certain resources. Unauthorized access to higher-level privileges could lead to the compromise of the entire system. Memory protection mechanisms, including access control lists (ACLs) and user privilege management, play a crucial role in enforcing these permissions and preventing unauthorized users or processes from gaining elevated access.

The protection of memory is also closely tied to the broader concept of access control, which encompasses authentication and authorization. Authentication ensures that only legitimate users gain access to a system, verifying their identity through credentials such as usernames and passwords. Authorization, on the other hand, determines the level of access and permissions granted to authenticated users. Memory protection integrates with access control mechanisms to enforce the principle of least privilege, ensuring that users and processes only have access to the resources and memory space necessary for their intended tasks.

In addition to protecting against external threats, memory protection is equally vital in mitigating the risks associated with insider threats. Insiders, whether malicious or unintentional, may attempt to access or modify data in ways that could jeopardize the integrity and confidentiality of the system. Robust memory protection measures are essential for detecting and preventing unauthorized actions by individuals with legitimate access to the system. This involves auditing and monitoring memory access patterns to identify anomalous behavior indicative of potential security breaches.

Compliance with regulatory frameworks and privacy standards further underscores the significance of memory protection. Governments and industry regulators impose strict requirements on organizations to safeguard sensitive information, and violations can result in legal consequences, financial penalties, and damage to an organization's reputation. Memory protection measures, including encryption, secure coding practices, and access controls, are essential components of compliance strategies designed to meet these stringent requirements.

The increasing prevalence of cloud computing adds another layer of complexity to the significance of memory protection. In cloud environments, where data and applications are hosted on shared infrastructure, robust memory protection is imperative to ensure the security and confidentiality of each tenant's information. Cloud service providers implement sophisticated memory isolation mechanisms to prevent one customer's data or processes from being accessed by another, reinforcing the trustworthiness of cloud computing platforms.

In conclusion, the significance of protecting memory from unauthorized access permeates all facets of computing, from personal devices to enterprise systems and cloud environments. Memory contains the lifeblood of digital operations, storing sensitive information and facilitating the execution of software. The consequences of unauthorized access to memory can be severe, encompassing privacy breaches, financial losses, intellectual property theft, and compromises to system integrity. Memory protection mechanisms, including encryption, access controls, virtual memory, and secure coding practices, form a multifaceted defense against a diverse array of cyber threats. As technology evolves and cyber threats become increasingly sophisticated, the ongoing emphasis on robust memory protection remains a cornerstone of cybersecurity efforts to ensure the trust, integrity, and confidentiality of digital systems.

Preventing data corruption and security breaches.

Preventing data corruption and security breaches is a critical imperative in the realm of information technology, encompassing a multifaceted approach that addresses various vulnerabilities, emerging threats, and the complex landscape of modern computing environments. At the forefront of these efforts is the implementation of robust security measures that safeguard data integrity, confidentiality, and availability.

One fundamental aspect of preventing data corruption and security breaches involves the establishment of secure communication channels. Encryption plays a pivotal role in securing data in transit, ensuring that information exchanged between systems, devices, or users remains confidential and tamper-proof. Employing strong encryption algorithms and implementing secure communication protocols, such as Transport Layer Security (TLS) for web traffic, mitigates the risk of eavesdropping and man-in-the-middle attacks, preserving the integrity of sensitive data during transmission.

The protection of data at rest, stored on devices or servers, is equally crucial. Encryption technologies, such as full disk encryption and file-level encryption, provide a robust defense against unauthorized access and data tampering. By encrypting data at rest, organizations can mitigate the impact of physical theft, unauthorized access to storage devices, or insider threats. Coupled with secure access controls and authentication mechanisms, encryption contributes to a layered defense strategy, reinforcing the resilience of stored data against various attack vectors.

Access controls and user authentication mechanisms form the backbone of data security, preventing unauthorized users from gaining entry to sensitive information. Strong and multifactor authentication protocols bolster the integrity of user identities, reducing the risk of unauthorized access. Role-based access controls (RBAC) and least privilege principles ensure that users or processes only have access to the data and resources necessary for their specific roles, minimizing the potential for security breaches resulting from overprivileged accounts.

To further fortify the defense against security breaches, organizations implement intrusion detection and prevention systems. These systems continuously monitor network traffic, system logs, and user activities to identify anomalous patterns indicative of unauthorized access attempts or malicious activities. Intrusion prevention mechanisms can automatically respond to detected threats by blocking suspicious network traffic or isolating compromised systems, mitigating the risk of data corruption or exfiltration.

Security patching and regular software updates are integral components of preventing security breaches. Vulnerabilities in software and operating systems are a common target for attackers seeking to exploit weaknesses and compromise data integrity. Timely application of security patches, coupled with a robust patch management process, helps close these vulnerabilities and fortify the overall security posture of systems. Regular updates also extend to antivirus and antimalware software, ensuring that systems are equipped with the latest threat intelligence to detect and neutralize emerging malware threats.

A proactive stance on security involves continuous monitoring and threat intelligence analysis. Security information and event management (SIEM) systems aggregate and analyze logs from various sources, providing insights into potential security incidents. Real-time monitoring allows organizations to detect and respond promptly to security events, preventing data corruption or unauthorized access before substantial damage occurs. Threat intelligence feeds enable organizations to stay informed about evolving threats and adjust their security posture accordingly.

In the context of web applications, secure coding practices and adherence to industry-standard security frameworks, such as OWASP (Open Web Application Security Project), are paramount in preventing security breaches. By designing applications with security in mind, developers can mitigate the risk of common vulnerabilities such as SQL injection, cross-site scripting (XSS), and cross-site request forgery (CSRF). Regular security audits and penetration testing further validate the resilience of web applications against potential exploitation, contributing to a robust defense against data corruption and unauthorized access.

Network segmentation and the implementation of firewalls enhance the security of internal networks, preventing lateral movement by attackers in the event of a successful breach. By dividing the network into isolated segments and enforcing strict access controls, organizations limit the potential impact of security incidents and safeguard critical data repositories. Firewalls serve as a perimeter defense, monitoring and filtering incoming and outgoing network traffic based on predefined security rules, preventing unauthorized access and protecting against external threats.

Human factors play a significant role in the prevention of data corruption and security breaches. Security awareness training for employees educates them on best practices, social engineering threats, and the importance of maintaining a security-conscious mindset. Phishing simulations and regular awareness campaigns empower users to recognize and report suspicious activities, reducing the likelihood of falling victim to social engineering attacks that could compromise sensitive data.

Endpoint security measures, including the deployment of antivirus software, endpoint detection and response (EDR) solutions, and mobile device management (MDM) systems, contribute to preventing security breaches originating from end-user devices. These measures protect against malware, unauthorized access attempts, and the loss or theft of devices containing sensitive data. Endpoint security solutions also facilitate the enforcement of security policies, ensuring that devices adhere to predefined configurations and compliance standards.

In the evolving landscape of cybersecurity, threat hunting and incident response capabilities are indispensable for organizations seeking to prevent and mitigate security breaches. Threat hunting involves actively searching for signs of malicious activities within an environment, proactively identifying potential threats before they escalate. Incident response plans outline predefined steps to be taken in the event of a security incident, ensuring a swift and coordinated response to contain and remediate the impact, thereby preventing further data corruption or unauthorized access.

Cloud security measures play a crucial role, especially as organizations increasingly adopt cloud services and infrastructures. Cloud providers offer a range of security features, including encryption, identity and access management (IAM), and security monitoring tools. Ensuring proper configuration and adherence to best practices when deploying resources in the cloud reinforces the protection of data against unauthorized access or corruption.

Compliance with regulatory frameworks and data protection laws adds a layer of accountability in the efforts to prevent data corruption and security breaches. Regulations such as the General Data Protection Regulation (GDPR) and the Health Insurance Portability and Accountability Act (HIPAA) outline specific requirements for the protection of personal and sensitive data. Adhering to these regulations not only helps avoid legal consequences but also fosters a culture of responsible data stewardship, reinforcing the commitment to safeguarding information integrity.

The significance of preventing data corruption and security breaches extends beyond the confines of individual organizations, encompassing collaborative efforts within the broader cybersecurity community. Information sharing, collaborative threat intelligence platforms, and industry alliances contribute to a collective defense against evolving threats. By fostering a collaborative approach, organizations can benefit from shared insights, early warnings, and collective responses to emerging security challenges, amplifying the overall resilience of the digital ecosystem.

In conclusion, preventing data corruption and security breaches is a multifaceted and ongoing endeavor that demands a holistic and proactive approach. From encryption and access controls to threat intelligence and human-centric security awareness programs, organizations must deploy a comprehensive array of measures to fortify their defenses. The ever-evolving nature of cyber threats necessitates continuous adaptation and innovation, with a commitment to staying ahead of potential adversaries. By embracing a culture of security, investing in technological defenses, and fostering collaboration, organizations can navigate the complex landscape of cybersecurity, thereby safeguarding the integrity, confidentiality, and availability of their critical data assets.

Balancing security with system performance.

Balancing security with system performance is a delicate and essential undertaking in the realm of information technology, where the imperative to safeguard digital assets must coexist with the demand for efficient and responsive computing environments. Achieving this equilibrium requires a nuanced approach that addresses the intricate interplay between security measures and the need for optimal system functionality.

One cornerstone of this delicate balance lies in the implementation of robust authentication mechanisms. While strong and multifactor authentication protocols contribute significantly to bolstering system security, they can potentially introduce performance overhead. The challenge lies in striking a balance between the level of authentication required and the impact on user experience and system responsiveness. Deploying adaptive authentication mechanisms that dynamically adjust the level of scrutiny based on contextual factors, such as user behavior and the sensitivity of the accessed resources, can be instrumental in optimizing the trade-off between security and performance.

Similarly, access controls play a pivotal role in shaping the security posture of systems, yet their implementation must be judiciously calibrated to prevent hindrances to performance. Restrictive access controls that overly constrain user permissions may impede the efficiency of legitimate operations. Employing a principle of least privilege, where users are granted only the permissions necessary for their specific roles, becomes a strategic approach to mitigate the risk of unauthorized access without unnecessarily compromising system performance.

Encryption, a cornerstone of data security, introduces both security benefits and computational overhead. While encrypting data at rest and in transit is imperative for safeguarding confidentiality, the cryptographic processes involved can impact system performance. Selecting appropriate encryption algorithms and key management strategies becomes crucial in finding the right compromise between data security and computational efficiency. Hardware-accelerated encryption, using specialized cryptographic processors or instructions, represents one avenue to mitigate the performance impact associated with encryption.

In the context of network security, firewalls and intrusion detection systems are indispensable components of defense against external threats. However, the stringent enforcement of security policies by firewalls can potentially introduce latency, especially in high-traffic environments. Balancing the need for comprehensive network security with the imperative to maintain low-latency communication requires careful tuning of firewall rules, prioritizing critical traffic, and considering innovative approaches such as deep packet inspection for more efficient threat detection.

Patch management presents another dimension of the delicate balance between security and performance. Timely application of security patches is imperative to close vulnerabilities and fortify the resilience of systems against emerging threats. However, the process of patching can disrupt system operations and requires careful planning to minimize downtime. Striking a balance between the urgency of patching to address security vulnerabilities and the need to avoid disruptions to critical services becomes an ongoing challenge in maintaining a secure and performant computing environment.

The prevalence of security measures in the design and development of software is a critical aspect of the security-performance equilibrium. Secure coding practices, adherence to industry-standard security frameworks, and the integration of security into the software development lifecycle contribute to building resilient and robust applications. However, the rigorous scrutiny introduced by security measures, such as static code analysis and security testing, can potentially introduce delays in the software development lifecycle. Adopting agile and DevSecOps methodologies becomes essential to harmonize security considerations with the need for rapid software development cycles.

Endpoint security measures, encompassing antivirus software, endpoint detection and response (EDR) solutions, and mobile device management (MDM) systems, are vital components of the security-performance balance. These measures protect end-user devices against malware, unauthorized access attempts, and data breaches. However, the continuous monitoring and scanning processes involved can impact system resources and responsiveness. Implementing lightweight and efficient endpoint security solutions, coupled with intelligent threat detection algorithms, becomes imperative to minimize the performance footprint while maintaining robust security.

In cloud computing environments, where scalability and resource efficiency are paramount, the security-performance balance takes on added complexity. Cloud providers offer a range of security features, including identity and access management, encryption services, and security monitoring tools. However, the configuration of these services must align with security best practices while optimizing resource utilization. Leveraging cloud-native security controls and considering the shared responsibility model between cloud providers and customers becomes essential in achieving a harmonious equilibrium between security and system performance in the cloud.

The management of security logs and audit trails represents an often-overlooked aspect of the security-performance balance. While logging is critical for detecting and investigating security incidents, indiscriminate or overly verbose logging can impact system performance and generate unnecessary storage overhead. Implementing a tailored logging strategy, focusing on relevant security events and leveraging log compression techniques, helps maintain the integrity of security monitoring without unduly burdening system resources.

Machine learning and artificial intelligence (AI) introduce both security enhancements and computational demands. These technologies can bolster security measures by enabling advanced threat detection, anomaly identification, and predictive analysis. However, the resource-intensive nature of machine learning algorithms requires thoughtful consideration in the deployment of security solutions. Optimizing model training and inference processes, exploring hardware accelerators for AI workloads, and embracing edge computing paradigms represent strategies to strike a balance between leveraging advanced technologies for security and maintaining system performance.

Regulatory compliance introduces an additional layer of complexity to the security-performance equilibrium. Adhering to regulations such as the General Data Protection Regulation (GDPR) or the Health Insurance Portability and Accountability Act (HIPAA) is non-negotiable, yet the stringent requirements imposed by these regulations can impact system operations. Aligning security measures with regulatory mandates while minimizing disruptions to system performance involves a meticulous understanding of compliance requirements and the implementation of tailored controls.

The significance of user education and awareness in maintaining the security-performance balance cannot be overstated. Users, whether employees or end consumers, play a pivotal role in the security posture of systems. Security awareness training programs, phishing simulations, and regular communication about security best practices empower users to make informed decisions that enhance security while minimizing the risk of inadvertent actions that could impact system performance.

In conclusion, the delicate balance between security and system performance requires a strategic and holistic approach that encompasses various dimensions of information technology. From authentication and access controls to encryption, software development practices, and the deployment of advanced technologies like machine learning, organizations must navigate a complex landscape to fortify their systems against threats while maintaining optimal performance. The key lies in a nuanced understanding of the specific requirements and constraints of the environment, informed decision-making, and the continual adaptation of security measures to align with evolving threats and technological advancements. Striking this balance is an ongoing journey, a dynamic equilibrium that demands vigilance, adaptability, and a commitment to fostering a secure and high-performing digital ecosystem.

Understanding privilege levels in operating systems.

Understanding privilege levels in operating systems is fundamental to comprehending the hierarchical model through which access and control over system resources are managed. Privilege levels, often referred to as "rings" or "modes," define the scope of authority that an entity, such as a user or a process, possesses within the operating system. This concept is deeply ingrained in the design of modern operating systems, providing a mechanism to ensure the integrity, security, and stability of the system while accommodating the diverse needs of users and applications.

The concept of privilege levels traces its roots to early computer architectures, where the operating system's functions were divided into distinct layers of execution. These layers, commonly organized into four privilege levels, are often labeled as Ring 0 through Ring 3. Ring 0, also known as the kernel mode or supervisor mode, represents the highest privilege level. In this mode, the operating system's core functions, including memory management, process scheduling, and device access, are executed. Ring 0 has unrestricted access to system resources and is crucial for maintaining the overall system integrity.

Conversely, Ring 3, often referred to as the user mode, is the lowest privilege level. In this mode, user applications and processes execute, and their access to system resources is constrained to prevent unauthorized or unintended actions. User mode serves as a protective boundary that shields the operating system kernel and critical system functions from direct manipulation by applications. This strict separation enhances system stability and security by mitigating the impact of errors or malicious activities within user-mode processes.

In between Ring 0 and Ring 3, there exist intermediate privilege levels, namely Ring 1 and Ring 2, although these are less commonly used in contemporary operating systems. The additional privilege levels were initially conceived to accommodate certain specialized tasks or facilitate the transition from user mode to kernel mode. However, as operating systems evolved, the simplicity and efficiency of a two-ring model (Ring 0 and Ring 3) gained prevalence, and intermediate rings were largely deprecated in favor of a more streamlined design.

The division of privilege levels serves multiple purposes within the operating system architecture. Primarily, it acts as a protective barrier to shield critical system components from unintended or malicious interference. The kernel, residing in Ring 0, enjoys unrestricted access to hardware and system resources, allowing it to execute privileged instructions and manage the overall system state. The user mode, on the other hand, operates in a constrained environment, ensuring that applications cannot directly manipulate critical system functions or interfere with the stability of the operating system.

The transition between privilege levels is a carefully orchestrated process governed by the operating system's architecture. System calls, which allow user applications to request services from the operating system kernel, serve as the conduit for transitioning between user mode and kernel mode. When a user application invokes a system call, it triggers a transition to the kernel mode, where the requested operation is performed with elevated privileges. This controlled interaction between privilege levels balances the need for system functionality with the imperative to prevent unrestricted access that could compromise security and stability.

In addition to delineating access privileges, privilege levels contribute to the enforcement of memory protection mechanisms. Virtual memory, a crucial feature in modern operating systems, enables the illusion of a larger address space than physically available memory. The mapping of virtual addresses to physical memory locations is managed by the operating system's memory management unit (MMU). Privilege levels play a role in controlling access to different portions of virtual memory. Kernel memory, critical for storing the operating system's code and data, is reserved for Ring 0, while user-mode processes are confined to their designated address spaces.

The concept of rings is not limited to the x86 architecture but is a broader principle applicable to various computing platforms. Different architectures may have varying numbers of privilege levels or use alternative terms such as "modes." For example, ARM architecture employs a similar concept with four Exception Levels (EL0 to EL3), where EL0 corresponds to user mode, and EL3 represents the most privileged level, akin to kernel mode.

The significance of privilege levels extends beyond the traditional boundaries of personal computers to encompass diverse computing environments. In embedded systems, where real-time constraints and resource efficiency are paramount, privilege levels play a crucial role in balancing system responsiveness with security considerations. Similarly, in server environments and cloud computing platforms, the orchestration of privilege levels becomes integral to ensuring the isolation of virtualized instances and preventing unauthorized access to shared resources.

One notable challenge in managing privilege levels lies in the need to accommodate both the demands of security and the requirements of user applications. Striking the right balance involves crafting an operating system architecture that provides sufficient isolation between privilege levels while facilitating efficient communication and resource sharing. This equilibrium is particularly critical in scenarios where multiple users or applications coexist on a single system, such as in multi-user operating systems or virtualized environments.

The concept of privilege levels also intersects with the broader field of security. Security vulnerabilities often stem from unauthorized access or exploitation of elevated privileges. Privilege escalation, a common attack vector, involves exploiting vulnerabilities to gain unauthorized access to higher privilege levels, potentially compromising the entire system. Operating system designers and security professionals continually work to identify and mitigate vulnerabilities that could be exploited for privilege escalation, emphasizing the ongoing importance of this aspect in the evolving landscape of cybersecurity.

While the traditional ring model has proven effective for many decades, advancements in operating system design and security paradigms continue to shape the landscape. Concepts such as microkernels, which advocate for a minimalistic kernel design with core functions implemented in user space, challenge the conventional wisdom of privilege levels. Microkernels aim to reduce the attack surface by minimizing the privileged code running in kernel mode, potentially mitigating the impact of security vulnerabilities.

In conclusion, understanding privilege levels in operating systems is pivotal to grasping the foundational principles that govern access control, security, and resource management. The hierarchical model of privilege levels, whether expressed as rings or modes, serves as a cornerstone in the design of operating systems, providing a framework for balancing the need for system functionality with the imperative to safeguard against unauthorized access and malicious activities. As computing environments evolve, the exploration of alternative architectures and security models continues, underscoring the ongoing relevance and significance of privilege levels in shaping the landscape of operating system design and security.

Implementing access control mechanisms.

Implementing access control mechanisms is a multifaceted and crucial aspect of information security, encompassing a wide array of strategies and technologies aimed at regulating and managing the permissions granted to users, processes, or systems within an environment. Access control is fundamental to ensuring the confidentiality, integrity, and availability of sensitive data and critical resources. The implementation of robust access control mechanisms involves a comprehensive understanding of the organization's security requirements, the nature of the data being protected, and the operational context in which access is granted or denied.

One fundamental approach to access control is the principle of least privilege (PoLP). This principle dictates that users and processes should be granted the minimum level of access necessary to perform their assigned tasks. By adhering to the principle of least privilege, organizations can reduce the potential impact of security incidents and limit the scope of unauthorized access. This approach involves the careful evaluation of user roles and responsibilities, mapping them to specific access permissions, and continually monitoring and adjusting these permissions as needed to align with evolving business requirements.

Role-based access control (RBAC) is a widely adopted framework for implementing access controls, particularly in large and complex organizational structures. RBAC assigns roles to users based on their job functions, and these roles are associated with specific sets of permissions. This hierarchical structure simplifies access management, as permissions can be assigned at the role level, and users inherit the permissions associated with their assigned roles. RBAC streamlines the process of onboarding and offboarding employees, ensures consistency in access permissions, and facilitates auditability by providing a clear mapping of roles to permissions.

Access control lists (ACLs) represent another foundational mechanism for specifying and controlling access permissions. ACLs are lists associated with specific resources, such as files, directories, or network resources, and enumerate the users or groups and the corresponding permissions granted or denied. ACLs provide a granular level of control, allowing administrators to tailor access permissions based on individual users or groups. This fine-grained control is particularly valuable in environments where specific resources require unique access considerations.

In addition to RBAC and ACLs, attribute-based access control (ABAC) offers a more dynamic and context-aware approach to access management. ABAC considers a range of attributes, including user characteristics, environmental conditions, and resource attributes, to make access control decisions. This flexibility enables organizations to define policies based on a broader set of criteria, allowing for more adaptive and context-specific access controls. ABAC is well-suited for dynamic and complex environments where access requirements may vary based on contextual factors.

Mandatory access control (MAC) is a security model that enforces access controls based on system-wide policies set by the system administrator or security administrator. Unlike discretionary access control (DAC), where resource owners determine access permissions, MAC places restrictions on users and processes, regardless of individual user preferences. This centralized approach is often employed in environments with stringent security requirements, such as government or military systems, where the need for control overrides user discretion to ensure the highest levels of information assurance.

Implementing access controls at the network level is critical for safeguarding resources and preventing unauthorized access to sensitive data. Firewalls, intrusion detection and prevention systems, and virtual private networks (VPNs) are integral components of network access control. Firewalls, whether at the perimeter or distributed within the network, filter and monitor incoming and outgoing traffic based on predetermined security rules, effectively controlling which network packets are allowed or denied. Intrusion detection and prevention systems analyze network traffic for signs of malicious activity, helping to prevent security incidents before they escalate. VPNs secure communication channels over public networks, ensuring that data transmitted between endpoints remains confidential and protected from interception.

Authentication mechanisms play a pivotal role in access control by verifying the identity of users or systems attempting to access resources. Single sign-on (SSO) solutions streamline the authentication process by allowing users to log in once and gain access to multiple systems or applications without the need for repeated logins. Multi-factor authentication (MFA) enhances security by requiring users to provide multiple forms of identification, such as a password and a temporary code sent to their mobile device. Biometric authentication, based on physical or behavioral characteristics, offers an additional layer of security by uniquely identifying individuals based on traits like fingerprints, iris patterns, or voice recognition.

Access control is not limited to traditional computing environments but extends to cloud computing platforms, where organizations leverage Infrastructure as a Service (IaaS), Platform as a Service (PaaS), or Software as a Service (SaaS) offerings. Cloud access security brokers (CASBs) act as intermediaries between cloud service providers and users, enforcing access controls, data encryption, and other security policies. Identity and access management (IAM) solutions in the cloud enable organizations to manage user identities and access permissions across diverse cloud services efficiently.

The management of privileged access is a critical component of access control, as privileged accounts often have elevated permissions that, if misused, could result in significant security risks. Privileged access management (PAM) solutions help organizations secure, monitor, and audit activities associated with privileged accounts. PAM includes features such as just-in-time privileged access, session monitoring, and password vaulting to mitigate the risks associated with unauthorized or excessive access.

Access control must be complemented by robust monitoring and auditing mechanisms to detect and respond to unauthorized or suspicious activities. Security information and event management (SIEM) systems aggregate and analyze logs from various sources, providing insights into access patterns, authentication events, and potential security incidents. Regular audits of access controls, permissions, and user accounts are essential for identifying and correcting any discrepancies, ensuring that access policies align with organizational requirements.

Implementing access controls is an ongoing process that requires regular reviews and updates to adapt to changing business needs, compliance requirements, and the evolving threat landscape. Periodic access reviews, often conducted through access certification processes, involve validating and recertifying the access permissions of users and ensuring that they align with their current roles and responsibilities. Continuous monitoring of access controls and proactive threat hunting activities contribute to the early detection and mitigation of potential security risks.

Compliance with regulatory frameworks and industry standards plays a crucial role in shaping access control implementations. Regulations such as the General Data Protection Regulation (GDPR), the Health Insurance Portability and Accountability Act (HIPAA), or the Payment Card Industry Data Security Standard (PCI DSS) mandate specific access control measures to protect sensitive information. Organizations must tailor their access control mechanisms to align with these regulatory requirements and demonstrate compliance through regular audits and reporting.

In conclusion, implementing access control mechanisms is a foundational pillar of information security, contributing to the protection of critical assets, the prevention of unauthorized access, and the overall resilience of organizational environments. The diverse array of access control strategies, including RBAC, ACLs, ABAC, MAC, and network-level controls, allows organizations to tailor their approach based on specific requirements and operational contexts. As technology evolves, access control continues to adapt, incorporating innovations such as cloud security solutions, IAM in the cloud, and advanced authentication mechanisms. The dynamic and evolving nature of access control underscores the importance of a holistic and adaptive approach to safeguarding information assets in an ever-changing digital landscape.

Securing critical system resources through privilege management.

Securing critical system resources through privilege management is an indispensable facet of information security, focusing on the meticulous control and oversight of access rights to safeguard sensitive assets and ensure the overall integrity and functionality of an organization's computing environment. Privilege management involves the judicious allocation and restriction of permissions granted to users, processes, and systems, with a primary objective of mitigating the risks associated with unauthorized access, misuse, or compromise of critical resources. This multifaceted approach extends beyond traditional access controls, delving into the intricacies of managing elevated privileges, often associated with administrative or privileged accounts, that wield considerable influence over key system components.

One fundamental principle underlying privilege management is the principle of least privilege (PoLP), advocating for the assignment of the minimum level of access necessary for users or processes to fulfill their designated functions. By adhering to PoLP, organizations aim to minimize the potential impact of security incidents, limiting the exposure of critical resources to only those actions essential for operational tasks. This principle applies prominently to administrative or privileged accounts, which typically have broader access rights, as organizations seek to strike a delicate balance between empowering administrators to perform necessary duties and reducing the likelihood of inadvertent or malicious actions.

Privileged access management (PAM) emerges as a specialized discipline within privilege management, concentrating on the comprehensive control and monitoring of accounts with elevated privileges. PAM solutions play a pivotal role in securing critical system resources by enforcing stringent access controls, robust authentication mechanisms, and continuous monitoring of privileged activities. These solutions often include features such as just-in-time privilege elevation, session monitoring, and password vaulting, all aimed at mitigating the inherent risks associated with privileged accounts.

One core aspect of privilege management is the secure provisioning and deprovisioning of privileged accounts. The process of onboarding new administrators or employees with elevated privileges demands a meticulous approach to ensure that access is granted based on job roles and responsibilities. Conversely, when administrators or employees change roles, depart from the organization, or no longer require elevated privileges, prompt deprovisioning becomes imperative to mitigate the risk of lingering access that could be exploited. Automated provisioning and deprovisioning mechanisms streamline these processes, reducing the likelihood of oversights or delays in adjusting access rights.

Just-in-time privilege elevation represents a proactive strategy within PAM, allowing administrators to temporarily acquire elevated privileges only when necessary for specific tasks. This approach minimizes the window of opportunity for potential misuse, as administrators operate with elevated privileges for the shortest duration required to perform designated functions. Just-in-time elevation, coupled with robust audit trails and session monitoring, enhances accountability and transparency, enabling organizations to trace privileged activities back to specific individuals and instances.

Session monitoring and recording play a crucial role in privilege management, offering organizations visibility into the actions performed by privileged users during their sessions. Comprehensive logs capture commands executed, changes made to critical configurations, and other activities that could impact system resources. Real-time monitoring of privileged sessions facilitates the rapid detection of anomalous behavior, potential security incidents, or unauthorized access. Furthermore, recorded sessions serve as valuable forensic evidence in the event of a security incident or compliance audit, aiding in the investigation and analysis of potential security breaches.

Password management is a cornerstone of privilege management, as compromised or weak passwords present a significant risk to the security of privileged accounts. Password vaulting solutions secure and centrally manage passwords associated with privileged accounts, ensuring their complexity, rotation, and secure storage. Additionally, multi-factor authentication (MFA) enhances the security posture of privileged accounts by requiring multiple forms of identification, adding an extra layer of protection against unauthorized access or credential theft.

Beyond user-based privilege management, organizations must also address the challenges associated with managing privileges granted to applications, services, and systems. Understanding the principle of least privilege in the context of systems involves limiting the permissions assigned to applications and services to the minimum necessary for their proper functioning. This approach mitigates the potential impact of security vulnerabilities within applications or services, reducing the attack surface and limiting the scope of potential exploits.

Continuous monitoring and auditing of privileged activities are integral components of privilege management, enabling organizations to detect and respond swiftly to potential security incidents. Security information and event management (SIEM) systems aggregate logs from various sources, providing a centralized platform for analyzing privileged access patterns, detecting anomalies, and correlating events indicative of unauthorized access or malicious activities. Regular security audits and reviews of privileged access rights contribute to the ongoing refinement and optimization of privilege management strategies.

Privilege management extends its purview to the realm of cloud computing, where organizations leverage Infrastructure as a Service (IaaS), Platform as a Service (PaaS), or Software as a Service (SaaS) offerings. Cloud environments necessitate a comprehensive approach to managing privileged access, encompassing not only traditional on-premises systems but also cloud-based resources. Cloud identity and access management (IAM) solutions facilitate the management of privileged identities and permissions in cloud services, ensuring a consistent and secure approach to privilege management across diverse computing environments.

Securing critical system resources through privilege management aligns closely with the overarching goal of achieving a defense-in-depth strategy. By implementing multiple layers of security controls, organizations can create a robust security posture that guards against both internal and external threats. Privilege management, as a vital component of this strategy, integrates with other security measures such as network segmentation, endpoint protection, and encryption to form a comprehensive framework that addresses the diverse challenges posed by evolving threat landscapes.

The significance of privilege management is accentuated in sectors where regulatory compliance and adherence to industry standards are paramount. Regulations such as the Payment Card Industry Data Security Standard (PCI DSS), the Health Insurance Portability and Accountability Act (HIPAA), or the General Data Protection Regulation (GDPR) mandate stringent controls over privileged access to safeguard sensitive information. Effective privilege management becomes an integral component of organizations' compliance efforts, demonstrating a commitment to protecting critical system resources and sensitive data in alignment with regulatory requirements.

In conclusion, securing critical system resources through privilege management represents a pivotal aspect of modern cybersecurity strategies. The meticulous control and monitoring of privileged access, whether wielded by users or systems, contribute to the resilience, integrity, and confidentiality of critical assets. As organizations navigate complex and dynamic IT environments, privilege management remains a cornerstone, evolving to address emerging threats, technological advancements, and the ever-evolving landscape of information security. Balancing the need for operational efficiency with the imperative to mitigate security risks, privilege management emerges as a dynamic and adaptive discipline essential for safeguarding critical system resources in an interconnected and digitally-driven world.

Introduction to ASLR as a security measure.

Address Space Layout Randomization (ASLR) stands as a pivotal security measure within the realm of information technology, designed to enhance the resilience of computer systems against a variety of malicious exploits and attacks. ASLR operates on the premise that unpredictability in the memory layout of a process makes it significantly more challenging for attackers to successfully exploit vulnerabilities and execute their malicious code. This technique is particularly effective against a class of security threats known as memory-based attacks, where attackers seek to take advantage of the predictable memory addresses of certain system components or software to compromise the integrity of a system.

At its core, ASLR introduces a dynamic element to the allocation of memory addresses within a process's address space, aiming to thwart attackers who rely on the predictability of memory layouts to execute their malicious payloads. Traditionally, computer systems assigned memory addresses in a deterministic manner, with specific regions of memory allocated for executable code, libraries, and data. This predictable structure made it easier for attackers to locate and exploit vulnerabilities by leveraging knowledge of where certain functions or data structures were positioned in memory.

ASLR disrupts this predictability by introducing randomness into the memory allocation process. When a program or system component is loaded into memory, ASLR ensures that the base addresses of key elements, such as the executable code, libraries, and stack, are randomly chosen. This randomization occurs each time the program is executed or the system is booted, making it challenging for attackers to anticipate the exact memory addresses they need to target. Consequently, even if a vulnerability exists in a program, the dynamic nature of ASLR forces attackers to first discover the correct memory addresses before they can successfully exploit the vulnerability.

One of the primary goals of ASLR is to thwart buffer overflow attacks, a prevalent category of exploits where attackers attempt to overflow a program's buffer with malicious code to hijack the execution flow. By randomizing the memory layout, ASLR introduces uncertainty about the location of critical elements in the address space, making it significantly harder for attackers to precisely craft their payloads. Without knowledge of the exact memory addresses, successful exploitation becomes a much more formidable challenge.

ASLR is not a one-size-fits-all solution but rather a defense-in-depth measure that complements other security mechanisms. It is particularly effective when combined with technologies such as Data Execution Prevention (DEP) or No eXecute (NX), which prevent the execution of code in certain regions of memory. The synergy between ASLR and DEP reinforces the protection against memory-based attacks, as even if an attacker manages to discover a vulnerability, they are impeded by the inability to execute malicious code in the identified memory region.

Operating systems, compilers, and binary executables play integral roles in the effective implementation of ASLR. Modern operating systems, including Windows, Linux, and macOS, have integrated ASLR as a standard security feature. When an application is compiled with ASLR support, the operating system introduces randomization into the loading of its executable and shared libraries, thereby extending the protection to the entire software stack. Additionally, the use of Position-Independent Executables (PIE) further enhances ASLR by allowing the operating system to load the program at random base addresses during execution.

While ASLR significantly raises the bar for attackers, it is essential to acknowledge that it is not an absolute guarantee of security. Sophisticated attackers may employ techniques to circumvent ASLR, such as memory disclosure vulnerabilities that reveal the randomized addresses during runtime. Nevertheless, ASLR remains a valuable layer of defense, especially against less sophisticated threats and automated attacks that rely on a static understanding of memory layouts.

The effectiveness of ASLR is also contingent on the quality of its implementation. Strong ASLR implementations exhibit high entropy, meaning that the degree of randomness introduced into the memory layout is substantial. Low entropy can potentially undermine the effectiveness of ASLR, as attackers might find it easier to deduce the randomized addresses. Additionally, timely security updates and patches play a crucial role in maintaining the potency of ASLR, as the discovery of new vulnerabilities or exploitation techniques may necessitate adjustments to the randomization algorithms.

The adoption and effectiveness of ASLR have grown in prominence over the years, driven by the escalating sophistication of cyber threats. As part of a comprehensive security strategy, ASLR serves as a valuable tool in the arsenal of defense mechanisms, especially given the prevalence of memory-based attacks in the cybersecurity landscape. The continuous evolution of ASLR, coupled with advancements in hardware security features and threat intelligence, contributes to a more robust and adaptive security posture for organizations and end-users alike.

In conclusion, Address Space Layout Randomization stands as a pivotal defense mechanism in the ongoing battle to secure computer systems against memory-based attacks. By injecting unpredictability into the allocation of memory addresses, ASLR disrupts the predictability that attackers often exploit to compromise system integrity. While not a panacea, ASLR, when properly implemented and complemented by other security measures, significantly raises the bar for attackers, forcing them to contend with the challenges of navigating a dynamically randomized memory landscape. As the cyber threat landscape evolves, ASLR remains a critical component in the arsenal of security measures, contributing to the overarching goal of fortifying computer systems against a diverse array of malicious exploits.

How ASLR mitigates risks of memory-based attacks.

Address Space Layout Randomization (ASLR) is a powerful and proactive security measure designed to mitigate the risks associated with memory-based attacks, a prevalent category of exploits that target vulnerabilities within a program's memory space. Memory-based attacks, such as buffer overflow exploits, often rely on the predictability of memory layouts to execute malicious code, compromise system integrity, and potentially gain unauthorized access. ASLR introduces a dynamic and unpredictable element into the allocation of memory addresses within a process's address space, fundamentally altering the landscape that attackers must navigate to successfully exploit vulnerabilities.

One of the primary ways ASLR contributes to risk mitigation is by disrupting the predictability of memory layouts. In traditional computing environments without ASLR, memory addresses are typically assigned in a deterministic manner, allowing attackers to anticipate the location of critical elements such as executable code, libraries, and the stack. This predictability provides a roadmap for attackers to craft malicious payloads precisely tailored to exploit vulnerabilities at known memory addresses. ASLR disrupts this roadmap by introducing randomness into the memory allocation process, making it considerably more challenging for attackers to determine the exact locations they need to target.

The randomization introduced by ASLR occurs each time a program is executed or the system is booted. Consequently, even if a vulnerability exists within a program, the randomized memory addresses mean that attackers must first discover the correct addresses before they can successfully exploit the vulnerability. This hurdle adds a layer of complexity to the exploitation process, significantly increasing the effort and time required for attackers to craft successful exploits. ASLR does not eliminate vulnerabilities, but it raises the bar for attackers by making the exploitation process more intricate and resource-intensive.

One of the key targets of ASLR is buffer overflow attacks, a prevalent class of memory-based exploits where attackers attempt to overflow a program's buffer with malicious code, thereby hijacking the program's execution flow. By randomizing the memory layout, ASLR introduces uncertainty regarding the locations of critical elements within the address space, such as the return addresses on the stack or the positions of essential libraries. As a result, attackers attempting to exploit buffer overflows encounter a moving target, necessitating a precise understanding of the dynamic memory layout to achieve successful exploitation.

ASLR significantly contributes to the mitigation of buffer overflow attacks by making it difficult for attackers to craft payloads that reliably exploit vulnerabilities. Without knowledge of the precise memory addresses for critical functions, attackers must resort to trial and error, making their malicious payloads less effective. Furthermore, even if attackers manage to identify a vulnerability, the dynamic nature of ASLR necessitates the discovery of randomized memory addresses, introducing an element of unpredictability that adds to the complexity of successful exploitation.

The synergy between ASLR and other security mechanisms further enhances its risk mitigation capabilities. When coupled with technologies such as Data Execution Prevention (DEP) or No eXecute (NX), which prevent the execution of code in certain regions of memory, ASLR forms a potent defense-in-depth strategy. DEP complements ASLR by ensuring that even if an attacker identifies a vulnerability and crafts a malicious payload, the execution of that payload in non-executable regions of memory is thwarted. The combination of ASLR and DEP creates a formidable barrier against memory-based attacks, reinforcing the overall security posture of the system.

The implementation of ASLR is not uniform across all computing environments; its effectiveness relies on the quality of its implementation, commonly measured by the level of entropy introduced into the memory layout. High entropy indicates a greater degree of randomness, making it more challenging for attackers to predict memory addresses accurately. Strong ASLR implementations strive to maximize entropy, ensuring that the randomized memory layout provides robust protection against exploitation attempts. Conversely, low entropy may potentially undermine the effectiveness of ASLR, as attackers might find it easier to deduce the randomized addresses through brute force or other techniques.

Timely security updates and patches play a critical role in maintaining the potency of ASLR. The discovery of new vulnerabilities or exploitation techniques may prompt adjustments to the randomization algorithms employed by ASLR. Regular updates ensure that the randomness introduced into the memory layout remains effective in thwarting emerging threats. As the cybersecurity landscape evolves, the adaptability and responsiveness of ASLR to newly identified risks are crucial for sustaining its effectiveness as a protective measure against memory-based attacks.

The adoption and effectiveness of ASLR have grown in prominence over the years, propelled by the escalating sophistication of cyber threats. Operating systems, compilers, and binary executables play integral roles in the successful implementation of ASLR. Modern operating systems, including Windows, Linux, and macOS, have integrated ASLR as a standard security feature. When an application is compiled with ASLR support, the operating system introduces randomization into the loading of its executable and shared libraries, extending the protection to the entire software stack.

In addition to its role in mitigating the risks of memory-based attacks at the user and application levels, ASLR also extends its protective measures to the realm of system libraries and shared objects. The randomization of memory addresses for dynamic link libraries (DLLs) in Windows or shared objects in Linux makes it challenging for attackers to reliably predict the location of critical functions and data structures, further enhancing the overall security posture of the system.

While ASLR significantly raises the bar for attackers, it is essential to acknowledge that it is not an absolute guarantee of security. Sophisticated attackers may employ advanced techniques to circumvent ASLR, such as leveraging memory disclosure vulnerabilities that reveal the randomized addresses during runtime. Additionally, side-channel attacks or information leakage from other sources may potentially aid attackers in deducing the randomized memory layout. However, such advanced exploitation techniques are typically reserved for high-profile and high-value targets, and ASLR remains a valuable layer of defense, especially against less sophisticated threats and automated attacks that rely on a static understanding of memory layouts.

In conclusion, ASLR serves as a cornerstone in the arsenal of security measures aimed at mitigating the risks associated with memory-based attacks. By injecting randomness into the allocation of memory addresses, ASLR disrupts the predictability that attackers exploit to compromise system integrity. While not a silver bullet, ASLR significantly raises the complexity and resource requirements for attackers attempting to exploit vulnerabilities. Its effectiveness lies in its ability to create a dynamic and unpredictable memory landscape, fortifying computer systems against a diverse array of malicious exploits. As the cybersecurity landscape continues to evolve, ASLR remains a critical component in the ongoing efforts to bolster the security of computer systems against memory-based attacks.

Challenges and considerations in ASLR implementation.

The implementation of Address Space Layout Randomization (ASLR) is a critical undertaking in bolstering the security posture of computer systems; however, it is not without its challenges and considerations. One of the primary challenges in ASLR implementation is achieving a balance between security and compatibility. While randomizing the memory layout enhances security, it can potentially introduce compatibility issues with certain applications that rely on static memory addresses. Compatibility concerns necessitate careful testing and validation to ensure that ASLR does not disrupt the functionality of essential software or lead to unforeseen errors, striking a delicate equilibrium between security improvements and operational stability.

Moreover, the effectiveness of ASLR hinges on the quality of its randomization, commonly referred to as entropy. High entropy ensures a greater degree of randomness in memory address allocation, making it more challenging for attackers to predict addresses accurately. However, achieving high entropy is not trivial, and low entropy levels may compromise the efficacy of ASLR. Striking the right balance and implementing robust randomization algorithms demand a nuanced understanding of the system's architecture, compiler capabilities, and the dynamic loading of libraries, presenting a formidable technical challenge in ASLR deployment.

ASLR's impact on performance is another consideration that organizations must weigh during implementation. The randomization of memory addresses introduces a level of overhead, as the operating system must calculate and manage the randomized addresses dynamically. This overhead can result in a marginal increase in memory usage and may impact system performance, especially in resource-constrained environments. Consequently, organizations need to assess the trade-off between the security benefits of ASLR and its potential impact on system efficiency, ensuring that the implementation strikes an optimal balance without adversely affecting overall performance.

Interoperability across different operating systems and software environments poses additional challenges in ASLR implementation. While major operating systems such as Windows, Linux, and macOS have incorporated ASLR as a standard security feature, disparities in the implementation details and the availability of support for ASLR-aware applications can create challenges in achieving a consistent security posture across diverse computing environments. Ensuring seamless interoperability requires collaboration among software vendors, operating system developers, and the broader cybersecurity community to establish standardized practices and promote a unified approach to ASLR.

Another critical consideration in ASLR implementation is its potential susceptibility to attacks that seek to bypass or undermine its protective measures. Sophisticated attackers may employ techniques such as memory disclosure vulnerabilities, which reveal randomized addresses during runtime, or conduct side-channel attacks to deduce the layout of memory. As a result, organizations must continually assess and update ASLR implementations to address emerging threats and evolving exploitation techniques. Regular security updates and patches become imperative to reinforce ASLR's resilience against advanced attacks and to adapt its randomization mechanisms in response to newly identified risks.

While ASLR is a potent defense against memory-based attacks, it is not a standalone solution. The efficacy of ASLR is maximized when integrated into a comprehensive defense-in-depth strategy that includes other security measures such as Data Execution Prevention (DEP), strict access controls, and regular security audits. Organizations need to consider how ASLR aligns with existing security measures and ensures that it complements, rather than duplicates, the protective functions of other security technologies.

Moreover, the deployment of ASLR introduces a unique set of considerations in virtualized or cloud environments. Virtualization abstracts the underlying hardware, and ASLR mechanisms must account for this abstraction to ensure consistent and effective randomization across virtual machines. Cloud service providers play a pivotal role in supporting ASLR, and organizations must collaborate with providers to ensure that the security benefits of ASLR are extended seamlessly to virtualized environments.

The collaborative nature of ASLR implementation extends beyond individual organizations to the broader cybersecurity community. The sharing of best practices, threat intelligence, and research findings fosters a collective effort to strengthen ASLR and address emerging challenges. Community collaboration can lead to the identification and resolution of vulnerabilities, the development of standardized ASLR implementation guidelines, and the dissemination of knowledge to enhance the overall resilience of computer systems against memory-based attacks.

Accessibility and inclusivity are critical considerations in ASLR implementation, especially in environments where legacy systems or specialized applications may pose constraints on the adoption of modern security features. Organizations must devise strategies to gradually implement ASLR while accounting for the constraints of legacy systems, ensuring a phased and tailored approach that accommodates diverse computing environments.

Furthermore, considerations related to user awareness and education are paramount in ASLR implementation. End-users should be informed about the security benefits of ASLR and understand its role in enhancing the overall resilience of the computing environment. Training programs, informational materials, and communication strategies contribute to a culture of security awareness, empowering users to recognize the importance of ASLR in thwarting memory-based attacks.

In conclusion, while ASLR stands as a formidable security measure, its implementation is not without challenges and considerations. Achieving the delicate balance between security and compatibility, maximizing entropy for effective randomization, addressing performance implications, ensuring interoperability across diverse environments, and guarding against potential bypass techniques are critical aspects of successful ASLR deployment. Collaboration within the cybersecurity community, continuous adaptation to emerging threats, and a comprehensive defense-in-depth strategy contribute to the overall efficacy of ASLR in mitigating the risks associated with memory-based attacks. As technology evolves, organizations must remain vigilant in refining and optimizing their ASLR implementations to adapt to the dynamic landscape of cybersecurity.

Explaining buffer overflow vulnerabilities.

Buffer overflow vulnerabilities represent a significant and pervasive security risk in computer systems, arising from the unintended consequences of programming errors and the exploitation of memory management intricacies. At their core, buffer overflows occur when a program writes more data to a designated memory buffer than it can accommodate, leading to an overflow into adjacent memory regions. This overflow can result in unpredictable behavior, crashes, or, critically, exploitation by attackers who deliberately craft input to manipulate program execution. Understanding the anatomy of buffer overflows necessitates an exploration of memory organization, programming languages, and the intricate dance between software and hardware components.

In the context of buffer overflows, memory organization plays a central role. Memory in a computer system is typically divided into segments, including the stack, heap, data section, and code section. The stack is a region of memory used for function call management, local variables, and control flow information. The heap, on the other hand, is a dynamic memory area where programs allocate memory during runtime. The data section stores global and static variables, while the code section contains the program's executable instructions. A buffer, often an array or a string, is a contiguous block of memory within these sections, and its boundaries must be carefully managed to prevent unintended overflow.

Programming languages, particularly those that allow direct memory manipulation like C and C++, are susceptible to buffer overflow vulnerabilities. In these languages, developers have a high degree of control over memory operations, but this control comes with the responsibility of ensuring proper bounds checking. A buffer overflow typically occurs when a program writes more data to a buffer than its allocated size, causing the excess data to spill over into adjacent memory locations. This overflow can lead to a corruption of critical data structures, alteration of function return addresses on the stack, or injection of malicious code into the program's memory space.

The exploitation of buffer overflow vulnerabilities often follows a predictable pattern. Attackers leverage input mechanisms, such as user inputs or network data, to inject excessive data into a program's buffers. If the program fails to validate and constrain these inputs, the excess data can overflow into adjacent memory regions. One common target for attackers is the stack, where they seek to overwrite function return addresses. By strategically manipulating these addresses, attackers can redirect the program's execution flow to arbitrary locations, including portions of memory containing malicious code.

A key enabler of buffer overflow exploitation is the absence or improper implementation of bounds checking mechanisms. Bounds checking involves verifying that data written to a buffer does not exceed its allocated size. In the absence of rigorous bounds checking, attackers can manipulate input to overflow buffers and compromise the integrity of the program's memory space. The infamous "shellcode" is a common payload in buffer overflow attacks, representing a sequence of carefully crafted instructions that grant the attacker unauthorized access or control over the compromised system.

The stack-based buffer overflow, a classic variant of this vulnerability, exploits the stack's structure and function call mechanisms. When a function is called, its local variables and function parameters are allocated on the stack. If these allocations are not properly bounded, an attacker can overflow a buffer in one function to overwrite the return address of the calling function. Subsequent execution then jumps to the manipulated return address, leading to the execution of injected malicious code. Defending against stack-based buffer overflows requires implementing proper bounds checking, adopting safer programming practices, and incorporating technologies like stack canaries to detect and thwart such attacks.

Heap-based buffer overflows, another prevalent variant, target dynamically allocated memory in the heap. Programs often use functions like `malloc()` to dynamically allocate memory at runtime. If developers fail to validate the size of data being written to dynamically allocated buffers, heap overflows can occur. In these scenarios, attackers exploit vulnerabilities in memory allocation functions to overwrite adjacent heap structures, potentially altering critical data or redirecting program execution. Mitigating heap-based buffer overflows requires diligent memory management practices, stringent bounds checking, and the use of memory-safe programming languages that automate memory allocation and deallocation.

An essential component of buffer overflow exploitation is the understanding of memory layout and the manipulation of function return addresses. Return-oriented programming (ROP) is a sophisticated technique wherein attackers leverage existing snippets of code, known as "gadgets," present in the program's code section. By chaining these gadgets together, attackers construct a malicious payload without injecting new code. ROP is particularly effective in circumventing countermeasures like Data Execution Prevention (DEP), which seeks to prevent the execution of data in certain memory regions. Crafting a successful ROP chain requires a deep understanding of the program's memory layout, available gadgets, and the ability to navigate the intricacies of the program's control flow.

Buffer overflow vulnerabilities are not confined to low-level programming languages; they can also manifest in higher-level languages through various vectors. For instance, web applications written in languages like PHP, Python, or JavaScript may encounter buffer overflow vulnerabilities in the context of string manipulation, especially when handling user inputs. These vulnerabilities, often termed "string-based" or "buffer manipulation" vulnerabilities, can expose applications to remote code execution or unauthorized access. Addressing these vulnerabilities involves adopting secure coding practices, input validation, and the use of secure coding libraries.

The pervasiveness of buffer overflow vulnerabilities underscores the ongoing challenge of securing software systems. While the industry has made strides in adopting safer programming languages and incorporating security measures, legacy codebases and the complexity of modern software development continue to expose systems to these risks. Security professionals employ a variety of techniques to detect and prevent buffer overflows, including static analysis tools, code reviews, and runtime protections like Address Space Layout Randomization (ASLR) and stack canaries. Additionally, security researchers and software vendors collaborate to identify and patch vulnerabilities, releasing updates and patches to mitigate the risk of exploitation.

In conclusion, buffer overflow vulnerabilities pose a persistent and serious threat to the security of computer systems. Stemming from the interplay of memory organization, programming languages, and the intricate dance between software and hardware components, buffer overflows can lead to unintended consequences, crashes, and exploitation by malicious actors. Understanding the nuances of these vulnerabilities, their exploitation patterns, and adopting proactive security measures are imperative for mitigating the risks they pose. The ongoing evolution of secure coding practices, the adoption of memory-safe languages, and the collaborative efforts of the cybersecurity community contribute to a more resilient defense against buffer overflow vulnerabilities in the ever-changing landscape of information technology.

Chapter 6: Parallel Processing and Memory Management

The role of multitasking in modern computing.

Multitasking stands as a foundational and transformative concept in modern computing, shaping the way users interact with and harness the power of computer systems. At its essence, multitasking refers to the concurrent execution of multiple tasks or processes within a computing environment. This capability has become synonymous with the efficiency and productivity that users expect from contemporary computing devices, from personal computers to smartphones and servers. The evolution of multitasking is deeply intertwined with advancements in hardware architecture, operating systems, and the ever-expanding demands of users for seamless and responsive computing experiences.

In the early days of computing, systems were primarily designed to execute a single task at a time. The concept of a single-user, single-tasking environment prevailed, where the entire computational resources of a system were dedicated to executing a solitary program. This approach, while functional for certain applications, lacked the flexibility and responsiveness demanded by users as computing needs diversified and expanded. The emergence of multitasking marked a paradigm shift, allowing systems to juggle multiple tasks concurrently, thereby enhancing overall system utilization and user experience.

A pivotal factor enabling multitasking is the evolution of hardware architectures. Early computers were characterized by single-core processors, limiting their ability to execute multiple tasks simultaneously. The advent of multi-core processors represented a monumental leap, providing the capability for parallel processing. Multi-core processors contain multiple processing units on a single chip, allowing them to execute multiple tasks concurrently. This parallelism forms the bedrock of modern multitasking, enabling systems to allocate computational resources efficiently and cater to the diverse demands of users running multiple applications simultaneously.

Operating systems play a pivotal role in orchestrating multitasking capabilities. The transition from single-user, single-tasking operating systems to multi-user, multitasking environments marked a transformative phase in computing history. Modern operating systems, such as Windows, Linux, macOS, and various flavors of Unix, have robust multitasking capabilities ingrained in their design. These operating systems employ scheduling algorithms to allocate processor time to different tasks, ensuring fairness, responsiveness, and optimal resource utilization. Time-sharing, a fundamental concept in multitasking operating systems, enables the interleaved execution of tasks, giving users the illusion of concurrent execution even in single-core environments.

The user interface is a critical aspect of multitasking, providing users with intuitive ways to interact with and manage concurrent tasks. Graphical user interfaces (GUIs) have played a pivotal role in enhancing the user experience of multitasking. Windowed environments, taskbars, and desktop management features empower users to seamlessly switch between applications, monitor ongoing processes, and organize their computing environment. These visual cues are integral to the user's perception of multitasking and contribute significantly to the overall usability of modern computing systems.

Multitasking manifests in various forms, accommodating a spectrum of user needs and preferences. Preemptive multitasking, a prevalent approach in modern operating systems, allows the system to interrupt and suspend the execution of a task, allocating processor time to another task in a seemingly seamless manner. This preemptive nature ensures that no single task monopolizes system resources, contributing to system stability and responsiveness. Cooperative multitasking, another approach, relies on tasks voluntarily yielding control to the operating system, necessitating a higher degree of cooperation from individual programs but offering simplicity in certain contexts.

The scope of multitasking extends beyond personal computing to server environments and distributed computing systems. In server environments, multitasking facilitates the concurrent execution of diverse services, from handling user requests to managing background tasks. The advent of virtualization technologies has further elevated multitasking capabilities in server environments, enabling the creation of virtual machines that run multiple operating systems or instances concurrently on a single physical server. This consolidation enhances resource utilization and scalability, catering to the dynamic demands of modern data centers.

The proliferation of mobile devices, especially smartphones, exemplifies the ubiquity and indispensability of multitasking in modern computing. Smartphones seamlessly handle a myriad of tasks concurrently, from running applications and handling communication to managing background processes and notifications. The ability to switch between applications effortlessly, receive real-time updates, and engage in multitasking gestures has become integral to the user experience, shaping user expectations and influencing the design of mobile operating systems.

Multitasking is not merely a convenience for end-users; it also plays a pivotal role in optimizing resource utilization and system efficiency. The ability to run multiple tasks concurrently ensures that idle computing resources are minimized, fostering a more efficient use of processing power, memory, and storage. This efficiency is particularly crucial in resource-constrained environments, where multitasking enables systems to deliver optimal performance despite limitations.

Despite its undeniable advantages, multitasking also poses challenges and considerations. Resource contention, where multiple tasks compete for limited resources, can lead to performance degradation and increased response times. Scheduling algorithms must strike a balance between fairness and efficiency, optimizing task execution while preventing monopolization of resources. Context switching overhead, incurred when the system transitions between different tasks, introduces complexities in managing system resources and can impact overall system responsiveness.

Security considerations also come into play in multitasking environments. The concurrent execution of multiple tasks introduces the potential for security vulnerabilities, such as unauthorized access to data or the exploitation of inter-process communication channels. Isolation mechanisms, such as process sandboxing and user privilege separation, are crucial in mitigating these risks and ensuring the integrity and security of multitasking environments.

The evolution of multitasking continues to be shaped by emerging technologies and evolving user needs. Cloud computing, with its distributed and scalable architecture, introduces new dimensions to multitasking by enabling users to offload tasks to remote servers. Edge computing, with its focus on processing data closer to the source, emphasizes the need for efficient multitasking at the edge of networks. Artificial intelligence and machine learning algorithms leverage multitasking capabilities to parallelize computations, accelerating the training of complex models.

In conclusion, multitasking stands as a cornerstone in modern computing, influencing the design of hardware, operating systems, and user interfaces. From the early days of single-tasking systems to the current era of multi-core processors and sophisticated scheduling algorithms, multitasking has become synonymous with efficiency, responsiveness, and user empowerment. Its ubiquity in personal computing, mobile devices, and server environments underscores its transformative impact on how users interact with and extract value from computing systems. As technology continues to advance, the evolution of multitasking will remain intertwined with the ever-expanding possibilities and demands of the digital landscape.

Parallel processing as a key aspect of system efficiency.

Parallel processing stands as a pivotal and transformative paradigm in computing, representing a key aspect of system efficiency that has revolutionized the way computational tasks are executed. At its core, parallel processing involves the simultaneous execution of multiple tasks or processes, leveraging the power of concurrency to enhance overall system performance. This concept has become increasingly indispensable as computing demands have grown exponentially, pushing the boundaries of traditional sequential processing. The evolution of parallel processing is deeply intertwined with advancements in hardware architectures, programming models, and the pursuit of harnessing computational power at scale.

The traditional model of sequential processing, where a single processor executes instructions in a linear fashion, faced limitations in meeting the escalating computational demands of complex applications and massive datasets. The rise of parallel processing was propelled by the recognition that concurrency, achieved through the simultaneous execution of multiple tasks, could unlock new dimensions of computational power. Hardware architects responded by introducing parallelism at various levels, from multi-core processors on a single chip to clusters of interconnected processors and specialized accelerators like graphics processing units (GPUs).

Multi-core processors, a fundamental manifestation of parallel processing, feature multiple processing units (cores) on a single chip. This architectural shift marked a departure from the era of single-core dominance, allowing systems to execute multiple tasks concurrently. The advantages of multi-core processors are evident in their ability to distribute the computational workload across cores, enabling tasks to be processed in parallel and reducing overall processing time. This parallelization is particularly advantageous for computationally intensive applications such as scientific simulations, data analytics, and image processing.

Parallel processing extends beyond individual processors to encompass clustered and distributed computing environments. Clusters, comprising multiple interconnected computers, collaborate to execute tasks in parallel, sharing the computational load and providing a scalable solution to complex problems. Distributed computing leverages a network of geographically dispersed machines, each contributing to the parallel execution of tasks. These architectures, facilitated by advancements in networking technologies, offer a means to tackle large-scale problems that surpass the capabilities of a single machine.

The programming model plays a critical role in realizing the potential of parallel processing. Parallel programming involves the explicit expression of concurrency in software, enabling developers to design algorithms that can be executed concurrently. Traditional sequential programming models often struggle to exploit the full power of parallel architectures. As a result, parallel programming paradigms, such as message passing and shared-memory models, have emerged to facilitate the coordination and communication between parallel tasks. Languages like OpenMP and MPI (Message Passing Interface) have become instrumental in enabling developers to harness the potential of parallel processing for scientific simulations, numerical computations, and other parallelizable workloads.

Parallel processing has redefined the landscape of high-performance computing (HPC), enabling the execution of simulations and calculations at unprecedented scales. HPC applications, ranging from weather forecasting and molecular simulations to financial modeling, rely on parallel architectures to deliver results in a timely manner. The quest for exascale computing, where systems are capable of performing a billion billion calculations per second, underscores the importance of parallel processing in pushing the boundaries of computational capabilities.

Graphics Processing Units (GPUs) exemplify a specialized form of parallel processing that has found widespread adoption in diverse domains. Originally designed for rendering graphics, GPUs excel at performing parallel computations due to their numerous cores optimized for floating-point operations. The emergence of General-Purpose GPU (GPGPU) computing has expanded the role of GPUs beyond graphics rendering, allowing them to tackle complex parallel workloads in fields such as scientific research, machine learning, and artificial intelligence. The parallel architecture of GPUs is particularly well-suited for parallelizable algorithms, offering a significant boost in computational efficiency.

Parallel processing is instrumental in addressing the challenges posed by big data analytics. The explosion of data generated in various domains necessitates scalable and efficient processing frameworks. Technologies like Apache Hadoop and Apache Spark leverage parallelism to distribute and process large datasets across clusters of machines. Parallel databases and data warehouses exploit parallel processing to execute complex queries concurrently, accelerating data retrieval and analysis. The ability to parallelize data processing tasks is indispensable in navigating the complexities of modern data landscapes.

The advent of parallel processing has also redefined the field of machine learning, providing the computational power required for training complex models. Deep learning, a subfield of machine learning, benefits significantly from parallel architectures, particularly GPUs, which excel at handling the matrix-based computations inherent in neural network training. Parallelization techniques, such as data parallelism and model parallelism, allow machine learning frameworks to distribute the training process across multiple processors or devices, expediting the convergence of models and enabling the exploration of larger model architectures.

Efforts to advance parallel processing have extended to exploring novel architectures and computing paradigms. Quantum computing, a groundbreaking field, seeks to leverage the principles of quantum mechanics to perform parallel computations at an astronomical scale. Quantum bits (qubits), unlike classical bits, can exist in multiple states simultaneously, enabling quantum computers to explore multiple solutions in parallel. While quantum computing is in its infancy, it holds the potential to revolutionize parallel processing by solving certain problems exponentially faster than classical computers.

Despite its transformative impact, parallel processing introduces challenges and considerations that require careful attention. The intricacies of coordinating parallel tasks, managing shared resources, and minimizing communication overhead are critical aspects of designing efficient parallel algorithms. Load balancing, the equitable distribution of computational tasks among processors, is essential to ensure that no processor remains idle while others are overloaded. Scalability, the ability of a parallel system to maintain or improve performance as the problem size increases, is a key metric in assessing the effectiveness of parallel processing solutions.

Synchronization and communication between parallel tasks become crucial factors in determining overall system efficiency. Shared-memory parallelism relies on efficient synchronization mechanisms to avoid conflicts and ensure data consistency. Message passing, a common approach in distributed computing, requires effective communication protocols to exchange information between nodes. These challenges underscore the importance of a holistic approach to parallel processing, considering both hardware and software aspects to achieve optimal performance.

In conclusion, parallel processing stands as a cornerstone of modern computing, driving advancements in hardware architectures, programming models, and computational efficiency. From multi-core processors and clusters to GPUs and emerging paradigms like quantum computing, the evolution of parallel processing has transformed the landscape of high-performance computing, big data analytics, and machine learning. Its role in tackling complex problems, leveraging the power of concurrency, and pushing the boundaries of computational capabilities underscores its significance in shaping the future of computing. As technology continues to evolve, parallel processing will remain a driving force in unlocking new frontiers of computational efficiency and addressing the ever-growing demands of the digital age.

Challenges and advantages of concurrent memory management.

Concurrent memory management, a critical aspect of modern computing systems, presents both significant advantages and notable challenges. This approach to memory management is designed to facilitate the concurrent execution of multiple threads or processes, allowing them to share and access memory resources simultaneously. The advantages of concurrent memory management are rooted in its ability to enhance system performance, responsiveness, and overall resource utilization. However, the complexities of coordinating memory access among concurrent entities introduce challenges related to data consistency, synchronization, and potential contention. A nuanced exploration of the advantages and challenges of concurrent memory management is essential to understanding its impact on the efficiency and reliability of contemporary computing systems.

One of the primary advantages of concurrent memory management lies in its capacity to improve overall system performance by maximizing the utilization of available resources. In a concurrent environment, multiple threads or processes can execute simultaneously, enabling the system to handle a greater number of tasks concurrently. This parallelism is particularly beneficial in scenarios where computational workloads can be divided into independent tasks, allowing them to progress concurrently and achieve a collective reduction in processing time. Concurrent memory management, when implemented effectively, ensures that memory resources are shared efficiently among concurrent entities, contributing to enhanced system throughput and responsiveness.

Another notable advantage of concurrent memory management is its ability to support multi-threaded and multi-process applications, a prevalent paradigm in modern software development. Applications designed to run concurrently benefit from the shared memory model, allowing threads or processes to communicate and exchange data seamlessly. This concurrent access to shared memory enables collaborative and resource-efficient execution, fostering the development of responsive and scalable applications. In scenarios where tasks can be decomposed into parallelizable components, concurrent memory management empowers developers to exploit the full potential of multi-core processors and distributed computing environments.

Concurrent memory management also plays a pivotal role in mitigating bottlenecks and enhancing scalability. In traditional single-threaded or single-process environments, contention for shared resources, such as memory, can lead to performance bottlenecks and hinder scalability. Concurrent memory management mechanisms, by facilitating simultaneous access to memory resources, reduce contention and allow systems to scale more effectively. Scalability is particularly crucial in contemporary computing, where the volume and complexity of data continue to grow, and applications need to adapt to varying workloads and user demands.

Moreover, concurrent memory management contributes to improved responsiveness in interactive applications. In scenarios where user interfaces or real-time systems are critical, the ability to concurrently execute tasks and access shared memory ensures that the system remains responsive to user inputs and external stimuli. Concurrent processing enables applications to maintain a level of interactivity, even when handling computationally intensive tasks, enhancing the user experience and meeting the expectations of modern computing environments.

Despite these advantages, concurrent memory management introduces a set of challenges that demand careful consideration and effective solutions. One of the primary challenges is ensuring data consistency in the face of concurrent memory access. When multiple threads or processes are accessing and modifying shared data concurrently, the potential for data corruption or inconsistencies arises. Synchronization mechanisms, such as locks, semaphores, and atomic operations, are employed to coordinate access to shared data and prevent race conditions. However, designing effective synchronization strategies requires a deep understanding of the application's requirements and careful consideration of potential contention points.

Concurrency control mechanisms introduce the challenge of contention, where multiple threads or processes compete for access to shared resources. Excessive contention can lead to performance degradation, as threads may spend a significant amount of time waiting for access to critical sections. Striking a balance between synchronization and minimizing contention is crucial for optimizing the performance of concurrent systems. Additionally, contention management becomes increasingly complex in scenarios where the granularity of synchronization is not appropriately chosen, potentially leading to either overly conservative locking, hindering parallelism, or insufficient synchronization, risking data inconsistencies.

Furthermore, concurrent memory management introduces the possibility of deadlocks and livelocks, complex scenarios where threads or processes are unable to make progress. Deadlocks occur when multiple entities are waiting for each other to release resources, resulting in a standstill. Livelocks, on the other hand, involve threads continually reacting to each other's actions without making progress. Mitigating deadlocks and livelocks requires meticulous design of synchronization protocols, careful consideration of resource acquisition order, and the implementation of deadlock detection and resolution strategies.

The issue of cache coherence presents another challenge in concurrent memory management, particularly in multi-processor or multi-core systems. Caches, utilized to speed up memory access, introduce the risk of inconsistent views of shared data among different processors or cores. Cache coherence protocols, such as MESI (Modified, Exclusive, Shared, Invalid), are employed to maintain consistency across caches. However, implementing effective cache coherence introduces complexities, including increased interprocessor communication overhead and potential performance bottlenecks, necessitating thoughtful trade-offs in system design.

Concurrency control mechanisms also need to contend with the trade-off between synchronization overhead and parallelism. Overly conservative synchronization, intended to ensure data consistency, can lead to performance bottlenecks and limit the scalability of concurrent systems. Conversely, insufficient synchronization may compromise data integrity, introducing subtle bugs that are challenging to detect and reproduce. Striking the right balance requires a thorough understanding of the application's requirements, careful profiling, and iterative refinement of synchronization strategies based on observed system behavior.

Despite these challenges, the advantages of concurrent memory management underscore its significance in modern computing. As hardware architectures continue to evolve with an emphasis on parallelism, the effective management of concurrent access to memory resources becomes increasingly vital. Techniques such as lock-free data structures, transactional memory, and fine-grained synchronization aim to address some of the challenges associated with concurrent memory management, providing alternative approaches to achieving data consistency and mitigating contention.

In conclusion, concurrent memory management represents a double-edged sword in modern computing, offering substantial advantages in terms of performance, responsiveness, and scalability, but also introducing complex challenges related to data consistency, synchronization, and contention. The effectiveness of concurrent memory management hinges on thoughtful system design, the judicious application of synchronization mechanisms, and an in-depth understanding of the application's requirements. As computing systems continue to embrace parallelism, the pursuit of efficient and reliable concurrent memory management remains a critical aspect of ensuring the optimal performance and responsiveness of contemporary software applications.

Understanding shared memory systems.

Shared memory systems represent a fundamental architecture in modern computing, providing a shared address space that allows multiple processors or cores to access and modify data concurrently. At the heart of a shared memory system is the concept of a common pool of memory accessible by all processing units, fostering communication and collaboration among them. This architecture, often found in multi-core processors, symmetric multiprocessing (SMP) systems, and certain parallel computing environments, offers advantages in terms of simplicity, ease of programming, and efficient data sharing. Understanding shared memory systems requires delving into their architecture, mechanisms for synchronization, and the challenges associated with concurrent access to shared resources.

The architecture of shared memory systems revolves around a central memory unit that is accessible by all processing units within the system. Each processor or core has direct access to this shared memory space, allowing for the seamless sharing of data and information. This shared address space simplifies communication among processors, as they can exchange information by reading from and writing to shared locations in memory. The unifying memory architecture eliminates the need for explicit data transfer mechanisms, streamlining the programming model and enhancing the system's overall simplicity.

Shared memory systems are often implemented in multi-core processors, where each core has its own cache but shares a common main memory. This arrangement exploits the benefits of parallelism inherent in multiple processing units while facilitating efficient communication through the shared memory space. In symmetric multiprocessing (SMP) systems, the architecture extends to multiple processors, each with its own set of cores, all interconnected to a central memory unit. The symmetry in access to memory ensures that any processor can access any portion of the shared memory, creating a uniform and cohesive computing environment.

One of the key advantages of shared memory systems lies in their ease of programming. The shared address space simplifies the coordination and communication between different threads or processes running on distinct processors or cores. Threads can communicate by reading and writing to shared memory locations, enabling straightforward implementation of parallel algorithms and concurrent data structures. This simplicity in programming facilitates the development of multi-threaded applications, making it more accessible for developers to harness the power of parallel processing.

Synchronization mechanisms play a crucial role in shared memory systems to ensure the orderly and consistent access to shared resources. Concurrent access to shared data by multiple processors raises the possibility of race conditions, where the final state of the data depends on the order of operations executed by the processors. Mutexes (mutual exclusion locks), semaphores, and other synchronization primitives are employed to control access to critical sections of code or shared data. These mechanisms prevent multiple processors from simultaneously modifying the same data, mitigating the risk of data corruption and ensuring data consistency.

The concept of atomic operations is central to maintaining consistency in shared memory systems. Atomicity ensures that an operation appears to occur instantaneously from the perspective of other processors, avoiding interleaved or partially completed operations that could lead to inconsistent states. Atomic operations, such as compare-and-swap (CAS), provide a means to update shared data atomically without the need for locks, reducing contention and improving the overall efficiency of concurrent algorithms. However, careful consideration is required to select appropriate atomic operations and ensure their correct usage in the context of the application.

Cache coherence is a critical aspect of shared memory systems, especially in multi-core processors. Caches, employed to speed up memory access, introduce the challenge of maintaining consistency across different caches that may contain copies of the same data. Cache coherence protocols, such as MESI (Modified, Exclusive, Shared, Invalid), are employed to manage cache states and ensure that all processors have a consistent view of shared data. These protocols detect and handle situations where a processor modifies a cached copy of data, ensuring that other processors are aware of the change and preventing inconsistencies.

Challenges in shared memory systems arise from the complexities of coordinating access to shared resources among multiple processors. Contentions for shared data, particularly in scenarios where multiple processors attempt to modify the same data concurrently, can lead to performance bottlenecks. Striking a balance between maximizing parallelism and minimizing contention requires thoughtful consideration of synchronization strategies and the granularity of shared data access. Fine-grained synchronization can reduce contention but introduces additional overhead, while coarse-grained synchronization may limit parallelism and responsiveness.

Deadlocks represent another challenge in shared memory systems, occurring when multiple processors are blocked, each waiting for a resource held by another. The intricacies of managing locks and ensuring a consistent order of resource acquisition are crucial in preventing deadlocks. Deadlock detection mechanisms and careful design practices, such as avoiding circular dependencies in resource acquisition, are employed to mitigate the risk of deadlocks and ensure the robustness of shared memory systems.

Efficient load balancing is essential in shared memory systems to ensure that processing units are utilized optimally. Load imbalances, where certain processors are underutilized while others are overloaded, can lead to suboptimal performance. Dynamic load balancing techniques, such as work stealing or task migration, aim to distribute computational workloads evenly among processors, promoting efficient resource utilization and scalability. Balancing the computational load becomes particularly crucial in applications with irregular or dynamic workloads.

The scalability of shared memory systems is a key consideration, especially as the number of processors or cores increases. Achieving scalable performance requires addressing challenges related to contention, synchronization, and cache coherence. Scalability testing, profiling, and performance analysis are integral to identifying and mitigating bottlenecks that may impede the efficient utilization of shared resources. Effective scalability ensures that shared memory systems can adapt to growing computational demands without sacrificing performance.

In conclusion, understanding shared memory systems involves grasping the fundamental architecture of a common memory space accessible by multiple processors or cores, fostering collaboration and communication. The simplicity of the programming model, ease of coordination through shared memory, and advantages in parallel processing make shared memory systems an attractive choice for various computing environments. However, challenges related to synchronization, cache coherence, contention, and scalability necessitate careful consideration and application of synchronization mechanisms, coherence protocols, and efficient load balancing strategies. Shared memory systems continue to play a crucial role in modern computing, providing a versatile and accessible platform for concurrent programming and parallel processing.

Implementing memory management for shared resources.

Implementing memory management for shared resources is a nuanced and crucial aspect of designing modern computing systems, where multiple processing units or entities need to efficiently access and manipulate shared data. This endeavor involves creating a robust framework that facilitates the concurrent and coordinated use of memory resources by different components within the system. The implementation must address various challenges, including ensuring data consistency, managing synchronization, handling contention, and optimizing performance. A thorough exploration of the principles and strategies involved in the implementation of memory management for shared resources provides insights into how these systems operate and deliver efficient, reliable, and scalable performance.

At the core of memory management for shared resources is the need to establish a shared address space accessible by all relevant entities within the system. This shared memory space serves as the medium through which different processing units can communicate and exchange data seamlessly. The implementation should define a clear and well-structured address space that accommodates the shared data structures, variables, and communication channels required for collaboration. The architecture of this shared memory space sets the foundation for efficient data sharing and manipulation across diverse components, whether they are threads, processes, or other entities.

Synchronization mechanisms play a pivotal role in ensuring orderly and consistent access to shared resources. Concurrent access by multiple entities introduces the risk of race conditions, where the final state of shared data depends on the interleaved execution of operations. Mutexes, semaphores, and other synchronization primitives are implemented to control access to critical sections of code or shared data. The choice of synchronization mechanisms depends on the nature of the shared resources and the desired level of coordination. Implementing effective synchronization strategies requires a deep understanding of the application's requirements and potential contention points.

A critical consideration in memory management for shared resources is achieving atomicity in operations. Atomic operations ensure that certain actions on shared data appear instantaneous from the perspective of other entities, preventing interleaved or partially completed operations that could lead to inconsistent states. Techniques such as compare-and-swap (CAS) are commonly employed to implement atomic operations without the need for locks. The careful selection and correct usage of atomic operations contribute to reducing contention and improving the overall efficiency of concurrent algorithms. However, it is essential to consider the trade-offs and limitations of different atomic operations in the context of the application's requirements.

Cache coherence emerges as a significant challenge in the implementation of memory management for shared resources, especially in systems with multiple processors or cores. Caches, designed to accelerate memory access, introduce the risk of inconsistent views of shared data among different caches. Cache coherence protocols, such as MESI, are implemented to manage cache states and ensure that all processors have a consistent view of shared data. The implementation of cache coherence protocols requires careful consideration of cache invalidation, updates, and communication overhead. Striking the right balance between cache coherence and performance is essential for optimizing the efficiency of memory management in shared resource environments.

Effective error handling and recovery mechanisms are integral to robust memory management implementations. Shared resources are susceptible to unexpected events, such as hardware failures, software errors, or communication disruptions. Implementing mechanisms for error detection, reporting, and recovery ensures the resilience of the system and prevents catastrophic failures that could compromise data integrity. The design of error-handling strategies should consider the impact on performance, the ability to isolate faulty components, and the overall reliability of the shared memory environment.

Addressing the challenge of contention is a key aspect of implementing memory management for shared resources. Contentions for shared data, especially in scenarios where multiple entities attempt to modify the same data concurrently, can lead to performance bottlenecks. Implementing effective strategies for contention management involves carefully choosing synchronization mechanisms and optimizing the granularity of shared data access. Fine-grained synchronization can reduce contention but introduces additional overhead, while coarse-grained synchronization may limit parallelism and responsiveness. The implementation must strike a balance that ensures optimal performance under varying workloads and access patterns.

Implementing load balancing mechanisms is crucial for optimizing the performance of memory management in shared resource environments. Uneven distribution of computational workloads among processing units can lead to underutilization of some entities and overloading of others, resulting in suboptimal performance. Dynamic load balancing techniques, such as work stealing or task migration, are implemented to distribute computational workloads evenly among entities, promoting efficient resource utilization and scalability. The implementation of load balancing strategies involves monitoring system metrics, identifying imbalances, and dynamically redistributing tasks to maintain optimal performance.

Scalability is a fundamental consideration in the implementation of memory management for shared resources, particularly as the system size grows. Scalable performance ensures that the system can adapt to increasing computational demands without sacrificing efficiency. Implementing scalability requires addressing challenges related to contention, synchronization, and cache coherence. Thorough scalability testing, profiling, and performance analysis are integral to identifying and mitigating bottlenecks that may impede the efficient utilization of shared resources. The implementation should be designed to scale gracefully, providing consistent performance across varying numbers of processing units.

Deadlock prevention and detection mechanisms are critical components of a reliable memory management implementation. Deadlocks, where multiple entities are blocked, each waiting for a resource held by another, can bring the system to a standstill. Implementing strategies to prevent deadlocks involves careful design of synchronization protocols, avoiding circular dependencies in resource acquisition, and ensuring a consistent order of resource acquisition. Deadlock detection mechanisms can identify and resolve deadlocks when they occur, preventing prolonged system unresponsiveness. The implementation of deadlock prevention and detection strategies contributes to the robustness and reliability of shared resource environments.

Effective monitoring and profiling tools are essential in the implementation of memory management for shared resources. These tools provide insights into the system's behavior, performance metrics, and potential bottlenecks. Implementing monitoring mechanisms allows administrators and developers to track resource usage, detect anomalies, and optimize the system configuration. Profiling tools aid in identifying areas of the code that may benefit from optimization, guiding the refinement of synchronization strategies, and fine-tuning the memory management implementation for improved efficiency.

In conclusion, implementing memory management for shared resources involves a comprehensive and carefully crafted approach to address various challenges and leverage the advantages of shared memory environments. The architecture must provide a shared address space, synchronization mechanisms, and atomic operations to facilitate seamless collaboration among processing units. Strategies for cache coherence, contention management, and load balancing must be implemented to optimize performance. Robust error handling, deadlock prevention, and scalability mechanisms contribute to the reliability and efficiency of the implementation. Monitoring and profiling tools aid in fine-tuning and optimizing the system for diverse workloads. The success of memory management implementation lies in striking a delicate balance between simplicity, efficiency, and reliability in the context of shared resource environments.

Optimizing performance in shared memory environments.

Optimizing performance in shared memory environments is a multifaceted endeavor that requires a deep understanding of the underlying architecture, efficient utilization of resources, and careful consideration of synchronization, cache coherence, and contention management. In shared memory systems, where multiple processing units concurrently access and modify shared data, achieving optimal performance involves addressing challenges and leveraging opportunities inherent in this collaborative paradigm.

The foundation of performance optimization in shared memory environments lies in the effective management of the shared address space. Designing a well-structured and organized shared memory layout is critical for minimizing contention, streamlining data access, and facilitating efficient communication among processing units. A thoughtful architectural approach that considers the nature of shared data, access patterns, and the overall communication flow is essential. By optimizing the layout of shared memory, applications can reduce access latencies and enhance the overall efficiency of data exchange.

Synchronization mechanisms play a pivotal role in achieving performance optimization. The judicious selection and implementation of synchronization primitives, such as mutexes, semaphores, and atomic operations, influence the coordination of access to critical sections of code or shared data. Fine-tuning synchronization strategies involves minimizing the use of locks to avoid unnecessary contention, exploring lock-free or lockless algorithms where appropriate, and optimizing the granularity of synchronization. By carefully balancing the need for coordination with the desire for parallelism, performance gains can be realized in shared memory environments.

Cache coherence poses a significant challenge to performance optimization in shared memory systems, especially in multi-core processors. Caches, designed to accelerate memory access, introduce the risk of inconsistent views of shared data among different cores. Implementing efficient cache coherence protocols, such as MESI, is crucial for maintaining a consistent state across caches and preventing unnecessary cache invalidations or updates. Strategies for cache-friendly data access, cache-conscious algorithms, and minimizing cache contention contribute to optimizing performance in shared memory environments. Additionally, considering the placement of shared data in memory to align with cache line sizes can enhance cache utilization and reduce access latencies.

Contention management is another critical aspect of performance optimization in shared memory environments. Contention for shared data, particularly in scenarios where multiple processing units attempt to modify the same data concurrently, can lead to performance bottlenecks. Strategies for contention management involve carefully selecting synchronization mechanisms, optimizing the granularity of shared data access, and employing techniques such as lock-free data structures or optimistic concurrency control. By minimizing contention through efficient synchronization strategies, applications can exploit the full potential of parallelism and achieve improved performance.

Fine-tuning atomic operations is an integral part of performance optimization in shared memory environments. Atomic operations, such as compare-and-swap (CAS), play a crucial role in achieving consistency without the need for locks. However, the performance impact of different atomic operations must be carefully considered. Optimizing the usage of atomic operations involves selecting the most appropriate operations for the specific application requirements, considering the underlying hardware architecture, and exploring alternatives, such as double-checked locking or other lock-free patterns, to reduce contention and enhance performance.

Load balancing emerges as a key strategy for optimizing performance in shared memory systems, ensuring that processing units are utilized optimally. Uneven distribution of computational workloads among cores or processors can result in underutilization of some units and overloading of others, leading to suboptimal performance. Dynamic load balancing mechanisms, such as work stealing or task migration, enable the redistribution of tasks to maintain an even workload distribution. Efficient load balancing strategies contribute to improved resource utilization, reduced idle times, and enhanced scalability, all of which are vital components of performance optimization in shared memory environments.

Scalability is a fundamental consideration in the pursuit of performance optimization, particularly as the system size grows.

Achieving scalable performance ensures that the system can adapt to increasing computational demands without sacrificing efficiency. Strategies for scalability involve addressing challenges related to contention, synchronization, and cache coherence. Thorough scalability testing, profiling, and performance analysis are integral to identifying and mitigating bottlenecks that may impede the efficient utilization of shared resources. Effective scalability ensures that shared memory systems can provide consistent and efficient performance across varying numbers of processing units.

Reducing overhead associated with synchronization is essential for achieving performance optimization in shared memory environments. While synchronization is necessary to ensure data consistency and coordination, excessive use of locks or overly conservative synchronization strategies can introduce unnecessary overhead and limit parallelism. Optimizing synchronization overhead involves minimizing the duration of critical sections, exploring lock-free or fine-grained synchronization approaches, and considering adaptive synchronization mechanisms that adjust to changing workloads. By striking the right balance between ensuring correctness and minimizing synchronization overhead, applications can achieve improved performance in shared memory systems.

Effective profiling and monitoring tools are invaluable for performance optimization in shared memory environments. Profiling tools provide insights into the system's behavior, identifying areas of code that may benefit from optimization. Monitoring tools enable real-time tracking of performance metrics, resource usage, and potential bottlenecks. By leveraging these tools, developers and system administrators can pinpoint performance hotspots, measure the impact of optimizations, and iteratively refine the shared memory implementation for improved efficiency. Continuous monitoring and profiling contribute to the ongoing process of performance optimization, allowing for adaptive adjustments based on observed system behavior.

In conclusion, optimizing performance in shared memory environments is a multifaceted challenge that involves addressing synchronization, cache coherence, contention, load balancing, and scalability considerations. A holistic approach that combines thoughtful architectural design, efficient synchronization mechanisms, cache-conscious strategies, and load balancing techniques is essential. Fine-tuning the usage of atomic operations, minimizing synchronization overhead, and leveraging profiling tools contribute to achieving improved performance. As shared memory systems continue to play a crucial role in modern computing, the pursuit of performance optimization remains a dynamic and ongoing process, driven by the need for efficiency, scalability, and responsiveness in shared resource environments.

Overview of distributed memory architectures.

Distributed memory architectures represent a fundamental paradigm in the design of modern computing systems, revolutionizing the way computational resources are organized and utilized. Unlike shared memory systems where multiple processors access a common address space, distributed memory architectures involve a network of independent processing units, each with its own local memory. This network allows for the seamless distribution of computation across nodes, providing scalability, fault tolerance, and the ability to tackle complex problems that demand vast computational resources. The overview of distributed memory architectures encompasses a deep dive into their key components, communication models, challenges, advantages, and the role they play in addressing the evolving landscape of computational needs.

At the heart of distributed memory architectures is the concept of decentralization, where processing units, often referred to as nodes or compute elements, are interconnected through a communication network. Each node possesses its own dedicated memory, and communication between nodes is achieved through explicit message passing. This departure from shared memory systems introduces challenges and opportunities associated with managing data distribution, synchronization, and efficient communication. Distributed memory architectures are often employed in high-performance computing (HPC) environments, scientific simulations, and large-scale data processing applications.

The communication model in distributed memory architectures relies on passing messages between nodes to facilitate coordination and data exchange. This model is in contrast to shared memory architectures where communication is implicit through the shared address space. In distributed memory systems, explicit communication is necessary for nodes to share information, synchronize computations, and collaborate on complex tasks. Message passing interfaces (MPI) have become a standard in the development of distributed memory applications, providing a set of protocols and functions that enable nodes to exchange messages and coordinate their activities. The use of MPI allows for the creation of scalable and parallel applications that harness the collective power of distributed computing resources.

One of the defining characteristics of distributed memory architectures is the decentralization of memory resources. Unlike shared memory systems where all processors can access a common pool of memory, each node in a distributed memory system has its own local memory, and data must be explicitly exchanged between nodes when needed. This distribution of memory poses challenges in terms of data locality, as the efficient use of data often requires careful consideration of where computations are performed and where data resides. However, this decentralization also contributes to scalability, allowing distributed memory systems to seamlessly scale to larger problem sizes by adding more nodes to the network.

The scalability of distributed memory architectures is a key factor in their widespread adoption for high-performance computing applications. As computational demands continue to grow exponentially, the ability to scale a system by adding more nodes becomes crucial. Distributed memory systems excel in this regard, allowing organizations to build supercomputers with thousands or even millions of processors, collectively providing immense computational power. Scalability is not only about increasing the number of processing units but also about efficiently distributing the workload and managing communication overhead to ensure that the overall performance scales with the size of the system.

Efficient load balancing is a significant consideration in the design and utilization of distributed memory architectures. The uneven distribution of computational tasks among nodes can result in some nodes being underutilized while others are overloaded, leading to suboptimal performance. Dynamic load balancing techniques, such as task migration or work stealing, are employed to redistribute computational workloads across nodes dynamically. This ensures that each node contributes proportionally to the overall computation, maximizing resource utilization and maintaining a balanced distribution of tasks. Load balancing strategies play a crucial role in achieving optimal performance in large-scale distributed memory systems.

The fault tolerance inherent in distributed memory architectures is a notable advantage, particularly in large-scale and mission-critical applications. With the decentralization of memory and computation, the failure of a single node does not necessarily lead to a catastrophic failure of the entire system. Redundancy and replication techniques, such as checkpointing and message logging, are often employed to recover from node failures gracefully. The fault tolerance capabilities of distributed memory systems make them well-suited for applications where reliability and continuous operation are paramount, such as scientific simulations, weather forecasting, and large-scale data processing.

Despite the advantages, the communication overhead in distributed memory architectures poses a challenge that must be addressed for optimal performance. Explicit message passing introduces latency and bandwidth considerations, and the efficiency of communication patterns significantly influences the overall system performance. Designing algorithms and applications that minimize communication or overlap it with computation becomes essential. Additionally, optimizing the network infrastructure and considering the topology of the interconnection network can contribute to reducing communication bottlenecks. As the scale of distributed memory systems increases, careful attention to communication patterns becomes increasingly critical for achieving high performance.

Programming models for distributed memory architectures often involve a combination of low-level message passing interfaces, such as MPI, and higher-level abstractions that simplify the development of parallel and distributed applications. Parallel programming languages like OpenMP and frameworks like Apache Hadoop or Apache Spark provide tools and libraries that abstract the intricacies of distributed computing, enabling developers to focus on the algorithmic aspects of their applications. These programming models aim to make distributed memory architectures more accessible to a broader range of developers and facilitate the development of scalable and efficient distributed applications.

The role of distributed memory architectures in addressing the computational challenges of contemporary applications is ever-expanding. In the era of big data, machine learning, and complex simulations, distributed memory systems provide the computational power necessary to process vast amounts of data and perform intricate computations. Applications in scientific research, climate modeling, financial simulations, and large-scale data analytics benefit from the scalability, fault tolerance, and parallel processing capabilities of distributed memory architectures. The ongoing evolution of these architectures is closely tied to advancements in network technologies, interconnectivity, and the development of programming models that empower a diverse range of applications to harness the potential of distributed computing.

In conclusion, distributed memory architectures represent a pivotal paradigm in modern computing, offering scalability, fault tolerance, and parallel processing capabilities. The overview of these architectures encompasses their decentralized nature, the explicit message passing communication model, scalability considerations, efficient load balancing strategies, fault tolerance mechanisms, and the challenges associated with communication overhead. The role of distributed memory systems in addressing contemporary computational needs, coupled with ongoing advancements in programming models and network technologies, underscores their significance in powering large-scale simulations, data processing, and scientific research.

Coordinating memory across multiple processing units.

Coordinating memory across multiple processing units represents a complex and crucial aspect of parallel and distributed computing, where the seamless sharing of data among disparate units is essential for collaborative and efficient computation. This coordination involves addressing challenges related to data consistency, synchronization, communication overhead, and the optimal utilization of resources. The overarching goal is to ensure that each processing unit, whether within a shared memory or distributed memory architecture, has coherent and timely access to the shared data, fostering parallelism and scalability in a computing system.

In shared memory architectures, coordinating memory access among multiple processing units revolves around the concept of a common address space. All processors share access to a unified memory pool, and coordination is achieved implicitly through the use of shared variables and data structures. The challenge lies in maintaining data consistency as different processors read from and write to shared memory locations concurrently. Synchronization mechanisms, such as locks, mutexes, and atomic operations, are employed to control access to critical sections of code or shared data, preventing race conditions and ensuring that modifications are coordinated to avoid conflicts. Effective coordination in shared memory systems is essential for harnessing the benefits of parallel processing while maintaining the integrity of shared data.

In contrast, distributed memory architectures introduce explicit coordination challenges, as each processing unit operates with its own local memory, necessitating communication for data exchange. The coordination of memory across distributed nodes is often achieved through message passing, where processors send and receive messages to share information and synchronize their activities. Message passing interfaces (MPI) and other communication protocols provide the foundation for coordinating memory access in distributed memory systems. The challenge here lies in minimizing communication overhead and ensuring that data is transferred efficiently among nodes to support collaborative computation. Coordinating distributed memory access is crucial for achieving parallelism, load balancing, and fault tolerance in large-scale computing environments.

Efficient synchronization mechanisms play a central role in coordinating memory access across both shared and distributed memory architectures. In shared memory systems, synchronization ensures that multiple processors do not simultaneously modify the same shared data, preventing inconsistencies. In distributed memory systems, synchronization mechanisms are vital for orchestrating the order of execution among nodes to maintain a globally consistent view of shared data. Achieving synchronization involves a careful balance between enforcing coordination to maintain data integrity and allowing parallelism to optimize performance. Adaptive synchronization strategies, where the granularity of synchronization is dynamically adjusted based on workload and communication patterns, contribute to efficient coordination in diverse computing environments.

Coordinating memory access also entails addressing the challenge of data consistency, particularly in distributed memory architectures where each node has its own local memory. Consistency models define the order in which memory operations appear to be executed globally across all processing units. Striking the right balance between strong consistency, which ensures a strict global order of operations, and weak consistency, which allows for more flexibility but may introduce ambiguity, depends on the application's requirements. Coordinating data consistency is essential for guaranteeing that all processing units observe a coherent view of shared data, preventing divergence in computation outcomes.

In shared memory systems, where coordination is implicit, the design of efficient and scalable parallel algorithms plays a pivotal role in coordinating memory access. Parallel algorithms determine how computation is decomposed and how data is distributed among processors to maximize parallelism. Load balancing techniques are employed to ensure that each processor's workload is proportionate to its computational capacity, preventing idle time or overloading. Coordination in shared memory systems involves carefully crafting algorithms that exploit parallelism, minimize communication bottlenecks, and optimize the use of shared resources. Effective coordination enhances the scalability of shared memory systems, allowing them to adapt to varying computational demands.

In distributed memory systems, coordinating memory access often involves addressing the challenge of data movement between nodes. Efficient data distribution and communication patterns play a critical role in minimizing the impact of data transfer on overall system performance. Partitioning data across nodes, optimizing the placement of computation relative to data, and leveraging collective communication operations contribute to efficient coordination. Load balancing becomes even more crucial in distributed memory systems, as the coordination of memory access relies on ensuring that each node is contributing equally to the overall computation. Dynamic load balancing strategies, such as task migration or work stealing, help maintain an even distribution of workloads, optimizing the efficiency of memory coordination.

Achieving fault tolerance is an integral aspect of coordinating memory access across multiple processing units, especially in distributed memory architectures where nodes may experience failures. Redundancy and replication strategies, such as checkpointing and message logging, are employed to recover from node failures and ensure the integrity of shared data. Coordinated fault tolerance mechanisms prevent the propagation of errors and enable the system to continue functioning even in the presence of node failures. The coordination of fault tolerance and memory access is critical for maintaining the reliability and continuous operation of parallel and distributed computing systems.

The role of programming models and languages cannot be overstated in coordinating memory access across multiple processing units. Parallel programming languages and frameworks, such as OpenMP, CUDA, MPI, and Apache Spark, provide abstractions and tools that simplify the development of parallel and distributed applications. These programming models encapsulate the intricacies of memory coordination, communication, and synchronization, allowing developers to focus on algorithmic aspects and application logic. Coordinated use of programming models ensures that memory access is managed efficiently, and applications can seamlessly scale across diverse computing environments.

The evolution of hardware architectures, including multi-core processors, accelerators, and high-performance interconnects, introduces new dimensions to the coordination of memory access. Coordinating memory across heterogeneous architectures requires careful consideration of data movement, synchronization mechanisms, and the effective utilization of specialized processing units. Hybrid memory architectures, combining shared and distributed memory paradigms, further complicate coordination strategies. Coordinating memory access in these advanced architectures involves exploring adaptive algorithms, optimizing communication patterns, and leveraging the unique features of each hardware component to achieve optimal performance.

In conclusion, coordinating memory access across multiple processing units is a multifaceted challenge that spans shared and distributed memory architectures. Whether implicit in shared memory systems or explicit in distributed memory systems, effective coordination involves addressing challenges related to synchronization, data consistency, communication overhead, load balancing, and fault tolerance. The development and application of efficient parallel algorithms, the selection of appropriate programming models, and the consideration of evolving hardware architectures contribute to successful memory coordination. As parallel and distributed computing continue to be at the forefront of addressing computational demands, the ongoing refinement of coordination strategies remains integral to achieving scalable, reliable, and efficient memory access in diverse computing environments.

Scalability and challenges in distributed memory management.

Scalability and challenges in distributed memory management represent two intertwined facets of the intricate landscape of parallel and distributed computing, where the effective coordination and utilization of memory resources across multiple nodes define the system's ability to handle increasingly larger computational workloads. Scalability, a cornerstone in the design of distributed memory systems, refers to the system's capacity to seamlessly expand and adapt as the computational demands grow, offering performance improvements without sacrificing efficiency. This scalability is vital for addressing complex problems and large-scale simulations, enabling distributed systems to leverage the collective power of numerous processing units. However, the pursuit of scalability is accompanied by a host of challenges, including those related to data consistency, communication overhead, load balancing, fault tolerance, and the intricacies of managing memory in a decentralized environment.

Scalability in distributed memory management begins with the ability to efficiently distribute and balance computational workloads across numerous nodes. As the size of the system grows, achieving an even distribution of tasks becomes increasingly challenging. Load balancing, a critical component of scalability, involves dynamically redistributing computational work to ensure that each processing unit contributes proportionally to the overall computation. Dynamic load balancing techniques, such as work stealing or task migration, become essential to mitigate the impact of imbalanced workloads, preventing certain nodes from being underutilized while others are overloaded. The scalability of a distributed memory system relies on the effectiveness of load balancing mechanisms to maintain optimal performance across diverse workloads and system sizes.

Data consistency, a fundamental aspect of distributed memory management, poses a considerable challenge to scalability. In a distributed memory system, each node operates with its local memory, necessitating explicit communication for data exchange. The challenge lies in coordinating the order of memory operations to maintain a globally consistent view of shared data across all nodes. As the system scales, ensuring data consistency becomes more complex, and the choice of consistency models, ranging from strong to weak consistency, involves trade-offs between coherence and flexibility. Achieving scalability while preserving data consistency requires meticulous design considerations and synchronization mechanisms to prevent conflicts and inconsistencies in the distributed memory environment.

Communication overhead emerges as a significant bottleneck in the pursuit of scalability in distributed memory systems. Explicit message passing between nodes introduces latency and consumes valuable bandwidth, impacting overall system performance. The challenge is to minimize communication overhead while ensuring efficient coordination and data exchange among nodes. Optimizing communication patterns, leveraging collective communication operations, and exploring advanced interconnect technologies are strategies employed to address this challenge. The scalability of a distributed memory system is intricately linked to the ability to manage and reduce communication overhead, allowing the system to scale gracefully without being hampered by increasing data exchange requirements.

The fault tolerance inherent in distributed memory systems, while crucial for ensuring continuous operation in the face of node failures, introduces additional challenges to scalability. As the system scales, the probability of node failures increases, necessitating robust fault tolerance mechanisms. Redundancy, replication, and recovery strategies, such as checkpointing and message logging, are employed to detect and recover from node failures gracefully. The challenge is to design fault tolerance mechanisms that scale seamlessly with the size of the system, minimizing the impact on overall performance while providing reliable and continuous operation. Achieving fault tolerance without sacrificing scalability requires a delicate balance between redundancy, recovery mechanisms, and the overall system architecture.

Efficient memory allocation and management across distributed nodes present another set of challenges to scalability. Allocating memory dynamically in a distributed environment involves considerations such as the fragmentation of memory space, efficient garbage collection, and the optimization of memory access patterns. As the system scales, these challenges become more pronounced, and traditional memory management strategies may need to be adapted or augmented to accommodate the increased complexity. Scalability in distributed memory management demands innovative approaches to memory allocation and recycling, considering the diverse memory access patterns and resource utilization characteristics of a large-scale distributed system.

Scalability challenges also extend to the complexities introduced by heterogeneous architectures in modern distributed memory systems. The inclusion of diverse processing units, accelerators, and specialized hardware components adds an additional layer of intricacy to achieving seamless scalability. Hybrid memory architectures, combining shared and distributed memory paradigms, further complicate the scalability equation. Coordinating memory access efficiently across diverse hardware components involves exploring adaptive algorithms, optimizing communication patterns, and leveraging the unique features of each processing unit. Achieving scalability in heterogeneous distributed memory systems requires a nuanced approach that considers the varying capabilities and characteristics of the underlying hardware.

The dynamic nature of workloads and the evolving landscape of computational demands introduce an ongoing challenge to scalability in distributed memory management. As applications and algorithms adapt to changing requirements, the system must be able to scale not only in terms of the number of nodes but also in response to shifting computational patterns. Scalability testing, profiling, and performance analysis become integral aspects of system development, allowing for the identification and mitigation of bottlenecks that may impede efficient scalability. The challenge is to design distributed memory systems that can adapt and scale gracefully in response to the evolving needs of diverse applications, ensuring long-term viability and performance.

Security considerations add another layer of complexity to scalability challenges in distributed memory systems. As the system scales, the attack surface increases, and managing access control, protecting sensitive data, and ensuring the integrity of memory become paramount. Coordinating secure memory access across multiple nodes involves implementing robust authentication and authorization mechanisms, encryption strategies, and intrusion detection systems. Scalability in the context of security necessitates the development of adaptive security protocols that can scale seamlessly with the growth of the distributed system while providing comprehensive protection against potential threats.

In conclusion, scalability and challenges in distributed memory management are intrinsically linked, defining the landscape of parallel and distributed computing. The pursuit of scalability involves addressing challenges related to load balancing, data consistency, communication overhead, fault tolerance, memory allocation, and the complexities introduced by heterogeneous architectures. Achieving seamless scalability requires a holistic approach that considers the interplay of these challenges, employing adaptive algorithms, innovative memory management strategies, and robust fault tolerance mechanisms. As distributed memory systems continue to play a pivotal role in addressing the computational demands of diverse applications, the ongoing refinement of scalability strategies remains integral to ensuring efficient, reliable, and scalable performance in large-scale distributed computing environments.

Techniques for managing concurrent access to shared resources.

Managing concurrent access to shared resources is a fundamental challenge in the realm of parallel and concurrent computing, where multiple threads or processes seek to access and modify shared data simultaneously. This challenge becomes particularly pronounced in multi-threaded or distributed systems, where efficient coordination is essential to ensure data consistency, prevent race conditions, and maximize parallelism. A myriad of techniques has been developed to address the complexities of managing concurrent access, encompassing synchronization mechanisms, transactional memory, lock-free and wait-free algorithms, as well as approaches to mitigate contention and enhance scalability.

Synchronization mechanisms are cornerstone techniques for managing concurrent access to shared resources. Mutexes, or mutual exclusion locks, are among the most prevalent synchronization tools. By enforcing mutual exclusion, mutexes allow only one thread or process to access the shared resource at a time, preventing data corruption due to simultaneous modifications. Semaphores extend this concept, providing a more flexible mechanism to control access to a resource by allowing a specified number of threads to acquire the semaphore simultaneously. While these mechanisms provide effective serialization of access, they may introduce contention, leading to performance bottlenecks and decreased parallelism. Careful consideration of granularity, or the size of the critical section protected by a lock, is crucial to strike a balance between avoiding contention and allowing for sufficient parallelism.

Transactional memory is an innovative technique aimed at simplifying the management of concurrent access by providing a higher-level abstraction. In a transactional memory system, a set of operations on shared data is grouped into a transaction, ensuring that either all operations within the transaction are executed, or none of them are. This atomicity property simplifies the programming model by eliminating the need for explicit locks, allowing developers to reason about shared data access in a more straightforward manner. However, the effectiveness of transactional memory relies on efficient hardware support and careful consideration of transaction boundaries to minimize conflicts and contention. While transactional memory simplifies programming, its applicability may be limited by hardware constraints and the overhead associated with ensuring transactional integrity.

Lock-free and wait-free algorithms represent a class of techniques that aim to manage concurrent access without relying on locks, mitigating contention and promoting scalability. Lock-free algorithms guarantee that at least one thread will make progress in a finite number of steps, even in the presence of contention. Wait-free algorithms take this a step further, ensuring that every thread will complete its operation in a finite number of steps, irrespective of contention levels. These algorithms often leverage low-level atomic operations, such as compare-and-swap (CAS), to achieve thread-safe updates to shared data without the need for locks. While lock-free and wait-free algorithms can enhance parallelism and scalability, designing them requires careful consideration of correctness, performance, and the specific characteristics of the underlying hardware architecture.

Contention management techniques are essential for optimizing concurrent access to shared resources, especially in scenarios where multiple threads compete for the same resource simultaneously. Backoff strategies, such as exponential backoff, provide a mechanism for threads to yield and retry access after a short delay, reducing contention and preventing unnecessary thrashing. Adaptive techniques dynamically adjust to the current contention level, altering strategies based on observed patterns to optimize access. Furthermore, techniques like optimistic concurrency control allow multiple threads to perform operations concurrently without blocking, with conflicts resolved at the end of the operation. These contention management strategies contribute to efficient resource utilization and can be crucial for systems with varying workloads and contention levels.

Scalability considerations play a pivotal role in the management of concurrent access, particularly as systems grow in size and complexity. Scalable techniques aim to ensure that the performance of the system improves proportionally with the increase in the number of threads or processes. Fine-grained locking, where locks protect smaller sections of shared data, can reduce contention and enhance scalability by allowing more threads to operate concurrently. Additionally, approaches like lock striping, where locks are applied to distinct portions of the shared data, can further mitigate contention and improve scalability by reducing the likelihood of multiple threads contending for the same lock. Scalable techniques necessitate careful design and consideration of the system architecture to balance synchronization and parallelism effectively.

Parallel algorithms and data structures are instrumental in managing concurrent access by facilitating efficient and coordinated computation across multiple threads or processes. Parallel algorithms divide computational tasks into smaller, independent units that can be executed concurrently, promoting parallelism and optimizing resource utilization. Concurrent data structures, such as lock-free or wait-free queues and hash tables, are designed to allow simultaneous access by multiple threads without the need for locks. Well-designed parallel algorithms and data structures enhance the overall efficiency of concurrent systems by enabling threads to perform independent operations, minimizing contention, and maximizing parallelism.

Asynchronous programming models represent a paradigm shift in managing concurrent access by decoupling the execution of tasks from the order in which they are initiated. In asynchronous models, tasks are initiated independently, and the system schedules their execution based on availability and readiness. This approach allows for efficient use of resources, as threads are not blocked waiting for the completion of specific tasks. Asynchronous programming is well-suited for scenarios with potentially long-running or blocking operations, enabling the system to progress and remain responsive. However, asynchronous programming introduces its own set of challenges, such as managing callback-based interactions and handling potential race conditions, requiring careful design to ensure correctness and maintainability.

Cache-conscious programming techniques are crucial for optimizing concurrent access by considering the underlying cache hierarchy of modern processors. Efficient cache utilization becomes particularly important in shared-memory architectures, where multiple threads share the same cache. Techniques such as thread affinity, where threads are bound to specific processor cores, aim to minimize cache contention and enhance data locality. Additionally, cache-aware data structures and access patterns, which consider the size and associativity of the cache, can significantly improve the overall performance of concurrent systems by reducing cache misses and optimizing memory access.

In conclusion, managing concurrent access to shared resources is a multifaceted challenge that demands a nuanced understanding of synchronization mechanisms, transactional memory, lock-free and wait-free algorithms, contention management, scalability considerations, parallel algorithms, asynchronous programming models, and cache-conscious programming techniques. The choice of technique depends on the specific characteristics of the application, the desired level of parallelism, the architecture of the underlying system, and the trade-offs between simplicity, performance, and scalability. Effective management of concurrent access is essential for developing robust, efficient, and scalable concurrent systems that can leverage the full potential of modern computing architectures.

Chapter 7: Real-time Memory Management

Understanding the demands of real-time systems.
Real-time systems, encompassing a diverse array of applications ranging from embedded systems to critical infrastructure, are characterized by their stringent temporal constraints, demanding precise and predictable responses within predefined time intervals. At their core, these systems prioritize the timely execution of tasks, where latencies and delays can have profound implications on functionality and, in some cases, safety. The fundamental challenge lies in orchestrating the myriad processes and operations with clockwork precision, necessitating an intricate understanding of the system's architecture, hardware, and the underlying software.

In the realm of real-time systems, the concept of determinism takes center stage, reflecting the imperative for predictable and reproducible behavior. This determinism extends across various dimensions, encompassing not only the execution time of individual tasks but also the system's response to external stimuli. This predictability is especially crucial in applications such as avionics, automotive systems, and industrial automation, where deviations from expected timings can result in catastrophic consequences. Achieving determinism requires careful consideration of factors like task scheduling, interrupt handling, and resource management.

Scheduling, a cornerstone of real-time systems, involves the allocation of resources to tasks in a manner that ensures deadlines are met consistently. There exist various scheduling algorithms, each tailored to specific application domains and system architectures. The choice between preemptive and non-preemptive scheduling, for instance, hinges on the nature of the tasks and their criticality. In preemptive systems, tasks can be interrupted to allow higher-priority tasks to execute, introducing complexities in managing shared resources and potential race conditions.

Interrupt handling further complicates the real-time landscape by introducing asynchronous events that necessitate immediate attention. Balancing the need for responsiveness to interrupts with the overarching goal of determinism is a delicate task. Carefully crafted interrupt service routines (ISRs) are essential, often requiring minimal execution time to guarantee that the system can promptly resume its normal operations. Additionally, prioritizing interrupts and managing their potential conflicts contribute to the intricacies of real-time system design.

Resource management poses another significant challenge, especially in systems with constrained resources such as memory and processing power. Real-time operating systems (RTOS) play a pivotal role in this regard, offering specialized mechanisms for resource allocation and protection. Efficient memory management, considering factors like fragmentation and allocation delays, becomes paramount in maintaining the system's predictability. Moreover, the judicious use of synchronization mechanisms, like semaphores and mutexes, is crucial to prevent data inconsistencies and ensure the integrity of shared resources.

The hardware platform on which a real-time system operates adds another layer of complexity. Processors with predictable instruction execution times, minimal interrupt latency, and dedicated features for real-time tasks are often preferred. In some cases, specialized hardware accelerators or coprocessors may be employed to offload specific tasks, enhancing overall system performance. The interplay between the software and hardware components requires a holistic design approach, with each facet optimized to complement the other in achieving the desired level of determinism.

Communication between different components within a real-time system introduces yet another dimension of consideration. Interprocess communication (IPC) mechanisms must be designed with low latency and high reliability in mind. In distributed real-time systems, where components may be physically separated, network protocols and communication delays become critical factors. The choice of communication patterns, such as publish-subscribe or client-server models, impacts the overall system architecture and its ability to meet stringent timing requirements.

Testing and validation in real-time systems present unique challenges, necessitating comprehensive methodologies to ensure that the system behaves as intended under various scenarios. Traditional testing approaches may not suffice, and techniques like worst-case execution time (WCET) analysis become essential to establish the upper bounds of task execution times. Real-world testing in environments that simulate operational conditions allows for the identification of potential bottlenecks and unforeseen interactions, contributing to the robustness of the system.

In safety-critical real-time systems, adherence to industry standards and certification processes is imperative. Regulatory bodies often define stringent requirements and guidelines to ensure the reliability and safety of systems deployed in sectors such as aviation, healthcare, and automotive. Compliance with standards like ISO 26262 in automotive systems or DO-178C in avionics is not only a legal requirement but also a testament to the system's reliability and adherence to best practices in real-time design.

As the landscape of real-time systems continues to evolve, emerging technologies like edge computing, artificial intelligence, and the Internet of Things (IoT) introduce new opportunities and challenges. Edge computing, for instance, brings computation closer to the source of data, reducing communication latencies but necessitating reevaluation of real-time strategies. The integration of AI algorithms introduces non-deterministic elements, requiring innovative approaches to harmonize the inherently unpredictable nature of machine learning with the deterministic demands of real-time systems.

In conclusion, the demands of real-time systems emanate from the intricate interplay of hardware and software, necessitating a meticulous understanding of the underlying principles and challenges. Achieving determinism, managing resources judiciously, navigating the complexities of interrupt handling, and ensuring compliance with industry standards are vital facets of real-time system design. The continuous evolution of technology introduces both new possibilities and complexities, underscoring the need for adaptive and innovative approaches to meet the ever-growing demands of real-time applications across diverse domains.

The critical role of memory management in meeting deadlines.

Memory management plays a pivotal and often underestimated role in the realm of meeting deadlines within the dynamic landscape of computing systems. In the intricate dance of hardware and software, the efficient utilization of memory resources emerges as a critical factor influencing the overall performance and responsiveness of a system. As applications grow in complexity and demand for computational power rises, the careful orchestration of memory becomes imperative to ensure that deadlines are met with precision and reliability.

At its core, memory management involves the allocation and deallocation of memory resources to different processes or tasks within a computing environment. The seamless execution of these operations is fundamental to the stability and efficiency of a system. In the context of meeting deadlines, the significance of memory management becomes increasingly evident as it directly impacts the ability of a system to handle concurrent processes and optimize resource utilization. A judicious allocation of memory enables the parallel execution of tasks, preventing bottlenecks that could impede the timely completion of critical operations.

One of the key challenges in meeting deadlines lies in the efficient handling of memory leaks – a phenomenon where a program fails to release allocated memory, resulting in a gradual depletion of available resources. Memory leaks not only compromise the stability of a system but also lead to performance degradation over time. Timely identification and mitigation of memory leaks are, therefore, essential to maintain the integrity of a computing environment and uphold the reliability required to meet stringent deadlines.

In real-time systems, where deadlines are not just goals but strict requirements, the role of memory management takes on heightened importance. Real-time applications demand a predictable and deterministic response from the underlying system, necessitating precise control over memory allocation and deallocation. In scenarios where tasks are time-sensitive, any inefficiency in memory management can introduce unpredictable delays, potentially jeopardizing the successful accomplishment of deadlines.

The intricacies of memory fragmentation further underscore the critical nature of memory management in deadline-oriented environments. Fragmentation occurs when the available memory is divided into small, non-contiguous blocks, making it challenging to allocate contiguous chunks of memory for larger tasks. This phenomenon can impede the smooth execution of processes and, in extreme cases, lead to memory exhaustion. Implementing effective memory compaction strategies becomes essential to mitigate fragmentation-related issues and maintain an environment conducive to meeting deadlines without compromise.

Furthermore, the symbiotic relationship between memory management and system architecture plays a vital role in determining the efficiency of a computing system. Modern architectures often employ hierarchical memory structures, including caches and virtual memory, to enhance performance. The judicious utilization of these structures requires sophisticated memory management algorithms that consider factors such as cache coherence, page replacement policies, and efficient mapping of virtual to physical memory. A harmonious interplay between hardware and software in managing these aspects is indispensable to achieving optimal performance and, consequently, meeting deadlines in resource-intensive applications.

The advent of multi-core processors and parallel computing introduces another layer of complexity to memory management. Coordinating memory access across multiple cores demands synchronization mechanisms and memory consistency models that ensure the integrity of shared data. The intricacies of managing shared memory spaces and avoiding race conditions become paramount in scenarios where parallelism is harnessed to meet deadlines through concurrent processing.

In the context of memory-intensive applications, such as large-scale data processing or scientific simulations, the optimization of memory access patterns becomes a critical aspect of meeting deadlines. Efficient algorithms and data structures tailored to the specific memory hierarchy of the underlying architecture can significantly enhance the performance of memory-bound tasks. Striking the right balance between computation and memory access is essential to prevent latency issues that could impede the timely completion of critical computations.

Beyond the technical intricacies, memory management also intersects with the broader landscape of software development methodologies. Adopting memory-efficient coding practices and incorporating tools for memory profiling and analysis contribute to the proactive identification and resolution of potential bottlenecks. The integration of memory management considerations into the software development life cycle becomes imperative, ensuring that applications are not only functionally robust but also optimized for meeting deadlines under varying workloads.

In conclusion, the critical role of memory management in meeting deadlines cannot be overstated in the ever-evolving landscape of computing. As applications become more intricate, and the demand for computational power continues to escalate, the efficient orchestration of memory resources emerges as a linchpin for system performance and responsiveness. From mitigating memory leaks to addressing fragmentation challenges, and from accommodating real-time constraints to optimizing memory access patterns, the multifaceted aspects of memory management converge to shape the success or failure of meeting deadlines in computing systems. As we look to the future, the synergy between hardware advancements, sophisticated algorithms, and conscientious software development practices will undoubtedly continue to define the landscape of memory management, influencing the ability of systems to navigate the complex terrain of deadlines with unwavering precision.

Balancing efficiency with predictability in real-time environments.

The delicate equilibrium between efficiency and predictability in real-time environments forms the cornerstone of achieving optimal performance while meeting stringent temporal requirements. Real-time systems, where tasks are not only expected to produce accurate results but also to do so within predetermined timeframes, necessitate a meticulous balance between the pursuit of computational efficiency and the imperative of predictable, deterministic behavior. This intricate dance becomes particularly pronounced in domains such as industrial automation, avionics, autonomous vehicles, and other mission-critical applications, where deviations from expected execution times can have severe consequences.

Efficiency in a real-time context entails the judicious allocation of computing resources to maximize the throughput of tasks and processes. It involves optimizing algorithms, leveraging parallelism, and harnessing the full potential of hardware capabilities to ensure that computations are executed swiftly and with minimal latency. The pursuit of efficiency is often driven by the desire to achieve higher computational throughput, allowing real-time systems to process larger volumes of data or handle more complex tasks within the confines of tight deadlines.

However, the quest for efficiency must be tempered by the need for predictability, a quality paramount in real-time environments. Predictability implies that the system's behavior is consistent and deterministic, exhibiting a reliable response to input stimuli under varying conditions. In the context of real-time systems, predictability is synonymous with meeting deadlines consistently and ensuring that critical tasks are executed within specified time bounds. This demand for predictability introduces a layer of complexity, as it requires mitigating uncertainties and avoiding non-deterministic behaviors that could compromise the system's ability to meet stringent temporal constraints.

One of the primary challenges in balancing efficiency with predictability lies in the inherent trade-offs between these two objectives. Efficient algorithms and data structures may introduce non-deterministic elements, such as dynamic memory allocation or complex scheduling policies, which can make it challenging to guarantee consistent execution times. Striking the right balance involves carefully navigating these trade-offs, making informed design choices, and selecting algorithms that prioritize both speed and reliability in the specific context of real-time requirements.

In the realm of real-time operating systems (RTOS), which are tailored to support time-critical applications, the challenge becomes even more pronounced. These specialized operating systems prioritize predictability and responsiveness, often employing techniques like fixed-priority scheduling, time-driven scheduling, and deterministic resource allocation to ensure that tasks meet their deadlines consistently. However, the implementation of these mechanisms requires a deep understanding of the underlying hardware architecture and trade-offs, as excessive constraints can lead to underutilization of resources and, paradoxically, reduced efficiency.

Efficient memory management is a crucial aspect of balancing efficiency with predictability in real-time environments. Memory allocation and deallocation operations, if not carefully managed, can introduce unpredictable delays, leading to variations in task execution times. Real-time systems often employ static memory allocation strategies to avoid the runtime overhead associated with dynamic memory management, thereby contributing to predictability. However, this static allocation comes at the cost of potentially underutilizing memory resources, highlighting the need for a nuanced approach that considers the specific requirements of the application.

In parallel processing environments, the challenge is amplified as the efficient distribution of tasks across multiple cores must be reconciled with the demand for predictable inter-process communication and synchronization. While parallelism can enhance overall system throughput, it introduces the complexity of managing shared resources, avoiding race conditions, and ensuring that tasks are synchronized in a manner consistent with real-time constraints. Techniques such as task partitioning, load balancing, and synchronization mechanisms must be orchestrated to maintain both efficiency and predictability in parallel real-time systems.

The advent of multicore processors adds another layer of complexity to the efficiency-predictability balance. While multicore architectures offer the potential for parallelism and increased computational power, coordinating tasks across multiple cores requires sophisticated scheduling algorithms and synchronization mechanisms to avoid contention and ensure predictable task execution. Striking the right balance involves optimizing task allocation to cores, considering cache coherence, and managing shared resources to prevent bottlenecks that could undermine predictability.

In safety-critical applications, such as those found in automotive systems or medical devices, the balance between efficiency and predictability takes on heightened significance. These systems must not only meet stringent real-time requirements but also adhere to safety standards and certifications. Achieving this delicate balance involves not only selecting efficient algorithms and optimizing resource usage but also incorporating fault-tolerant mechanisms, redundancy, and rigorous testing to ensure that the system operates predictably even in the face of unforeseen failures.

The integration of machine learning and artificial intelligence into real-time systems introduces a new dimension to the efficiency-predictability trade-off. While these technologies offer the potential for adaptive and intelligent behavior, they often rely on complex, data-driven algorithms that may exhibit non-deterministic characteristics. Balancing the benefits of AI-driven decision-making with the need for predictability requires careful consideration of algorithmic choices, model complexity, and the impact on real-time performance. Techniques such as model quantization, hardware acceleration, and real-time inference optimizations become essential to strike a balance that aligns with the specific requirements of the application.

In conclusion, the delicate balance between efficiency and predictability in real-time environments is a multifaceted challenge that requires a holistic and nuanced approach. The pursuit of computational efficiency must be tempered by a steadfast commitment to deterministic behavior and adherence to strict temporal constraints. Whether in the design of real-time operating systems, the orchestration of parallel processing, or the integration of emerging technologies, the quest for this equilibrium demands a deep understanding of the application's requirements, careful consideration of trade-offs, and a willingness to navigate the intricate interplay between efficiency and predictability. As real-time systems continue to evolve in complexity and scope, the ability to strike this balance will remain a defining factor in their success across diverse domains where precision, reliability, and performance converge in the pursuit of meeting stringent temporal requirements.

Techniques for partitioning memory in real-time applications.

Partitioning memory in real-time applications is a crucial aspect of system design, playing a pivotal role in ensuring deterministic behavior and meeting stringent temporal requirements. The allocation and organization of memory resources directly impact the predictability and reliability of real-time systems, influencing their ability to execute critical tasks within specified deadlines. Several techniques and strategies have been developed to address the unique challenges posed by real-time applications, each tailored to strike a balance between efficient memory utilization and the imperative of meeting strict temporal constraints.

One fundamental approach to memory partitioning in real-time applications involves the division of memory into fixed-size blocks or partitions. This strategy, often referred to as fixed partitioning, allocates a predetermined amount of memory to each task or process in the system. The fixed nature of these partitions contributes to simplicity and predictability, as the system can ascertain in advance the maximum memory requirements of each task. However, this approach has limitations in terms of flexibility and efficient resource utilization, as tasks may not always fully utilize their allocated partitions, leading to potential memory wastage.

In contrast, dynamic partitioning techniques aim to address the limitations of fixed partitioning by allowing memory partitions to be allocated and deallocated dynamically based on the evolving requirements of tasks. This approach offers more flexibility, enabling tasks to adapt to changing memory demands. Dynamic partitioning can be implemented using algorithms like the buddy system, which divides memory into variable-sized partitions that can be merged or split dynamically. While dynamic partitioning provides greater adaptability, it introduces challenges related to fragmentation, both external and internal, which can impact memory utilization efficiency and, consequently, the ability to meet real-time deadlines consistently.

Another prevalent memory partitioning strategy in real-time applications involves the use of fixed-priority scheduling combined with fixed-size memory partitions. This approach aligns the allocation of memory with the scheduling priority assigned to each task. High-priority tasks are allocated larger memory partitions, reflecting their critical nature and ensuring that they have the necessary resources to meet their deadlines. Lower-priority tasks, on the other hand, receive smaller memory partitions, fostering a hierarchical structure that aligns with the task priority levels. While this strategy enhances predictability, it necessitates a careful calibration of the memory allocation to prevent resource contention and ensure optimal efficiency.

In multiprocessor real-time systems, memory partitioning takes on an added layer of complexity as tasks may need to be allocated across multiple cores. This requires not only spatial partitioning of memory but also a consideration of inter-core communication and synchronization. Techniques such as space-partitioned scheduling allocate dedicated memory regions to each processor core, isolating their memory spaces to prevent interference. Time-partitioned scheduling, another multiprocessor memory partitioning technique, involves assigning specific time intervals to each processor core for exclusive memory access, reducing contention and enhancing predictability. Balancing the trade-offs between spatial and time partitioning is crucial in achieving efficient and predictable memory access in multiprocessor real-time systems.

Affinity-based memory partitioning is another strategy that leverages the concept of task affinity to enhance memory access efficiency in real-time applications. This technique involves assigning specific memory regions to tasks based on their affinity for certain data or resources. By aligning memory access patterns with task affinities, the system can reduce cache misses and improve overall performance. However, implementing affinity-based memory partitioning requires a deep understanding of task behavior and may involve dynamic adjustments to adapt to changing execution patterns.

In safety-critical real-time systems, where fault tolerance is paramount, the concept of memory protection and isolation becomes integral to memory partitioning strategies. Memory protection mechanisms aim to prevent unauthorized access or modification of memory regions, enhancing the security and reliability of the system. Isolation techniques, such as memory protection units (MPUs) or memory protection keys, enforce strict boundaries between tasks, minimizing the impact of faults or errors in one task on the integrity of others. These mechanisms contribute to the robustness of real-time systems, allowing them to maintain predictable behavior even in the face of unexpected events.

Temporal partitioning is a specialized memory partitioning technique designed for systems with both hard and soft real-time tasks. In temporal partitioning, time is partitioned into fixed intervals, and tasks are assigned to specific time slots. Each task is allocated both processing time and memory resources within its designated time slot, ensuring temporal isolation between tasks. This approach enhances predictability by preventing long-term interference between tasks and accommodating both hard and soft real-time requirements. However, temporal partitioning requires careful consideration of task deadlines, as the temporal boundaries must align with the critical time constraints of each task.

The integration of virtual memory concepts into real-time systems introduces a layer of abstraction that can complicate memory partitioning strategies. Real-time virtual memory management involves mapping virtual addresses to physical addresses in a manner that preserves temporal predictability. Techniques such as fixed mapping, where virtual-to-physical mappings are predetermined and do not change during task execution, contribute to the predictability of virtual memory in real-time systems. However, the overhead associated with virtual-to-physical address translation introduces challenges in meeting strict temporal constraints, requiring optimizations to strike a balance between the benefits of virtual memory and the demands of real-time performance.

In conclusion, the techniques for partitioning memory in real-time applications are diverse and multifaceted, each offering unique advantages and trade-offs. From fixed and dynamic partitioning strategies to affinity-based, temporal, and safety-critical memory protection mechanisms, the selection of an appropriate memory partitioning technique depends on the specific requirements and characteristics of the real-time system at hand. Achieving a delicate balance between efficient memory utilization and the predictability necessary to meet stringent temporal constraints is a complex task that demands a nuanced understanding of the application domain, careful consideration of trade-offs, and the application of tailored strategies to optimize memory access in the pursuit of deterministic and reliable real-time performance.

Guarantees and limitations of partitioned memory models.

Partitioned memory models, while providing certain guarantees in terms of predictability and isolation, also exhibit limitations that must be carefully considered in the design and implementation of real-time systems. These models, which involve dividing the system's memory into distinct partitions for different tasks or processes, offer a framework for managing memory resources in a way that aligns with the requirements of time-critical applications. However, a nuanced understanding of the guarantees and limitations associated with partitioned memory models is essential for architects and developers seeking to strike a balance between efficiency and the imperative of meeting stringent temporal constraints.

One of the primary guarantees of partitioned memory models is the predictability they afford to real-time systems. By assigning dedicated memory regions to individual tasks or processes, these models aim to prevent interference and contention, ensuring that each task can access its allocated memory space without unexpected delays or conflicts. This predictability is fundamental to meeting hard real-time requirements, where tasks must complete within specified deadlines to avoid system failures or compromise safety. The guarantee of predictability stems from the clear and static assignment of memory partitions, allowing the system to calculate and enforce worst-case execution times with a high degree of accuracy.

Moreover, partitioned memory models contribute to the isolation of tasks, a critical aspect of achieving system robustness in real-time environments. Each task operates within its designated memory partition, preventing unintended access or modification by other tasks. This isolation is particularly relevant in safety-critical systems, where faults or errors in one task should not propagate to others, maintaining the integrity of the overall system. The guarantees of isolation are often enforced through memory protection mechanisms, such as memory protection units (MPUs) or hardware-based memory protection keys, adding an additional layer of security to the partitioned memory model.

However, these guarantees come with certain limitations that must be carefully navigated. One significant limitation is the potential for underutilization of memory resources. In fixed partitioning models, where each task is allocated a predefined amount of memory, tasks may not always fully utilize their assigned partitions. This underutilization can lead to wasted memory space, reducing overall efficiency and potentially limiting the scalability of the system. Dynamic partitioning techniques attempt to address this limitation by allowing memory allocations to adapt dynamically to changing task requirements, but they introduce challenges related to fragmentation and may still result in suboptimal resource utilization.

Another limitation of partitioned memory models is the challenge of accommodating varying memory demands. In dynamic real-time systems where task requirements evolve dynamically, fixed-size partitions may prove inflexible. The rigid allocation of memory may lead to scenarios where certain tasks require more memory than initially allocated, leading to potential system failures or degraded performance. Dynamic partitioning attempts to address this limitation by allowing for adaptive adjustments, but it introduces complexities related to fragmentation, and efficient strategies for dynamic resizing must be carefully implemented to maintain predictability.

The temporal predictability guaranteed by partitioned memory models is contingent on static and fixed allocations. However, this predictability may be compromised in the face of dynamic events or unpredictable changes in task behavior. For example, if a task experiences a sudden increase in memory requirements due to unforeseen circumstances, the static nature of partitioned memory models may result in missed deadlines or degraded system performance. Achieving a balance between temporal predictability and the adaptability to dynamic changes remains a challenge in the design of real-time systems, particularly when utilizing partitioned memory models.

The guarantee of isolation in partitioned memory models, while essential for system robustness, can introduce challenges related to inter-task communication and coordination. Tasks operating within isolated memory spaces may need to communicate or share data, requiring well-defined mechanisms for inter-process communication (IPC). The design and implementation of IPC mechanisms add complexity to the system, and ensuring that they do not compromise the guarantees of isolation demands careful consideration. Balancing the need for task isolation with the practical requirements of communication is a delicate trade-off that influences the overall efficiency and effectiveness of partitioned memory models.

In multiprocessor systems, the guarantees of partitioned memory models extend to spatial isolation, where each processor core is assigned its dedicated memory regions. However, achieving temporal isolation in multiprocessor environments becomes a challenging task. Temporal partitioning, which allocates specific time intervals to each processor core, can enhance temporal predictability to a certain extent. Still, the coordination of tasks across multiple cores demands sophisticated scheduling algorithms and synchronization mechanisms to prevent contention and ensure predictable task execution. The limitations of achieving temporal isolation in multiprocessor partitioned memory models underscore the complexities introduced by parallel processing architectures.

Safety-critical applications, where the consequences of system failures can be severe, benefit from the guarantees of isolation provided by partitioned memory models. However, these systems must also contend with the limitation of fault tolerance. While memory protection mechanisms contribute to fault isolation, they may not be sufficient to address all potential sources of errors. Redundancy and fault-tolerant design strategies are often necessary to enhance the robustness of safety-critical systems, acknowledging that partitioned memory models alone may not provide a comprehensive solution to the challenges of fault tolerance.

In conclusion, the guarantees and limitations of partitioned memory models in real-time applications encapsulate a complex interplay between predictability, isolation, and resource efficiency.

While these models provide essential guarantees in terms of temporal predictability and task isolation, they must be carefully tailored to address the specific requirements of the application domain. The challenge lies in navigating the trade-offs between static and dynamic partitioning, ensuring efficient resource utilization while accommodating dynamic changes in task behavior. The limitations related to underutilization, adaptability, inter-task communication, and fault tolerance underscore the need for a nuanced and context-aware approach to the design and implementation of partitioned memory models in the ever-evolving landscape of real-time systems.

Adapting partitioning strategies to specific real-time requirements.

Adapting partitioning strategies to specific real-time requirements is a nuanced process that demands a deep understanding of the unique characteristics and constraints of the targeted application domain. Real-time systems span a diverse spectrum, from safety-critical applications in automotive and avionics to multimedia processing and industrial automation, each with its distinct set of temporal, reliability, and performance requirements. The effectiveness of partitioning strategies lies in their ability to align with and cater to these specific demands, ensuring that the memory architecture not only meets but optimally supports the stringent requirements of the real-time tasks at hand.

In safety-critical applications, where system reliability is paramount, adapting partitioning strategies involves a careful consideration of fault tolerance mechanisms. The guarantees of isolation provided by memory partitioning must be complemented with redundancy and error-detection strategies to enhance the system's robustness. Dual or triple modular redundancy, combined with fault-tolerant memory access patterns, can mitigate the impact of faults on critical tasks. The partitioning of memory should accommodate these fault-tolerant mechanisms, ensuring that redundant data structures or processes are isolated appropriately to prevent common-mode failures. Adapting partitioning to safety-critical requirements involves a holistic approach that considers not only temporal predictability and isolation but also the intricate landscape of fault tolerance.

In multimedia and graphics-intensive real-time systems, where the demand for computational throughput is high, partitioning strategies must be tailored to accommodate the specific memory access patterns of multimedia processing tasks. Streaming data, large buffers, and frequent data exchanges between tasks necessitate a memory architecture that minimizes contention and maximizes throughput. Spatial partitioning, where memory is allocated based on the spatial proximity of tasks, can enhance cache locality and reduce memory access times for multimedia processing. Efficient interprocess communication mechanisms, such as shared memory or direct memory access (DMA), should be integrated into the partitioning strategy to facilitate rapid data exchange. Adapting partitioning strategies to multimedia requirements involves optimizing not only for temporal predictability but also for the data flow patterns intrinsic to these applications.

In industrial automation, where real-time systems govern processes with strict timing constraints, adapting partitioning strategies involves a focus on deterministic behavior and efficient resource utilization. Tasks controlling sensors, actuators, and process control loops must operate within well-defined time bounds to ensure the stability and reliability of industrial processes. Fixed partitioning, where memory is statically allocated to tasks, can enhance predictability by avoiding the overhead of dynamic memory management. Additionally, affinity-based partitioning may be employed to align memory access patterns with the specific resources or data structures relevant to industrial automation tasks. The partitioning strategy must account for the critical nature of tasks controlling real-world processes, ensuring that the memory architecture facilitates timely and deterministic execution.

In the domain of autonomous vehicles, where real-time systems govern critical functions such as perception, decision-making, and control, adapting partitioning strategies involves addressing the diverse requirements of these tasks. Perception tasks, relying on sensor data processing, may benefit from spatial partitioning that optimizes memory access patterns for sensor data. Decision-making and control tasks, on the other hand, demand efficient inter-process communication and coordination, necessitating a memory architecture that enables seamless data exchange. Temporal partitioning may be employed to ensure that decision-making tasks have dedicated time intervals for processing, aligning with the real-time constraints of autonomous driving. Adapting partitioning strategies to autonomous vehicles requires a holistic understanding of the interplay between perception, decision-making, and control tasks, each with its unique memory requirements.

In the context of real-time operating systems (RTOS), which cater to a broad range of applications with diverse real-time requirements, adapting partitioning strategies involves providing a flexible framework that can be configured to suit specific application domains. RTOS platforms often incorporate both fixed and dynamic partitioning mechanisms to accommodate varying requirements. Parameters such as task priorities, scheduling policies, and memory allocation strategies can be configured based on the specific demands of the application. RTOS-based partitioning strategies must be adaptable to support both hard and soft real-time tasks, ensuring that critical tasks are allocated the necessary resources while allowing flexibility for less time-sensitive operations.

In safety-critical avionics systems, where compliance with stringent certification standards is essential, adapting partitioning strategies involves addressing not only the temporal predictability and isolation requirements but also the regulatory constraints. The DO-178C standard for avionics software, for instance, imposes stringent requirements on the verification and validation of software systems. Memory partitioning must be designed to facilitate the rigorous testing and analysis demanded by aviation certification authorities. Additionally, partitioning strategies must align with the safety-critical level of the avionics system, ensuring that memory access patterns and isolation mechanisms are in compliance with the prescribed safety standards.

For real-time systems in the Internet of Things (IoT), where a multitude of interconnected devices operate within constrained environments, adapting partitioning strategies involves considerations of resource efficiency, communication overhead, and power consumption. Memory partitioning in IoT devices must balance the need for predictability with the constraints of limited resources. Dynamic partitioning may be employed to adapt to varying workloads and optimize memory utilization. Additionally, communication mechanisms such as message-passing or shared memory should be tailored to minimize energy consumption and reduce latency. Adapting partitioning strategies to IoT requirements requires a holistic approach that addresses the challenges of resource-constrained devices operating in interconnected environments.

In high-frequency trading systems, where microseconds can have a significant impact on financial transactions, adapting partitioning strategies involves a relentless pursuit of low-latency memory access. Tasks responsible for algorithmic trading and order execution demand not only predictable execution times but also minimal memory access times. Spatial partitioning strategies that optimize cache locality and minimize contention become crucial in this context. The memory architecture must be tailored to support the rapid data access patterns intrinsic to high-frequency trading, ensuring that market data processing and order execution tasks operate with the lowest possible latency.

Adapting partitioning strategies to specific real-time requirements requires a context-aware approach that considers the unique characteristics and constraints of each application domain. Whether optimizing for fault tolerance in safety-critical systems, accommodating data flow patterns in multimedia processing, ensuring deterministic behavior in industrial automation, addressing the diverse requirements of autonomous vehicles, providing configurability in real-time operating systems, complying with aviation certification standards in avionics, optimizing for resource efficiency in IoT, or minimizing latency in high-frequency trading, the effectiveness of partitioning strategies hinges on their ability to align with the intricacies of the targeted real-time application. As real-time systems continue to evolve in complexity and diversity, the adaptability of partitioning strategies becomes a defining factor in their success across a wide range of domains and industries.

Impact of scheduling on real-time memory management.

The impact of scheduling on real-time memory management is a crucial and intricate aspect that shapes the overall performance, predictability, and efficiency of real-time systems. In the realm of real-time computing, where tasks must meet stringent temporal constraints, the coordination of memory management and scheduling is paramount to achieving the desired levels of responsiveness and reliability. Scheduling decisions, such as the allocation of CPU time to tasks and the order in which tasks are executed, intimately influence how memory resources are utilized and accessed, presenting a complex interplay that requires careful consideration.

Fixed-priority scheduling, a prevalent approach in real-time systems, establishes a predetermined priority for each task based on its criticality or time sensitivity. The impact of fixed-priority scheduling on memory management is profound, as it dictates the order in which tasks are executed and influences their access to memory resources. High-priority tasks are granted preferential access to memory, ensuring that they can meet their deadlines consistently. However, this prioritization introduces challenges, such as the potential for priority inversion, where a high-priority task is delayed by the execution of a lower-priority task holding a shared resource. The impact of fixed-priority scheduling on real-time memory management underscores the delicate balance required to ensure both temporal predictability and efficient resource utilization.

Another scheduling paradigm, dynamic priority scheduling, allows task priorities to change dynamically based on their execution history and behavior. The impact of dynamic priority scheduling on real-time memory management is characterized by increased adaptability but introduces challenges related to system complexity. Tasks with dynamically changing priorities may exhibit varying memory access patterns, necessitating memory management strategies that accommodate these fluctuations. The impact of dynamic priority scheduling extends beyond temporal considerations to influence the overall system behavior, emphasizing the need for memory management mechanisms that can flexibly adapt to evolving task requirements.

In multiprocessor real-time systems, the impact of scheduling becomes even more intricate as tasks are distributed across multiple cores. Spatial and temporal partitioning strategies, which allocate specific processors and time intervals to tasks, directly influence how memory is managed in a multiprocessor environment. Spatial partitioning ensures that each processor core has its dedicated memory regions, minimizing contention and enhancing predictability. However, the impact of spatial partitioning on real-time memory management involves careful consideration of inter-core communication and synchronization, as tasks may need to exchange data or coordinate their activities.

Temporal partitioning in multiprocessor systems involves assigning specific time intervals to each processor core for exclusive memory access. The impact of temporal partitioning on real-time memory management lies in its ability to isolate tasks temporally, preventing interference and contention. However, the impact of temporal partitioning extends to the efficient utilization of memory resources, as tasks must complete their memory operations within their allocated time intervals. The impact of scheduling choices in multiprocessor real-time systems underscores the need for a holistic approach that considers both spatial and temporal aspects, balancing the benefits of isolation with the demands of efficient resource utilization.

The integration of priority inheritance protocols into real-time scheduling has a significant impact on memory management in scenarios where shared resources are involved. Priority inheritance prevents priority inversion by temporarily boosting the priority of a task holding a shared resource to that of the highest-priority task waiting for the resource. The impact of priority inheritance on real-time memory management is evident in its role in mitigating priority inversion-related delays, ensuring that high-priority tasks can access shared resources promptly. However, the impact of priority inheritance introduces overhead in terms of additional scheduling complexities and potential increased memory requirements, emphasizing the importance of carefully considering trade-offs in real-time system design.

Cache-aware scheduling, an approach that considers the cache hierarchy of modern processors, has a profound impact on how memory is managed in real-time systems. The impact of cache-aware scheduling is rooted in its ability to optimize cache locality, reducing cache misses and improving overall performance. Tasks scheduled to run on the same processor core benefit from shared cache access, enhancing memory access efficiency. The impact of cache-aware scheduling extends to memory management decisions, as system designers must consider the cache behavior of tasks when allocating memory regions or deciding on the placement of data structures. The impact of cache-aware scheduling exemplifies the need for a holistic understanding of the hardware architecture and its interaction with memory management strategies in real-time systems.

The integration of real-time virtual memory management into scheduling decisions introduces a layer of complexity that directly impacts memory management strategies. Real-time virtual memory management involves mapping virtual addresses to physical addresses in a manner that preserves temporal predictability. The impact of real-time virtual memory management on scheduling is evident in the need for careful consideration of address translation overhead and the potential for unpredictable delays introduced by virtual-to-physical mapping. The impact of scheduling decisions becomes intertwined with the impact of virtual memory management, requiring an integrated approach to ensure both efficient memory utilization and temporal predictability.

The impact of priority inversion, a phenomenon where a high-priority task is delayed by a lower-priority task holding a shared resource, underscores the importance of employing priority inheritance or priority ceiling protocols in real-time scheduling. Priority inheritance ensures that the priority of a task holding a shared resource is temporarily boosted to that of the highest-priority task waiting for the resource, preventing priority inversion-related delays. The impact of priority inheritance on real-time memory management is evident in its role in mitigating priority inversion, enabling high-priority tasks to access shared resources promptly. However, the impact of priority inheritance introduces additional complexity to the scheduling algorithm, necessitating careful consideration of its implications on system behavior.

Temporal partitioning, a scheduling technique that assigns specific time intervals to each task for exclusive execution, impacts how memory is managed in real-time systems. The impact of temporal partitioning on memory management lies in its ability to provide temporal isolation between tasks, preventing interference and ensuring predictable execution times. However, the impact of temporal partitioning extends to the allocation of memory resources, as tasks must complete their memory operations within their designated time intervals. The impact of temporal partitioning on real-time memory management highlights the trade-offs between temporal predictability and efficient resource utilization, emphasizing the need for a balanced approach in system design.

In conclusion, the impact of scheduling on real-time memory management is multifaceted and central to the performance and predictability of real-time systems. Whether employing fixed-priority scheduling, dynamic priority scheduling, or cache-aware scheduling, the decisions made in the scheduling algorithm directly influence how memory resources are allocated, accessed, and shared among tasks. The impact of scheduling choices is particularly pronounced in multiprocessor systems, where spatial and temporal partitioning strategies introduce additional complexities related to inter-core communication and synchronization. The integration of priority inheritance, real-time virtual memory management, and considerations of cache behavior further emphasizes the intricate interplay between scheduling decisions and memory management strategies. As real-time systems continue to evolve, the impact of scheduling on memory management will remain a critical area of research and development, demanding a holistic and context-aware approach to ensure optimal performance, reliability, and efficiency in diverse real-time applications.

Deterministic and non-deterministic scheduling algorithms.
Deterministic and non-deterministic scheduling algorithms are fundamental components of operating systems, shaping how tasks are executed on computer systems and influencing overall system be-

havior. The essence of these scheduling algorithms lies in their approach to task execution, with deterministic algorithms providing a predictable and consistent order of task execution, while non-deterministic algorithms introduce variability and unpredictability into the scheduling process.

Deterministic scheduling algorithms are characterized by their ability to produce a predictable and reproducible order of task execution under the same set of conditions. One of the most common deterministic scheduling algorithms is the Fixed-Priority Scheduling algorithm. In this approach, each task is assigned a priority based on its criticality or time sensitivity, and tasks are scheduled for execution in order of their priority. The deterministic nature of fixed-priority scheduling ensures that tasks with higher priority always get preference over lower-priority tasks, promoting predictability in meeting deadlines. However, while deterministic scheduling algorithms offer reliability and consistent behavior, they may suffer from limitations such as priority inversion, where a low-priority task holds a shared resource and delays the execution of a higher-priority task.

Another deterministic scheduling algorithm is the Rate-Monotonic Scheduling (RMS) algorithm, which assigns priorities inversely proportional to the task periods. Tasks with shorter periods receive higher priorities, ensuring that tasks with tighter deadlines are scheduled more frequently. RMS is deterministic in nature, providing a clear order of task execution based on the fixed relationship between priorities and periods. While deterministic scheduling algorithms like RMS are effective in meeting real-time constraints and ensuring predictability, they may not always be the most optimal choice in scenarios with dynamic task characteristics or varying workloads.

Contrastingly, non-deterministic scheduling algorithms introduce an element of unpredictability into the task execution order, making it challenging to precisely anticipate the sequence of task executions. A notable example of a non-deterministic scheduling algorithm is the Round Robin Scheduling algorithm. In Round Robin, each task is assigned a fixed time quantum during which it can execute. When a task's time quantum expires, it is moved to the back of the queue, and the next task in line gets a turn. The non-deterministic nature of Round Robin arises from the potential variability in the order of task execution, depending on factors like task arrival times and quantum sizes. While non-deterministic scheduling algorithms offer fairness and prevent tasks from monopolizing resources, they may lead to less predictable task completion times, making them less suitable for real-time systems with stringent timing requirements.

Another non-deterministic scheduling algorithm is the Lottery Scheduling algorithm, which allocates tickets to tasks based on their priority or importance. During each scheduling event, a ticket is randomly drawn, and the task associated with that ticket is selected for execution. The probabilistic nature of Lottery Scheduling introduces variability into the selection process, making it challenging to precisely determine the order of task execution. While non-deterministic scheduling algorithms like Lottery Scheduling offer a degree of fairness and adaptability to dynamic workloads, they may lack the predictability required in real-time systems where tasks must meet strict deadlines.

Hybrid scheduling approaches combine elements of both deterministic and non-deterministic scheduling to achieve a balance between predictability and adaptability. Earliest Deadline First (EDF) scheduling, for instance, is a dynamic priority scheduling algorithm that is both deterministic and adaptable. In EDF, tasks are assigned priorities based on their absolute deadlines, and the task with the earliest deadline is scheduled for execution first. While EDF is deterministic in its adherence to deadlines, its adaptability arises from the dynamic nature of the priorities, which change as tasks progress through their execution phases. Hybrid scheduling algorithms aim to leverage the strengths of both deterministic and non-deterministic approaches, catering to diverse application scenarios with varying requirements.

Deterministic scheduling algorithms play a crucial role in real-time systems, where tasks must meet strict temporal constraints to ensure correct functionality and safety. These algorithms, such as Fixed-Priority Scheduling and Rate-Monotonic Scheduling, offer predictability by establishing a clear order of task execution based on priority assignments. In safety-critical applications like avionics or automotive control systems, where missing deadlines can have severe consequences, deterministic scheduling algorithms provide a reliable framework for meeting stringent timing requirements. The predictability offered by deterministic scheduling contributes to the assurance of system behavior, simplifying analysis and verification processes in safety-critical domains.

Non-deterministic scheduling algorithms, on the other hand, find applications in scenarios where adaptability and fairness are prioritized over strict predictability. In general-purpose operating systems or environments with dynamic workloads, non-deterministic algorithms like Round Robin or Lottery Scheduling help prevent task starvation and ensure that each task receives a fair share of CPU time. The inherent flexibility of non-deterministic scheduling algorithms makes them suitable for scenarios where precise task execution sequences are less critical, and the emphasis is on resource sharing and responsiveness.

Deterministic scheduling algorithms often rely on the concept of priority to establish a clear order of execution, with higher-priority tasks preempting lower-priority ones. While this ensures predictability, it may lead to priority inversion scenarios where a low-priority task holds a shared resource needed by a higher-priority task, causing delays. Priority Inheritance Protocols are mechanisms designed to mitigate priority inversion by temporarily boosting the priority of a task holding a shared resource to that of the highest-priority task waiting for the resource. These protocols represent an attempt to address limitations within deterministic scheduling, acknowledging the impact of resource sharing on the overall performance of the system.

Non-deterministic scheduling algorithms face challenges in meeting the stringent timing requirements of real-time systems. The inherent variability in task execution order and completion times introduces uncertainty that can be unacceptable in applications where deadlines must be met reliably. Real-time systems often rely on deterministic scheduling approaches to ensure that tasks complete within specified time bounds, reducing the risk of missed deadlines and potential system failures. While non-deterministic algorithms contribute to fairness and adaptability, their impact on temporal predictability limits their applicability in safety-critical or mission-critical domains where deterministic guarantees are essential.

The concept of preemption, inherent in many deterministic scheduling algorithms, allows higher-priority tasks to interrupt the execution of lower-priority tasks when necessary. This feature ensures that urgent or time-sensitive tasks can be promptly serviced, contributing to the predictability of task completion times. However, the impact of preemption introduces overhead and complexity, especially in systems with fine-grained time constraints. Scheduling decisions must be made judiciously to balance the benefits of preemption in meeting deadlines with the associated costs in terms of context switching and potential priority inversion scenarios.

The impact of scheduling algorithms extends beyond the realm of the CPU to influence memory management and overall system performance. Deterministic scheduling algorithms often cooperate with partitioned memory models, where memory is statically allocated to tasks based on priorities or time sensitivity. This collaboration ensures that high-priority tasks have dedicated memory regions, minimizing contention and enhancing temporal predictability. Non-deterministic scheduling algorithms, by introducing variability into task execution, may complicate memory management strategies, necessitating adaptive approaches to address dynamic resource requirements and access patterns.

In conclusion, the choice between deterministic and non-deterministic scheduling algorithms depends on the specific requirements of the application and the characteristics of the underlying system. Deterministic scheduling algorithms, with their emphasis on predictability and adherence to strict priorities, find favor in safety-critical real-time systems where meeting deadlines is paramount. Non-deterministic scheduling algorithms, offering fairness and adaptability, are suitable for general-purpose operating systems and environments with dynamic workloads. Hybrid approaches, such as EDF scheduling, attempt to strike a balance between the two paradigms, providing adaptability while maintaining deterministic guarantees. The impact of scheduling algorithms resonates throughout the layers of a computer system, influencing not only CPU execution but also memory management, responsiveness, and overall system behavior in diverse and evolving application domains.

Ensuring timely access to memory resources in real-time scenarios.

Ensuring timely access to memory resources in real-time scenarios is a critical aspect of system design, particularly in applications where tasks must meet stringent temporal constraints. The effectiveness of real-time systems relies heavily on the ability to access memory resources promptly and predictably to guarantee the timely execution of tasks. Real-time scenarios encompass a broad spectrum of applications, ranging from safety-critical systems in avionics and automotive control to multimedia processing, industrial automation, and beyond. Achieving timely access to memory resources involves a multifaceted approach that encompasses memory partitioning, scheduling algorithms, caching strategies, and consideration of the underlying hardware architecture.

Memory partitioning plays a pivotal role in ensuring timely access to memory resources in real-time scenarios. By allocating dedicated memory regions to individual tasks or processes, memory partitioning minimizes contention and interference, enhancing the predictability of memory access times. Fixed partitioning, where each task is assigned a predetermined portion of memory, provides simplicity and predictability. However, dynamic partitioning allows for adaptability to changing memory requirements, albeit with the challenge of fragmentation. The choice between fixed and dynamic partitioning depends on the specific demands of the real-time application, striking a balance between predictability and flexibility to meet temporal constraints effectively.

In the realm of scheduling algorithms, the choice profoundly influences the timely access to memory resources. Fixed-priority scheduling assigns priorities to tasks based on their criticality, allowing high-priority tasks to access memory promptly. Rate-Monotonic Scheduling, a fixed-priority algorithm, prioritizes tasks with shorter periods, emphasizing timely execution of recurrent tasks. On the other hand, dynamic priority scheduling algorithms, such as Earliest Deadline First (EDF), dynamically adjust priorities based on task deadlines. EDF prioritizes tasks with imminent deadlines, ensuring that tasks with the most imminent temporal constraints are granted expedited access to memory resources. The interplay between scheduling and memory access is integral to meeting real-time requirements, with the selected scheduling algorithm influencing the overall predictability and responsiveness of the system.

Cache management strategies are crucial for ensuring timely memory access, especially considering the hierarchical nature of modern processors. Cache-aware scheduling aims to optimize cache locality, reducing cache misses and improving overall performance.

In real-time scenarios, where latency is a critical concern, efficient use of caches can significantly impact the timely retrieval of data. Strategies like prefetching, where data is loaded into the cache ahead of time, and cache partitioning, which allocates cache space based on task priorities, contribute to minimizing memory access times. However, the trade-offs involved in cache management, such as increased complexity and potential contention, require careful consideration to strike the right balance for the specific real-time application.

Affinity-based memory partitioning is another strategy employed to enhance timely access to memory resources in real-time scenarios. This approach involves assigning specific memory regions to tasks based on their affinity for certain data or resources. By aligning memory access patterns with task affinities, the system can reduce cache misses and improve overall performance. Affinity-based memory partitioning is particularly relevant in scenarios where tasks exhibit predictable data access patterns, allowing for a targeted allocation of memory resources that optimally aligns with the tasks' requirements. However, implementing affinity-based partitioning necessitates a deep understanding of task behavior and may involve dynamic adjustments to adapt to changing execution patterns.

Temporal partitioning is a specialized technique designed to ensure timely memory access in systems with both hard and soft real-time tasks. In temporal partitioning, time is partitioned into fixed intervals, and tasks are assigned specific time slots. This temporal isolation prevents long-term interference between tasks, ensuring that each task has dedicated processing time and, consequently, timely access to memory resources. The alignment of temporal boundaries with critical time constraints enhances predictability, with tasks being guaranteed access to memory during their allocated time slots. However, the implementation of temporal partitioning requires careful consideration of task deadlines and efficient coordination to optimize memory access across different time intervals.

In safety-critical real-time systems, where reliability and fault tolerance are paramount, the concept of memory protection and isolation becomes integral to ensuring timely access to memory resources. Memory protection mechanisms, such as Memory Protection Units (MPUs) or Memory Protection Keys, aim to prevent unauthorized access or modification of memory regions, contributing to the security and integrity of the system. Isolation techniques enforce strict boundaries between tasks, minimizing the impact of faults or errors in one task on the integrity of others. The implementation of memory protection and isolation mechanisms adds an additional layer of complexity but is essential for maintaining reliable and timely access to memory in safety-critical applications.

In the context of multiprocessor real-time systems, ensuring timely access to memory resources becomes even more challenging due to the presence of multiple processor cores. Space-partitioned scheduling allocates dedicated memory regions to each processor core, minimizing contention and enhancing predictability. Time-partitioned scheduling assigns specific time intervals to each processor core for exclusive memory access, reducing interference during critical processing times. The coordination of memory access across multiple cores involves considerations of inter-core communication and synchronization to prevent conflicts and ensure timely data exchange. Balancing the trade-offs between spatial and time partitioning is crucial in achieving efficient and predictable memory access in multiprocessor real-time systems.

The integration of virtual memory concepts into real-time systems introduces a layer of abstraction that must be carefully managed to ensure timely access to memory resources. Real-time virtual memory management involves mapping virtual addresses to physical addresses in a manner that preserves temporal predictability. Fixed mapping, where virtual-to-physical mappings are predetermined and do not change during task execution, contributes to the predictability of virtual memory in real-time systems. However, the overhead associated with virtual-to-physical address translation introduces challenges in meeting strict temporal constraints. Optimizations, such as minimizing page faults and optimizing TLB (Translation Lookaside Buffer) usage, are crucial for ensuring timely access to memory resources while leveraging the benefits of virtual memory.

Ensuring timely access to memory resources in real-time scenarios requires a comprehensive understanding of the specific demands and constraints of the application domain. Safety-critical systems demand reliability and fault tolerance, driving the need for robust memory protection mechanisms and isolation strategies. Multimedia processing applications, on the other hand, may prioritize efficient use of caches and affinity-based memory partitioning to optimize for data access patterns. The choice of scheduling algorithm, whether fixed-priority, dynamic priority, or a hybrid approach, significantly influences the temporal predictability and responsiveness of memory access. The hierarchical nature of modern processors necessitates cache-aware scheduling and efficient cache management strategies to minimize latency. Ultimately, achieving timely access to memory resources in real-time scenarios involves a holistic and context-aware approach, carefully tailoring memory management strategies to the specific requirements of the application while navigating the trade-offs inherent in real-time system design.

The role of memory locking in real-time applications.

The role of memory locking in real-time applications is a critical facet that directly impacts the predictability, reliability, and performance of these systems. Memory locking, also known as memory pinning, involves reserving a specific region of memory in physical RAM, preventing it from being swapped out to secondary storage such as a hard disk or SSD. In real-time applications where meeting stringent timing constraints is paramount, the ability to control and manage memory access becomes a crucial factor in ensuring consistent and predictable system behavior.

One of the primary purposes of memory locking in real-time applications is to eliminate the non-deterministic delays introduced by virtual memory management, specifically paging and swapping. In traditional operating systems, virtual memory management allows pages of memory to be moved between physical RAM and secondary storage to optimize overall system performance. However, this introduces uncertainty in memory access times, as pages may be swapped in and out based on the operating system's decisions. In contrast, memory locking ensures that specific regions critical to real-time tasks remain in physical RAM at all times, eliminating the unpredictable delays associated with page faults and swaps.

In safety-critical systems, such as those found in avionics or automotive control, where tasks must meet stringent deadlines to ensure system stability and safety, memory locking plays a pivotal role in providing determinism. By preventing critical sections of code or data structures from being swapped out, memory locking guarantees that the necessary resources are readily available when needed. This determinism is essential for meeting real-time requirements, preventing potential interruptions that could lead to missed deadlines and jeopardize the correct functioning of safety-critical systems.

Memory locking is particularly relevant in scenarios where tasks involve real-time signal processing, multimedia applications, or control systems with precise timing requirements. In these applications, consistent and low-latency access to specific memory regions is crucial for maintaining the integrity of data processing or control algorithms. By locking the relevant memory areas, real-time tasks can access data with minimal variability in access times, facilitating the adherence to tight timing constraints and enhancing the overall reliability of the system.

However, the indiscriminate use of memory locking can have trade-offs and implications for overall system performance. While it ensures predictability and determinism, memory locking may lead to increased memory usage and potential fragmentation, especially in scenarios where large portions of memory need to be locked. The careful consideration of which parts of memory to lock, based on the criticality and timing requirements of tasks, becomes essential to strike a balance between predictability and resource efficiency.

In real-time applications where multi-threading or parallel processing is employed, the role of memory locking extends to synchronization and coordination between threads. Memory locking can be used to ensure that shared data structures critical for inter-process communication or coordination are consistently available in physical RAM. This is particularly relevant in scenarios where tasks must exchange data or synchronize their activities within strict time bounds. The predictability introduced by memory locking becomes instrumental in avoiding race conditions and ensuring that threads can access shared resources without the uncertainty introduced by dynamic memory management.

In the realm of real-time operating systems (RTOS), memory locking is often tightly integrated with the overall scheduling strategy. RTOS platforms, designed specifically for applications with stringent timing requirements, leverage memory locking to enhance predictability. Tasks with critical timing constraints may have their associated memory regions locked to ensure that they remain resident in physical RAM, ready for immediate access. This integration of memory locking into the scheduling framework contributes to the holistic approach required for meeting the diverse and demanding requirements of real-time applications.

In the context of high-performance computing, where real-time constraints may not be as stringent as in safety-critical systems but low-latency access to data remains crucial, memory locking plays a strategic role. Applications such as algorithmic trading, scientific simulations, or real-time analytics often demand rapid access to large datasets. Memory locking can be employed to keep these datasets in physical RAM, reducing access latency and contributing to the overall responsiveness of the system. The trade-offs between memory usage, fragmentation, and the benefits of low-latency access must be carefully evaluated to optimize the performance of high-performance computing applications.

In the domain of real-time multimedia processing, where tasks involve streaming and processing large volumes of data, memory locking becomes instrumental in ensuring continuous and uninterrupted data flow. By locking the memory regions involved in data processing and rendering, multimedia applications can minimize the risk of interruptions or glitches, enhancing the overall user experience. The role of memory locking in multimedia applications extends beyond meeting real-time deadlines; it directly influences the seamless and reliable delivery of multimedia content in various scenarios, from video conferencing to live streaming.

The impact of memory locking is also evident in scenarios where real-time tasks interface with external hardware or peripherals. In industrial automation, for example, where tasks must interact with sensors, actuators, or control systems in real-time, memory locking ensures that the data structures involved in these interactions remain resident in physical RAM. This guarantees timely access to the information necessary for controlling and monitoring industrial processes. The reliability introduced by memory locking becomes a critical factor in preventing delays or inconsistencies in the communication between real-time tasks and external devices.

In safety-critical avionics systems, where compliance with stringent certification standards is essential, memory locking contributes to meeting regulatory requirements. Certification standards, such as DO-178C, impose strict guidelines on the verification and validation of software systems. Memory locking aids in ensuring that critical software components essential for flight control or navigation remain in physical RAM, facilitating the thorough testing and analysis demanded by aviation certification authorities. The deterministic nature introduced by memory locking aligns with the rigorous safety standards, providing assurance in the reliability and predictability of avionics systems.

However, the role of memory locking is not without challenges, and its implementation requires a careful consideration of various factors. In scenarios where memory resources are limited, the indiscriminate use of memory locking may lead to increased contention for locked regions, potentially impacting overall system performance. Balancing the need for determinism with efficient resource utilization becomes a design consideration, and careful profiling and analysis are essential to identify which memory regions should be locked based on their criticality to real-time tasks.

In conclusion, the role of memory locking in real-time applications is multifaceted, addressing the fundamental need for predictability and determinism in scenarios where tasks must meet stringent temporal constraints. Whether in safety-critical systems, high-performance computing, multimedia processing, or industrial automation, memory locking contributes to the reliability and responsiveness of real-time applications. The careful consideration of which memory regions to lock, the trade-offs involved, and the integration with overall system design are critical aspects of leveraging memory locking effectively. As real-time systems continue to evolve and diversify, the role of memory locking remains a key element in the toolkit of strategies aimed at ensuring consistent and timely access to memory resources in the pursuit of reliable and predictable real-time performance.

Chapter 8: Future Trends in Memory Management

Overview of new and future memory technologies.

The landscape of memory technologies is undergoing a transformative phase, marked by the emergence of new and future technologies that promise to redefine the boundaries of computing and data storage. One of the most notable advancements is the development of Resistive Random-Access Memory (RRAM or ReRAM). RRAM utilizes the resistance change in a memory cell to store information, offering advantages such as high-speed read and write operations, low power consumption, and excellent scalability. With the potential to surpass traditional Flash memory in terms of performance and endurance, RRAM is a candidate for next-generation non-volatile memory solutions, particularly in applications demanding high-speed data access and lower energy consumption.

Another breakthrough in memory technology is the advent of Phase-Change Memory (PCM). PCM relies on the reversible phase transition of a chalcogenide glass material between amorphous and crystalline states to represent binary data. This non-volatile memory technology exhibits fast read and write speeds, high endurance, and compatibility with existing silicon manufacturing processes. PCM's ability to combine high-density storage with low-latency access makes it a compelling option for applications ranging from data centers to edge devices, where the demand for improved performance and energy efficiency is ever-growing.

Beyond traditional solid-state memory technologies, there is a surge in interest surrounding Storage-Class Memory (SCM). SCM, exemplified by Intel's Optane and Samsung's Z-NAND, aims to bridge the gap between dynamic random-access memory (DRAM) and conventional storage. SCM combines the non-volatility of storage with the speed and byte-addressability of DRAM, offering a compelling alternative for applications requiring large, persistent, and fast-access storage. The advent of SCM has the potential to re-shape the memory hierarchy in computing systems, providing a more unified and responsive storage architecture.

Memristors, short for memory resistors, represent a novel and promising avenue in memory technology. These devices exhibit non-volatile resistive switching properties, enabling them to function as both memory and logic elements. Memristors can potentially revolutionize neuromorphic computing by mimicking the synaptic plasticity observed in biological neural networks. This capability makes memristors a key player in the development of brain-inspired computing architectures, where they can facilitate the efficient processing and storage of information in a manner that parallels the human brain's neural connections.

In the pursuit of ever-increasing data transfer rates and bandwidth, High-Bandwidth Memory (HBM) has emerged as a cutting-edge memory technology. HBM stacks multiple memory dies vertically, providing a high-bandwidth interface between the memory and the processor. This three-dimensional stacking architecture, coupled with shorter interconnects, significantly enhances data transfer rates and reduces latency, making HBM particularly well-suited for graphics processing units (GPUs) and other high-performance computing applications.

The evolution of memory technologies is not limited to traditional electronic approaches. Photonic Memory, leveraging light instead of electrical signals, is a burgeoning field with the potential to revolutionize data transfer and storage. Optical memories utilize photons to encode and retrieve information, offering advantages such as high-speed data transmission, low power consumption, and resistance to electromagnetic interference. Photonic Memory holds promise for applications in data centers, telecommunications, and quantum computing, where the inherent properties of light can be harnessed to overcome current limitations in speed and bandwidth.

Quantum Random-Access Memory (qRAM) represents a futuristic and highly speculative avenue in the realm of memory technologies. As quantum computing gains traction, the concept of quantum memory becomes essential for storing and retrieving quantum states. QRAM, theoretically leveraging quantum superposition to store information in multiple states simultaneously, has the potential to complement quantum processors by facilitating faster and more efficient quantum data manipulation. However, practical implementations of qRAM are still in their infancy, with numerous challenges to overcome before they become viable in real-world quantum computing applications.

The advent of persistent memory technologies is also shaping the future of storage and computing. Persistent memory combines the speed of volatile memory with the non-volatility of traditional storage devices, blurring the lines between memory and storage. Technologies like Intel's Optane Persistent Memory exemplify this paradigm shift, enabling larger and more cost-effective in-memory databases, improved virtualization performance, and more efficient handling of large datasets.

In the pursuit of memory technologies with superior energy efficiency, researchers are exploring Ferroelectric Memory as a potential candidate. Ferroelectric memory relies on the polarization of ferroelectric materials to store information. It offers non-volatility, low power consumption, and fast switching times, making it suitable for applications where energy efficiency is a critical consideration. Ferroelectric memory's potential to operate at lower voltages and retain data without continuous power makes it an attractive option for battery-powered devices and energy-constrained environments.

Emerging Non-Volatile Memory technologies, such as Spin-Transfer Torque RAM (STT-RAM) and Magnetic RAM (MRAM), are gaining traction for their ability to combine non-volatility with fast access times and endurance. STT-RAM utilizes the spin of electrons to store information, offering advantages in terms of scalability and potential integration with existing semiconductor fabrication processes. MRAM, on the other hand, leverages the magnetic properties of materials to achieve non-volatile storage. These technologies show promise in various applications, from embedded systems to high-performance computing, where the need for reliable, fast, and energy-efficient non-volatile memory is ever-present.

As memory technologies continue to evolve, it is essential to address the challenges associated with their adoption and integration into existing computing architectures. Issues such as compatibility with legacy systems, scalability, manufacturing costs, and the development of effective memory management strategies become crucial considerations. Furthermore, the exploration of new materials, novel architectures, and innovative fabrication techniques will play a pivotal role in shaping the trajectory of memory technologies in the coming years. The synergistic integration of these advancements holds the potential to revolutionize not only the way data is stored and accessed but also the very fabric of computing itself, ushering in an era of unprecedented performance, efficiency, and versatility in memory technologies.

Non-volatile memory and its impact on system architecture.
Non-volatile memory (NVM) has emerged as a transformative force in computing, reshaping system architectures and fundamentally altering the way data is stored, accessed, and processed. Unlike traditional volatile memory such as DRAM, which loses its contents

when power is turned off, non-volatile memory retains data even in the absence of power. This characteristic introduces a paradigm shift in system design, impacting various aspects of computing from energy efficiency to overall system performance.

One of the key areas where non-volatile memory has a profound impact is in the domain of storage systems. Traditional storage solutions, like Hard Disk Drives (HDDs) and Solid State Drives (SSDs), have served as primary non-volatile storage devices. However, these technologies have inherent limitations in terms of access speed, endurance, and power consumption. The advent of novel non-volatile memory technologies, such as 3D XPoint (as exemplified by Intel's Optane), offers a compelling alternative. 3D XPoint combines the speed of DRAM with the non-volatility of traditional storage, blurring the lines between memory and storage. This convergence results in storage-class memory (SCM), a category of non-volatile memory that provides low-latency access, high endurance, and byte-addressability. SCM technologies bridge the performance gap between DRAM and conventional storage, enabling more responsive and efficient data storage solutions.

In the context of storage-class memory, the impact on system architecture is profound. The distinction between main memory and storage becomes less pronounced, leading to a more unified memory hierarchy. Traditional architectures, where data is transferred between storage and main memory, incur latency overheads. SCM, being non-volatile and offering near-DRAM speed, allows for in-memory processing, where computation occurs directly on the stored data without the need for frequent transfers. This paradigm shift in memory architecture has implications for database management systems, analytics, and applications requiring large, persistent datasets. In-memory databases, for instance, benefit significantly from SCM by reducing data access latencies, improving overall query performance, and enabling real-time analytics on massive datasets.

Non-volatile memory technologies also play a pivotal role in enhancing system resilience and reliability. The persistence of data in the absence of power eliminates the need for time-consuming data recovery processes after system reboots or power outages. In scenarios where downtime is costly or unacceptable, as in critical infrastructure, financial systems, or telecommunications, the resilience afforded by non-volatile memory becomes a crucial design consideration. Persistent memory technologies, such as Intel's Optane Persistent Memory, combine the capacity of storage with the speed of memory. This innovation enables large, persistent datasets to be stored closer to the processor, reducing the need for extensive data transfers between storage and main memory. The result is improved system reliability, reduced downtime, and enhanced fault tolerance, contributing to the overall robustness of critical systems.

Non-volatile memory's impact extends beyond traditional storage and into the realm of emerging technologies, such as edge computing and Internet of Things (IoT) devices. In edge computing scenarios, where processing occurs closer to the data source, non-volatile memory facilitates efficient data storage and retrieval. Edge devices often operate in resource-constrained environments, and the non-volatility of memory ensures data persistence despite intermittent power availability. This reliability is crucial for applications like autonomous vehicles, industrial automation, and remote monitoring, where edge devices must store and process data reliably in real-time. Additionally, non-volatile memory's ability to operate in low-power modes aligns with the energy-efficient requirements of IoT devices, contributing to prolonged device lifetimes and reduced maintenance needs.

The advent of non-volatile memory technologies also has implications for energy-efficient computing. The energy consumption associated with traditional storage solutions, especially in data-intensive applications with frequent disk accesses, poses a significant challenge. Non-volatile memory, with its lower power requirements and ability to operate in low-power states without sacrificing data persistence, offers a compelling solution. This is particularly relevant in mobile devices, where energy efficiency is a critical design consideration. The integration of non-volatile memory in smartphones and tablets not only improves storage performance but also contributes to longer battery life and enhanced user experience.

Non-volatile memory's impact on system architecture is further accentuated in the context of emerging computing paradigms, such as neuromorphic computing and in-memory computing. The non-volatility of memory is a key enabler for persistent storage of synaptic weights in neuromorphic systems, mimicking the plasticity observed in biological neural networks. This capability is essential for realizing energy-efficient and brain-inspired computing architectures, where non-volatile memory facilitates the retention of learned information even during power cycles. In-memory computing leverages the persistence of non-volatile memory to perform computations directly on the stored data, eliminating the need for frequent data transfers between memory and processing units. This architectural shift enhances computational efficiency and reduces latency, making in-memory computing well-suited for data-intensive tasks such as machine learning and data analytics.

Security considerations in system architecture are also influenced by the characteristics of non-volatile memory. The non-volatility of data introduces challenges in ensuring secure data erasure, especially in scenarios where storage devices may be repurposed or decommissioned. Secure data deletion becomes a critical concern to prevent sensitive information from being accessed by unauthorized entities. Additionally, the non-volatility of memory raises the bar for secure storage solutions, as the potential persistence of data across power cycles requires robust encryption and access control mechanisms. As non-volatile memory technologies continue to advance, addressing these security challenges becomes imperative to ensure the confidentiality and integrity of stored data.

The integration of non-volatile memory into traditional system architectures necessitates adaptations in operating systems and memory management strategies. Operating systems must be optimized to leverage the unique characteristics of non-volatile memory, such as its persistence and lower-latency access. Memory management algorithms need to evolve to exploit the capabilities of non-volatile memory for enhanced data storage, retrieval, and processing. File systems may require rethinking to accommodate the unified memory hierarchy introduced by SCM, allowing for more efficient utilization of storage-class memory alongside traditional DRAM.

Despite the myriad benefits, challenges remain in the widespread adoption of non-volatile memory technologies. Cost considerations, manufacturing challenges, and the need for industry standards pose hurdles that must be addressed to ensure the seamless integration of non-volatile memory into diverse computing environments. Additionally, the diverse range of non-volatile memory technologies, each with its own set of characteristics and trade-offs, requires careful consideration to match the technology with specific application requirements.

In conclusion, non-volatile memory stands as a transformative force in modern system architecture, influencing storage systems, resilience, energy efficiency, and emerging computing paradigms. From storage-class memory technologies that blur the lines between memory and storage to persistent memory solutions that enhance system reliability, non-volatile memory is reshaping the way computing systems are designed and operated. As technology continues to evolve, the integration of non-volatile memory into diverse computing environments promises to unlock new possibilities, ushering in an era where data persistence, energy efficiency, and system responsiveness converge to redefine the boundaries of computing architecture.

Evaluating the potential of emerging memory innovations.

Evaluating the potential of emerging memory innovations requires a comprehensive exploration of the transformative advancements poised to reshape the landscape of computing. One such innovation that holds immense promise is Resistive Random-Access Memory (RRAM or ReRAM). RRAM operates by utilizing the resistance change in a memory cell to store information. This novel non-volatile memory technology has garnered attention for its potential to outperform traditional Flash memory in terms of speed, energy efficiency, and scalability. With characteristics that include high-speed read and write operations, low power consumption, and compatibility with existing semiconductor manufacturing processes, RRAM emerges as a strong contender for next-generation memory solutions. Its potential impact spans a multitude of applications, ranging from edge computing and IoT devices to high-performance computing environments, where the need for faster, more energy-efficient, and scalable memory solutions is paramount.

Phase-Change Memory (PCM) stands as another groundbreaking innovation in the realm of emerging memory technologies. PCM relies on the reversible phase transition of a chalcogenide glass material between amorphous and crystalline states to store binary data. This non-volatile memory technology exhibits rapid read and write speeds, high endurance, and compatibility with existing silicon fabrication processes. PCM's unique blend of characteristics positions it as a compelling candidate for various applications, particularly in data-intensive tasks where speed and endurance are critical factors. The potential of PCM extends to storage-class memory (SCM), where its attributes enable the convergence of storage and memory, contributing to a more unified and efficient memory hierarchy. This convergence promises to bridge the gap between traditional memory and storage, revolutionizing the way data is processed and stored in computing systems.

The advent of Storage-Class Memory (SCM) is a paradigm shift that has the potential to redefine system architectures. SCM, exemplified by technologies such as Intel's Optane, represents a convergence of the best attributes of both traditional memory and storage. Operating at speeds close to DRAM while retaining data persistence, SCM introduces a new layer in the memory hierarchy that blurs the lines between volatile and non-volatile memory. This innovation has far-reaching implications for various computing domains, from data centers to edge devices. In data centers, SCM can be leveraged to enhance in-memory databases, accelerating data access and reducing latency. At the edge, where low-latency access to persistent data is crucial, SCM contributes to the efficient operation of IoT devices and other edge computing applications. The potential of SCM to reshape memory architectures lies in its ability to provide a balance between speed, endurance, and data persistence.

Memristors, short for memory resistors, represent a frontier in emerging memory technologies that combines memory and logic functionalities. Memristors exhibit non-volatile resistive switching properties, allowing them to store information and perform logic operations. This unique capability positions memristors as key elements in the development of neuromorphic computing, where the goal is to mimic the synaptic plasticity observed in biological neural networks. Memristors hold promise for energy-efficient computing by emulating the brain's ability to learn and adapt. Their potential impact spans applications such as artificial intelligence, pattern recognition, and cognitive computing, where the convergence of memory and processing in a single device can lead to unprecedented computational efficiency. While challenges in manufacturing and scalability remain, memristors represent a disruptive innovation that could revolutionize the way future computing systems operate.

High-Bandwidth Memory (HBM) is another innovation that significantly impacts memory architectures, particularly in graphics processing units (GPUs) and high-performance computing environments. HBM employs a three-dimensional stacking architecture to vertically integrate multiple memory dies, resulting in shorter interconnects and higher data transfer rates. This innovation addresses the growing demand for increased memory bandwidth in data-intensive applications, such as artificial intelligence, graphics rendering, and scientific simulations. The potential of HBM lies in its ability to deliver faster and more efficient data access, reducing latency and enhancing overall system performance. As applications continue to demand higher bandwidth, HBM stands as a critical innovation that enables the parallel processing power of modern GPUs and accelerators.

In the realm of optical memories, emerging technologies leverage light for data storage, retrieval, and processing. Photonic Memory, with its reliance on photons instead of electrical signals, introduces advantages such as high-speed data transmission, low power consumption, and resistance to electromagnetic interference. This innovation has the potential to revolutionize data transfer and storage, particularly in data centers and telecommunications. Photonic Memory's impact extends to quantum computing, where the use of light for data manipulation aligns with the principles of quantum mechanics. Although practical implementations of photonic memory are still evolving, the potential of this technology to overcome current limitations in speed and bandwidth marks it as a significant innovation in the landscape of emerging memory technologies.

Quantum Random-Access Memory (qRAM) represents a futuristic concept that aligns with the development of quantum computing. In the quantum realm, qRAM aims to store and retrieve quantum states efficiently. Quantum computing, with its potential to perform complex computations exponentially faster than classical computers, demands innovations in memory technologies that can keep pace with the unique requirements of quantum algorithms. While qRAM is still in the theoretical domain, its potential impact on the development of quantum computers is substantial. Quantum computers, when realized, could transform fields such as cryptography, optimization, and materials science, where memory innovations compatible with quantum principles are indispensable.

The advent of Persistent Memory technologies, such as Intel's Optane Persistent Memory, introduces a new dimension in the integration of storage and memory. Persistent Memory combines the speed of volatile memory with the non-volatility of storage devices, offering a middle ground between traditional DRAM and storage solutions. This innovation significantly impacts data-intensive applications, such as in-memory databases and analytics, where large datasets can be stored and accessed with lower latency. Persistent Memory also enhances system resilience by eliminating the need for time-consuming data recovery processes after power cycles. This innovation extends the potential for large, persistent datasets to be stored closer to the processor, reducing the latency associated with frequent data transfers between storage and main memory.

Ferroelectric Memory emerges as a potential candidate for energy-efficient computing solutions. This type of memory relies on the polarization of ferroelectric materials to store information. Ferroelectric Memory offers non-volatility, low power consumption, and fast switching times, making it suitable for applications where energy efficiency is a critical consideration. In scenarios such as battery-powered devices or energy-constrained environments, Ferroelectric Memory holds the potential to contribute to prolonged device lifetimes and reduced operational costs. While challenges in manufacturing and scalability need to be addressed, the unique combination of non-volatility and energy efficiency positions Ferroelectric Memory as a promising innovation for future computing systems.

Non-volatile memory technologies, including Spin-Transfer Torque RAM (STT-RAM) and Magnetic RAM (MRAM), offer a compelling blend of non-volatility, fast access times, and endurance. STT-RAM utilizes the spin of electrons to store information, providing advantages in terms of scalability and potential integration with existing semiconductor fabrication processes. MRAM, leveraging the magnetic properties of materials, achieves non-volatile storage with excellent endurance. These technologies find applications in diverse domains, from embedded systems to high-performance computing, where the need for reliable, fast, and energy-efficient non-volatile memory is essential. STT-RAM and MRAM represent innovations that bridge the gap between volatile and non-volatile memory, contributing to more resilient and energy-efficient computing architectures.

Despite the immense potential of emerging memory innovations, challenges exist that must be addressed for widespread adoption. Manufacturing costs, scalability, compatibility with existing architectures, and the need for standardized interfaces are critical factors that influence the feasibility of incorporating these innovations into diverse computing environments. Additionally, considerations related to security, reliability, and the development of efficient memory management strategies are essential to fully realize the potential benefits of these innovations.

In conclusion, the evaluation of emerging memory innovations reveals a landscape rich with transformative potential, influencing a broad spectrum of applications from traditional computing to quantum and neuromorphic systems. RRAM, PCM, SCM, memristors, HBM, photonic memory, qRAM, persistent memory technologies, Ferroelectric Memory, STT-RAM, and MRAM collectively represent a diverse array of innovations, each with its unique set of characteristics and potential applications. As technology continues to evolve, the integration of these emerging memory technologies into computing systems promises to unlock new capabilities, revolutionizing the way data is stored, accessed, and processed. The journey towards the realization of these innovations involves overcoming challenges, fostering collaboration across industries, and envisioning a future where memory technologies play a central role in advancing the frontiers of computational efficiency, energy sustainability, and technological possibilities.

Integrating machine learning techniques in memory management.

The integration of machine learning techniques into memory management represents a paradigm shift in optimizing the performance, efficiency, and adaptability of computing systems. Memory management, a critical aspect of operating systems, governs the allocation and deallocation of memory resources to different processes, ensuring efficient utilization of the available memory. Traditional memory management strategies often rely on static heuristics or predefined algorithms that may not fully adapt to the dynamic and diverse workloads encountered in modern computing environments. The infusion of machine learning into memory management seeks to address these limitations by enabling systems to learn and adapt based on observed patterns, thereby enhancing responsiveness, resource allocation, and overall system efficiency.

One of the key applications of machine learning in memory management is predictive analytics for memory usage patterns. Machine learning models can be trained to analyze historical data on memory usage and predict future patterns based on factors such as time of day, workload characteristics, and application behaviors. By leveraging techniques like time-series analysis and regression, these models can anticipate peak memory demands, enabling proactive memory allocation and deallocation strategies. This predictive capability is particularly valuable in scenarios where workloads exhibit temporal variability or are subject to periodic spikes, allowing the system to optimize memory allocation preemptively and avoid performance bottlenecks.

Another area of integration involves the use of machine learning algorithms to dynamically adjust memory allocation based on application behavior. Traditional static memory allocation may lead to inefficiencies when applications have varying memory requirements during their execution. Machine learning models, equipped with real-time monitoring capabilities, can adaptively adjust memory allocations for each application, considering factors such as historical usage, current demands, and predicted future requirements. Reinforcement learning, in particular, offers a framework where the system can learn from the consequences of its memory allocation decisions and continuously refine its strategies over time, maximizing overall system performance.

Machine learning techniques also find application in memory leak detection and resolution. Memory leaks, where programs fail to release allocated memory, can lead to degraded system performance and eventual instability. Traditional memory leak detection tools often rely on static analysis or runtime monitoring with fixed heuristics. Machine learning models, on the other hand, can be trained to recognize subtle patterns indicative of memory leaks by analyzing the relationships between variables, memory usage patterns, and the longevity of allocated memory blocks. Through supervised learning, these models can identify potential memory leaks with higher accuracy and lower false positive rates, facilitating more effective and automated memory management.

In virtualized and cloud computing environments, where multiple virtual machines or containers share physical resources, machine learning becomes instrumental in optimizing memory allocation across diverse workloads. Clustering algorithms can categorize similar workloads based on their memory usage characteristics, allowing the system to allocate resources more efficiently. Additionally, machine learning models can learn from the interactions and resource usage patterns of different virtual machines, enabling the prediction of optimal resource allocations for specific workloads in real-time. This adaptability is crucial in dynamic environments where the composition and characteristics of workloads may change rapidly.

Machine learning techniques are also leveraged in memory compression and caching strategies. Compression algorithms, traditionally designed based on predefined rules, can benefit from machine learning models that adapt to the specific data access patterns of applications. By learning from historical data and identifying recurring patterns, these models can dynamically adjust compression algorithms to maximize compression ratios while minimizing computational overhead. Similarly, machine learning-driven caching mechanisms can learn which data should be retained in memory based on usage patterns, application behavior, and the temporal locality of memory accesses. This adaptability enhances cache hit rates, reducing the need for fetching data from slower storage tiers and thereby improving overall system performance.

An innovative application of machine learning in memory management is the development of autonomous memory management agents. These agents, powered by reinforcement learning or autonomous decision-making algorithms, can continuously monitor system performance, analyze memory usage patterns, and dynamically adjust memory allocations without human intervention. This autonomous capability is particularly beneficial in large-scale distributed systems or edge computing environments where manual tuning of memory management parameters may not be practical. The agents can adapt to changing workloads, optimize resource utilization, and enhance the overall efficiency of the system without requiring explicit instructions.

In scenarios where stringent Quality of Service (QoS) requirements are essential, machine learning contributes to memory management strategies that prioritize critical tasks. Classification models can distinguish between different types of workloads based on their impact on system performance or user experience. This information is then used to allocate memory resources preferentially to mission-critical applications, ensuring that their performance is maintained within acceptable bounds. Such intelligent memory allocation mechanisms are crucial in real-time systems, where meeting deadlines and ensuring predictable performance are paramount.

The integration of machine learning in memory management also extends to the domain of energy-efficient computing. By learning from historical data and workload patterns, machine learning models can predict periods of low activity or reduced resource demand. During these periods, the system can employ strategies such as aggressive memory consolidation, dynamically adjusting the memory allocated to different applications or virtual machines, and placing unused memory regions into low-power states. This adaptive approach contributes to reduced energy consumption without compromising system responsiveness during periods of increased demand.

Moreover, machine learning techniques play a significant role in anomaly detection and mitigation in memory management. Anomalous memory behavior, whether caused by software bugs, security threats, or unexpected workload variations, can lead to system instability and performance degradation. Machine learning models can be trained to recognize patterns associated with anomalous behavior, enabling the system to detect and respond to deviations from expected memory usage. This proactive approach enhances system security and robustness by identifying and addressing potential threats or irregularities in real-time.

Despite the transformative potential of integrating machine learning into memory management, challenges and considerations exist. The interpretability of machine learning models is crucial for understanding the rationale behind their decisions, especially in critical systems where transparency is essential. Additionally, the overhead introduced by machine learning algorithms, both in terms of computational resources and training data requirements, must be carefully balanced to avoid performance degradation. Privacy concerns related to the collection and analysis of system data for training machine learning models also necessitate robust privacy-preserving mechanisms.

In conclusion, the integration of machine learning techniques into memory management represents a pioneering approach to enhancing the adaptability, efficiency, and responsiveness of computing systems. From predictive analytics for memory usage patterns to autonomous memory management agents, machine learning enables systems to learn, adapt, and optimize memory allocations dynamically. This innovation is particularly impactful in addressing the challenges posed by dynamic workloads, virtualized environments, and emerging computing paradigms. As machine learning continues to advance, its integration into memory management strategies holds the potential to revolutionize the way computing systems allocate, utilize, and optimize memory resources, paving the way for more intelligent, efficient, and adaptive memory management solutions in the evolving landscape of computing.

Adaptive memory allocation based on usage patterns.

Adaptive memory allocation based on usage patterns represents a dynamic and intelligent approach to managing memory resources in computing systems. Traditional memory allocation strategies often rely on fixed heuristics or predetermined algorithms that may not fully exploit the dynamic nature of application workloads. The concept of adaptive memory allocation introduces a paradigm shift, allowing systems to analyze real-time usage patterns, learn from historical data, and dynamically adjust memory allocations to optimize performance, responsiveness, and resource utilization.

One of the primary motivations behind adaptive memory allocation is the recognition that application workloads exhibit varying memory requirements throughout their execution. Traditional static memory allocation may lead to inefficiencies, as applications may experience periods of both increased and decreased memory demands. Adaptive memory allocation leverages machine learning techniques to continuously monitor and analyze the memory usage patterns of applications. By learning from historical data and considering factors such as application behavior, workload characteristics, and temporal trends, the system can make informed decisions on how to allocate memory resources in real-time.

Predictive analytics plays a pivotal role in adaptive memory allocation. Machine learning models can be trained to forecast future memory usage patterns based on historical data. These models utilize techniques such as time-series analysis, regression, and pattern recognition to identify trends and correlations in the memory usage behavior of applications. By understanding the temporal dynamics of memory demands, the system gains the ability to anticipate peak usage periods, allocate additional memory preemptively, and avoid potential performance bottlenecks during periods of heightened activity. This predictive capability enhances the system's responsiveness to dynamic workloads.

In the context of adaptive memory allocation, machine learning algorithms contribute to the development of intelligent memory management agents. These agents act as autonomous entities that continuously monitor the system's performance, analyze memory usage patterns, and dynamically adjust memory allocations without requiring explicit human intervention. Reinforcement learning, a subset of machine learning, is particularly relevant in this context. Memory management agents, powered by reinforcement learning algorithms, learn from the consequences of their memory allocation decisions. By receiving feedback on the impact of their actions in real-time, these agents can adapt and refine their strategies over time, maximizing overall system performance.

The adaptability introduced by adaptive memory allocation is especially beneficial in virtualized and cloud computing environments. In these settings, multiple virtual machines or containers often share physical resources, making it challenging to allocate memory efficiently. Adaptive memory allocation, informed by machine learning models, allows the system to categorize and understand different workloads based on their memory usage characteristics. Clustering algorithms can identify similar patterns among workloads, enabling the system to allocate resources more effectively. This adaptability is crucial in environments where the composition and characteristics of workloads may change rapidly, necessitating a flexible and intelligent approach to memory management.

Dynamic memory adjustment based on application behavior is a key facet of adaptive memory allocation. Traditional static allocation may result in underutilization of memory during periods of low demand or inefficient utilization during periods of peak demand. Adaptive memory allocation, however, enables the system to dynamically adjust memory allocations for each application based on its specific requirements. Machine learning models, equipped with real-time monitoring capabilities, continuously assess factors such as historical usage, current demands, and predicted future requirements. This adaptive approach ensures that each application receives an optimal amount of memory, maximizing the efficiency of resource utilization.

Moreover, adaptive memory allocation contributes to the detection and resolution of memory leaks. Memory leaks, where programs fail to release allocated memory, can lead to performance degradation and system instability. Traditional memory leak detection tools often rely on static analysis or runtime monitoring with fixed heuristics. In contrast, machine learning models can be trained to recognize subtle patterns indicative of memory leaks by analyzing the relationships between variables, memory usage patterns, and the longevity of allocated memory blocks. Through supervised learning, these models can identify potential memory leaks with higher accuracy and lower false positive rates, providing a more effective and automated approach to memory management.

In virtualized environments, where the number and types of applications running on a system can change dynamically, adaptive memory allocation becomes essential for efficient resource usage. Machine learning algorithms can continuously analyze the memory usage patterns of different virtual machines or containers, learning from their interactions and resource requirements. This learning process enables the system to predict optimal memory allocations for specific workloads in real-time, ensuring that resources are distributed effectively among the virtualized instances. The adaptability introduced by adaptive memory allocation is particularly valuable in cloud computing scenarios, where the allocation of memory resources needs to align with the evolving needs of diverse workloads.

Furthermore, adaptive memory allocation enhances system resilience by addressing the challenges posed by unpredictable workloads. In scenarios where applications exhibit bursty or sporadic memory usage patterns, traditional static allocation may lead to inefficient use of resources. Adaptive memory allocation, driven by machine learning insights, allows the system to dynamically adjust memory allocations to accommodate changing demands. This adaptability ensures that the system can effectively handle variations in workload characteristics, contributing to improved stability and robustness. In critical systems where reliability is paramount, adaptive memory allocation becomes a key factor in maintaining consistent performance.

In energy-efficient computing, adaptive memory allocation plays a crucial role in optimizing resource usage while minimizing power consumption. Machine learning models can predict periods of low activity or reduced resource demand by analyzing historical data and workload patterns. During these periods, the system can employ adaptive memory consolidation strategies, dynamically adjusting the memory allocated to different applications or virtual machines. Unused memory regions can be placed into low-power states, contributing to energy savings without compromising system responsiveness during periods of increased demand. This adaptive approach aligns with the broader goal of sustainable computing, where resource efficiency and energy conservation are central considerations.

Additionally, adaptive memory allocation has implications for optimizing cache usage and improving overall system performance. Machine learning-driven caching mechanisms can learn which data should be retained in memory based on usage patterns, application behavior, and the temporal locality of memory accesses. By analyzing real-time data access patterns, these models can dynamically adjust caching strategies, ensuring that frequently accessed data remains in the cache for faster retrieval. This adaptability enhances cache hit rates, reducing the need for fetching data from slower storage tiers and thereby improving overall system efficiency.

The integration of adaptive memory allocation into memory management strategies introduces a level of intelligence and responsiveness that aligns with the dynamic nature of modern computing environments. Whether in virtualized settings, cloud computing, or edge computing scenarios, the ability to dynamically adjust memory allocations based on real-time usage patterns is a powerful tool for optimizing system performance, resource utilization, and energy efficiency. As machine learning techniques continue to advance, the potential for adaptive memory allocation to revolutionize the way computing systems manage memory resources is poised to play a pivotal role in the evolving landscape of computing.

Enhancing efficiency through intelligent memory optimization.

Enhancing efficiency through intelligent memory optimization represents a transformative approach to managing memory resources in computing systems, with a focus on maximizing performance, responsiveness, and overall system efficiency. Traditional memory optimization techniques often rely on static algorithms or predetermined heuristics, which may not fully adapt to the dynamic and diverse workloads encountered in modern computing environments. Intelligent memory optimization leverages advanced techniques, including machine learning and adaptive strategies, to analyze real-time usage patterns, learn from historical data, and dynamically adjust memory allocations to align with the evolving needs of applications and workloads.

One key aspect of intelligent memory optimization lies in predictive analytics, where machine learning models are employed to forecast future memory usage patterns based on historical data. These models utilize advanced statistical techniques, time-series analysis, and pattern recognition to identify trends and correlations in the memory usage behavior of applications. By understanding the temporal dynamics of memory demands, the system gains the ability to anticipate peak usage periods and allocate additional memory preemptively. This proactive approach enhances responsiveness, reduces the risk of performance bottlenecks, and ensures that the system can adapt to the varying demands imposed by dynamic workloads.

In the realm of intelligent memory optimization, the development of autonomous memory management agents stands out as a significant innovation. These agents, driven by machine learning algorithms, continuously monitor the system's performance, analyze memory usage patterns, and dynamically adjust memory allocations without requiring explicit human intervention. Reinforcement learning, a subset of machine learning, is particularly relevant in this context. Memory management agents, powered by reinforcement learning algorithms, learn from the consequences of their memory allocation decisions. Through real-time feedback on the impact of their actions, these agents can adapt and refine their strategies over time, maximizing overall system performance.

Adaptive memory allocation, a key component of intelligent memory optimization, is instrumental in responding to the dynamic memory requirements of applications. Traditional static allocation may lead to underutilization of memory during periods of low demand or inefficient resource usage during peak demand. Adaptive memory allocation, informed by machine learning models, allows the system to dynamically adjust memory allocations for each application based on its specific requirements. Real-time monitoring of factors such as historical usage, current demands, and predicted future requirements enables the system to ensure that each application receives an optimal amount of memory, thereby maximizing the efficiency of resource utilization.

Furthermore, intelligent memory optimization plays a crucial role in virtualized and cloud computing environments, where multiple virtual machines or containers often share physical resources. Machine learning algorithms can categorize and understand different workloads based on their memory usage characteristics. Clustering techniques identify similar patterns among workloads, allowing the system to allocate resources more effectively. This adaptability is essential in environments where the composition and characteristics of workloads may change rapidly, necessitating a flexible and intelligent approach to memory management. In this context, intelligent memory optimization contributes to the efficient allocation of resources across diverse workloads, improving the overall efficiency of virtualized and cloud-based infrastructures.

Dynamic memory adjustment based on application behavior is another hallmark of intelligent memory optimization. Machine learning models, equipped with real-time monitoring capabilities, continuously assess factors such as historical usage, current demands, and predicted future requirements. This adaptive approach ensures that memory allocations are dynamically adjusted for each application, taking into account the specific needs of varying workloads. This capability is particularly valuable in scenarios where applications exhibit fluctuating memory requirements during their execution, allowing the system to respond dynamically and optimize resource usage based on the evolving demands of each application.

Intelligent memory optimization also addresses the critical issue of memory leaks, which can lead to performance degradation and system instability. Traditional memory leak detection tools often rely on static analysis or runtime monitoring with fixed heuristics. Machine learning models, however, can be trained to recognize subtle patterns indicative of memory leaks by analyzing the relationships between variables, memory usage patterns, and the longevity of allocated memory blocks. Through supervised learning, these models can identify potential memory leaks with higher accuracy and lower false positive rates, providing a more effective and automated approach to memory management. By addressing memory leaks proactively, intelligent memory optimization contributes to system stability and reliability.

In virtualized environments, where the characteristics of workloads can change dynamically, intelligent memory optimization becomes essential for efficient resource usage. Machine learning algorithms continuously analyze the memory usage patterns of different virtual machines or containers, learning from their interactions and resource requirements. This learning process enables the system to predict optimal memory allocations for specific workloads in real-time, ensuring that resources are distributed effectively among the virtualized instances. The adaptability introduced by intelligent memory optimization is particularly valuable in cloud computing scenarios, where the allocation of memory resources needs to align with the evolving needs of diverse workloads.

Energy-efficient computing benefits significantly from intelligent memory optimization strategies. Machine learning models can predict periods of low activity or reduced resource demand by analyzing historical data and workload patterns. During these periods, the system can employ adaptive memory consolidation strategies, dynamically adjusting the memory allocated to different applications or virtual machines. Unused memory regions can be placed into low-power states, contributing to energy savings without compromising system responsiveness during periods of increased demand. This adaptive approach aligns with the broader goal of sustainable computing, where resource efficiency and energy conservation are central considerations.

Moreover, intelligent memory optimization has implications for optimizing cache usage and improving overall system performance. Machine learning-driven caching mechanisms can learn which data should be retained in memory based on usage patterns, application behavior, and the temporal locality of memory accesses. By analyzing real-time data access patterns, these models can dynamically adjust caching strategies, ensuring that frequently accessed data remains in the cache for faster retrieval. This adaptability enhances cache hit rates, reducing the need for fetching data from slower storage tiers and thereby improving overall system efficiency.

The integration of intelligent memory optimization into memory management strategies introduces a level of intelligence and adaptability that aligns with the dynamic nature of modern computing environments. Whether in virtualized settings, cloud computing, or edge computing scenarios, the ability to dynamically adjust memory allocations based on real-time usage patterns is a powerful tool for optimizing system performance, resource utilization, and energy efficiency. As machine learning techniques continue to advance, the potential for intelligent memory optimization to revolutionize the way computing systems manage memory resources is poised to play a pivotal role in the evolving landscape of computing.

Quantum implications on memory storage and retrieval.

The advent of quantum computing brings forth profound implications for the storage and retrieval of information, fundamentally challenging classical paradigms and unlocking new frontiers in computational capabilities. Quantum memory, an integral component of quantum information processing, is not constrained by classical bits but instead relies on quantum bits or qubits, which can exist in superpositions of states. Quantum superposition allows qubits to represent multiple classical states simultaneously, offering an exponential increase in information storage capacity. Quantum memory, often realized through quantum registers, leverages the principles of superposition to encode and manipulate vast amounts of information in parallel.

Quantum superposition is a cornerstone for quantum memory's potential to revolutionize data storage. In classical computing, bits are either in a state of 0 or 1. However, qubits can exist in a superposition of both 0 and 1 states simultaneously, enabling the storage of a vast number of classical bit combinations in a single quantum state. This feature, known as quantum parallelism, opens up possibilities for quantum memory to process and store information more efficiently than classical memory systems. Quantum registers, formed by entangling qubits, further exploit this parallelism, allowing for the storage and retrieval of complex data structures in a fraction of the time it would take classical systems.

Quantum entanglement, another fundamental quantum phenomenon, introduces correlations between qubits that enable the creation of entangled quantum states. Entangled qubits exhibit instantaneous correlations, regardless of the physical distance between them. This property has intriguing implications for quantum memory as it offers the potential for distributed quantum storage networks. Quantum entanglement enables the synchronization of quantum states across spatially separated qubits, laying the foundation for novel approaches to collaborative and distributed quantum memory architectures. These architectures could facilitate the development of quantum memory networks that transcend the limitations of classical data transfer and storage systems.

Quantum coherence, a delicate state of quantum systems, is crucial for the stable storage and retrieval of quantum information. Quantum coherence refers to the phase relationships between different quantum states. Maintaining coherence is a significant challenge in quantum memory, as interactions with the external environment can lead to decoherence, causing the loss of quantum information. Quantum error correction techniques, a key focus in quantum computing research, aim to mitigate the impact of decoherence on quantum memory. By encoding redundant quantum information and implementing error correction algorithms, quantum memory systems can enhance the reliability of information storage and retrieval, paving the way for more robust quantum computing applications.

The concept of quantum superposition also has implications for the speed of memory retrieval in quantum systems. In classical computing, retrieving information involves sequentially checking each bit to determine its value. Quantum memory, with its ability to exist in superpositions of states, allows for the simultaneous evaluation of multiple possibilities. Quantum algorithms, such as Grover's algorithm, leverage this capability to search through unsorted databases exponentially faster than classical algorithms. The implications for memory retrieval are profound, as quantum systems can, in theory, provide near-instantaneous access to information stored in quantum memory registers, surpassing the computational efficiency of classical counterparts.

Quantum memory's impact on information density is evident in the realm of quantum data compression. Classical data compression techniques are limited by the requirement to preserve all possible classical states. In contrast, quantum data compression exploits the principles of quantum superposition and entanglement to represent information in a more compact form. Quantum compressed sensing techniques, for instance, leverage the intrinsic structure of quantum states to achieve efficient compression, reducing the amount of quantum memory required for storing information. This approach holds promise for optimizing quantum memory resources and addressing the challenges associated with limited qubit coherence times.

The development of quantum random access memory (qRAM) represents a significant stride in the quest for efficient memory storage and retrieval in quantum systems. qRAM aims to provide quantum algorithms with the ability to access and manipulate specific pieces of information directly, mimicking classical random access memory in a quantum context. Various proposals for qRAM architectures explore the use of quantum entanglement, superposition, and coherence to enable rapid and direct access to stored quantum information. While the realization of practical qRAM implementations is still an active area of research, the concept underscores the potential of quantum memory to revolutionize the efficiency of information retrieval in quantum computing applications.

Quantum memory's impact on cryptography is profound, particularly in the realm of quantum key distribution (QKD). QKD relies on the principles of quantum superposition and entanglement to secure communication channels by detecting any eavesdropping attempts. Quantum memory systems play a critical role in QKD protocols, enabling the storage and retrieval of quantum keys for secure communication. The use of quantum memory enhances the security of cryptographic systems by enabling the creation of long-distance entanglement and facilitating the distribution of quantum keys over quantum communication networks.

The exploration of quantum memory extends beyond conventional quantum bits to include higher-dimensional quantum states known as quantum dits. Quantum dits, analogous to classical dits or information units, introduce additional degrees of freedom for quantum information processing. Quantum memory systems capable of storing and manipulating quantum dits could enable more versatile and efficient representation of information. This concept aligns with the broader exploration of high-dimensional quantum systems, expanding the potential applications of quantum memory in quantum information processing tasks.

In quantum computing architectures, the role of quantum memory becomes increasingly pivotal as the scale of quantum processors grows. Quantum random access memory, in particular, is crucial for implementing quantum algorithms that require the manipulation of specific quantum states during computation. Quantum memory's ability to store and retrieve information in a superposition of states aligns with the principles of quantum parallelism, facilitating the execution of quantum algorithms at scales that surpass the capabilities of classical counterparts. This scalability is a key factor in realizing the full potential of quantum computing for solving complex problems in areas such as optimization, cryptography, and simulation.

The integration of quantum memory with quantum communication networks introduces novel possibilities for quantum information transfer. Quantum repeaters, a key component of quantum communication, rely on quantum memory to store and transmit entangled quantum states over long distances. The ability to extend quantum entanglement across vast quantum communication networks holds promise for secure quantum communication and the development of quantum internet architectures. Quantum memory's role in preserving and distributing quantum entanglement positions it as a cornerstone for the future development of quantum communication technologies.

Challenges, however, accompany the realization of efficient quantum memory systems. Decoherence, caused by interactions with the external environment, remains a significant hurdle in maintaining the stability and integrity of quantum information stored in quantum memory. Ongoing research focuses on developing error correction techniques, quantum error-resistant codes, and strategies to mitigate the impact of decoherence on quantum memory. Additionally, the physical implementation of quantum memory technologies, such as solid-state qubits, trapped ions, or superconducting circuits, demands advances in materials science, control technologies, and the mitigation of various noise sources to enhance the performance of quantum memory systems.

In conclusion, the implications of quantum memory on storage and retrieval transcend classical limitations, ushering in a new era of computational possibilities. Quantum superposition, entanglement, and coherence principles redefine the landscape of information storage by allowing for unprecedented information density, enhanced computational efficiency, and novel cryptographic applications. As quantum computing technologies advance, the development of robust and efficient quantum memory systems will play a pivotal role in unlocking the full potential of quantum information processing and quantum communication networks. The journey towards practical quantum memory solutions involves overcoming challenges, innovating in quantum error correction, and realizing the transformative promise of quantum technologies on a global scale.

Memory management challenges in quantum computing.

The advent of quantum computing heralds a new era in computational capabilities, promising to revolutionize information processing and solve complex problems that classical computers find intractable. However, the realization of practical quantum computing systems is accompanied by a myriad of memory management challenges that necessitate innovative solutions to harness the full potential of quantum technologies.

One of the fundamental challenges in quantum memory management stems from the fragile nature of quantum information. Unlike classical bits, which are stable and deterministic, quantum bits or qubits are susceptible to decoherence—a phenomenon where quantum states lose their coherence and become entangled with the external environment. Decoherence poses a significant hurdle for the stable storage and retrieval of quantum information, as maintaining the delicate quantum states necessary for computation is essential. Quantum memory systems must contend with the need for extended coherence times, requiring advancements in error correction techniques and the development of quantum memory technologies capable of preserving quantum information in the presence of environmental interactions.

The scalability of quantum memory systems presents another formidable challenge. Quantum computers aim to solve problems that scale exponentially with the size of the input space, demanding a correspondingly large number of qubits. However, as the number of qubits increases, so does the complexity of quantum memory management. Quantum entanglement, a key resource for quantum information processing, introduces correlations between qubits that demand sophisticated memory architectures to handle entangled quantum states efficiently. Scalable quantum memory solutions must grapple with the intricate task of preserving and manipulating entanglement across an expanding quantum register, requiring innovations in quantum error correction and the development of scalable quantum memory architectures.

Quantum error correction is pivotal in addressing the inherent susceptibility of quantum systems to errors and noise. Classical error correction relies on redundancy and parity checks to detect and correct errors in bits, but quantum error correction introduces unique challenges. Quantum information is delicate and subject to a broader array of errors, including bit flips, phase flips, and more complex correlated errors. Quantum error correction codes, such as the surface code, mitigate these errors by encoding quantum information redundantly and implementing error-detection circuits. However, these codes demand additional qubits for error correction, exacerbating the challenge of achieving fault-tolerant quantum memory with a sufficiently low error rate. Overcoming the complexities of quantum error correction is essential for the viability of quantum memory in large-scale quantum computing applications.

The exploration of various physical implementations for qubits introduces additional memory management challenges. Superconducting qubits, trapped ions, topological qubits, and other quantum technologies exhibit distinct characteristics, and their memory management requirements vary accordingly. Superconducting qubits, for instance, are sensitive to environmental factors such as temperature fluctuations, magnetic fields, and electromagnetic radiation. Quantum memory for superconducting qubits must contend with the need for cryogenic environments to maintain the necessary conditions for coherence. Trapped ions, on the other hand, face challenges related to the precision and stability of laser systems used for qubit manipulation. Memory management solutions must be tailored to the idiosyncrasies of each qubit technology, requiring a nuanced approach to address the diverse array of quantum hardware platforms.

The development of quantum random access memory (qRAM) is an area of active research with both theoretical and practical challenges. Classical computers use random access memory (RAM) to quickly retrieve specific bits of information, but quantum systems must grapple with the no-cloning theorem, which prohibits the exact duplication of an arbitrary unknown quantum state. Quantum algorithms requiring efficient random access to quantum states demand innovative solutions for qRAM. The development of practical qRAM implementations involves addressing the limitations imposed by quantum no-cloning, the trade-offs between precision and efficiency, and the integration of qRAM into larger quantum computing architectures. QRAM solutions must reconcile the need for rapid and direct access to quantum states with the constraints imposed by quantum mechanics.

The coherence time of quantum memory poses a significant challenge for quantum algorithms that require extended periods of stability for computation. Quantum systems are susceptible to noise and interactions with the environment, leading to the loss of coherence over time. Quantum error correction techniques, while essential, introduce additional overhead and may limit the effective coherence time of quantum memory. Innovations in preserving and extending coherence times, such as quantum dynamical decoupling techniques, quantum memories based on atomic ensembles, and hybrid quantum-classical approaches, are crucial for enabling the execution of more complex quantum algorithms that demand longer coherence times.

Quantum cache management is another facet of quantum memory challenges, particularly as quantum computers strive to solve problems with large datasets. Classical cache management strategies, such as prefetching and caching, are not directly transferable to quantum architectures due to the no-cloning theorem and the superposition principle. Quantum algorithms that rely on accessing specific quantum states from a larger dataset must grapple with the trade-offs between memory utilization and computational efficiency. Quantum cache management solutions must navigate the delicate balance between exploiting quantum parallelism and minimizing the impact of decoherence, presenting a unique set of challenges in the quest for efficient quantum memory systems.

The quantum-classical interface introduces challenges in hybrid quantum-classical systems, where quantum processors interact with classical components. Quantum memory management must navigate the intricacies of data transfer between quantum and classical registers, addressing issues such as latency, synchronization, and the overhead associated with quantum-classical communication. Quantum-classical systems demand seamless integration of quantum memory with classical memory management techniques, requiring the development of hybrid algorithms that optimize the interplay between quantum and classical resources.

Quantum data storage and retrieval in the presence of errors and noise are essential aspects of quantum memory management. Classical storage systems rely on redundant error correction codes, data replication, and backup strategies to ensure data integrity. Quantum memory systems, while leveraging quantum error correction, must contend with the limitations imposed by the no-cloning theorem and the principles of quantum mechanics. Strategies for efficient quantum data storage, retrieval, and error correction must be developed, accounting for the unique properties of quantum information and the challenges imposed by the quantum-classical transition.

Quantum networking and distributed quantum computing further amplify the challenges in quantum memory management. Quantum communication networks require robust quantum memory systems for storing and transmitting entangled quantum states over long distances. The development of quantum repeaters, quantum memories based on solid-state devices, and the exploration of quantum memories for quantum key distribution are areas of active research. Distributed quantum computing architectures, where quantum processors are interconnected for collaborative computation, introduce challenges in memory synchronization, error correction across distributed registers, and the efficient distribution of quantum states. Quantum memory solutions must adapt to the demands of quantum networking and distributed quantum computing, considering the implications of entanglement distribution, quantum communication delays, and the coordination of quantum information across multiple nodes.

In conclusion, the challenges in quantum memory management are intricate and multifaceted, spanning the realms of coherence preservation, error correction, scalability, hardware diversity, and the interplay between quantum and classical systems. Addressing these challenges requires a multidisciplinary approach that combines advances in quantum error correction, materials science for qubit technologies, algorithm design, and quantum-classical interface optimization. As quantum computing technologies continue to progress, overcoming these memory management challenges is essential for unlocking the transformative potential of quantum information processing in diverse fields, from cryptography and optimization to simulation and materials science. The journey towards practical and efficient quantum memory solutions involves navigating the complexities of quantum mechanics, developing robust error correction strategies, and envisioning the future landscape of quantum computing architectures.

Preparing for the integration of quantum principles in memory technologies.

Preparing for the integration of quantum principles in memory technologies represents a transformative journey at the intersection of quantum mechanics, information theory, and materials science. As the promise of quantum computing and quantum information processing looms on the horizon, the integration of quantum principles into memory technologies becomes a focal point for researchers and engineers alike. This paradigm shift introduces a profound departure from classical memory systems, necessitating a comprehensive understanding of quantum phenomena and the development of innovative memory architectures that harness the unique features of quantum mechanics.

At the heart of preparing for the integration of quantum principles lies the need for a foundational understanding of quantum information theory. Classical bits, the basic units of classical information, have deterministic values of 0 or 1. In the quantum realm, information is encoded in quantum bits or qubits, which can exist in superpositions of 0 and 1. Quantum superposition is a fundamental principle that underlies the potential of quantum memory to store exponentially more information than classical memory. To prepare for this integration, researchers delve into the theoretical aspects of quantum information, exploring the principles of superposition, entanglement, and quantum parallelism that characterize quantum information processing.

The concept of quantum entanglement emerges as a cornerstone for the development of quantum memory technologies. Entanglement allows qubits to become correlated in ways that defy classical intuition, with the state of one qubit instantaneously influencing the state of another, regardless of the physical separation between them. Quantum memory, leveraging entanglement, holds the promise of creating more robust and interconnected storage systems. Preparing for this integration involves not only harnessing the power of entanglement for enhanced memory capabilities but also understanding the challenges associated with preserving and manipulating entangled states over extended periods—a crucial consideration in the development of practical quantum memory technologies.

Quantum coherence, the delicate state of quantum systems where phase relationships between different quantum states are maintained, emerges as both a resource and a challenge in the integration of quantum principles into memory technologies. Coherence is essential for stable quantum computation and information storage. Quantum memory systems must be designed to preserve coherence, mitigating the effects of decoherence caused by interactions with the external environment. Researchers explore techniques such as quantum error correction and quantum dynamical decoupling to extend coherence times, laying the groundwork for the development of robust and reliable quantum memory.

Preparing for the integration of quantum principles in memory technologies necessitates a shift in the paradigm of memory architecture. Classical memory relies on binary encoding and deterministic operations, whereas quantum memory requires a more nuanced approach to accommodate the probabilistic nature of quantum states. Quantum memory architectures explore the use of quantum registers, which can hold a superposition of states, and entanglement-based storage schemes to enhance memory density and information retrieval efficiency. Hybrid memory architectures that integrate classical and quantum memory components are also considered, providing a bridge between existing technologies and the emerging quantum paradigm.

Materials science plays a pivotal role in preparing for the integration of quantum principles into memory technologies. Different physical implementations of qubits, such as superconducting circuits, trapped ions, and topological qubits, demand tailored memory solutions. Superconducting qubits, for example, require cryogenic environments to maintain coherence, influencing the design of quantum memory systems. Advances in materials science contribute to the development of stable and scalable qubit technologies, addressing the diverse requirements of quantum memory across various quantum computing platforms.

Quantum error correction emerges as a critical component in the preparation for quantum memory integration. The inherent susceptibility of quantum systems to errors and noise poses challenges to reliable information storage and retrieval. Quantum error correction techniques, inspired by classical error correction but adapted to the probabilistic nature of quantum information, are essential for mitigating the impact of errors in quantum memory. Researchers explore codes such as the surface code and cat codes to protect quantum information from decoherence and other sources of error, ensuring the reliability of quantum memory systems.

The development of quantum random access memory (qRAM) becomes a focal point in preparing for quantum memory integration, particularly for quantum computing applications that require efficient access to specific quantum states. Classical random access memory (RAM) relies on the ability to retrieve specific bits of information quickly. Quantum systems, constrained by the no-cloning theorem, demand innovative solutions for qRAM. Preparing for qRAM integration involves addressing the trade-offs between precision and efficiency, as well as exploring the possibilities of leveraging quantum parallelism for rapid and direct access to quantum states.

The exploration of quantum-classical interfaces is essential in preparing for the integration of quantum principles into memory technologies, especially in hybrid quantum-classical systems. Quantum processors interacting with classical components necessitate seamless integration of quantum and classical memory management techniques. Quantum-classical interfaces must be optimized to minimize latency, synchronize data transfer between quantum and classical registers, and manage the overhead associated with quantum-classical communication. The development of hybrid algorithms that leverage the strengths of both quantum and classical resources is a key aspect of preparing for quantum-classical integration in memory technologies.

Quantum networking and distributed quantum computing introduce additional challenges in preparation for quantum memory integration. Quantum communication networks demand robust quantum memory systems for storing and transmitting entangled quantum states over long distances. The development of quantum repeaters, solid-state quantum memories, and the exploration of quantum memories for quantum key distribution become integral components of preparing for quantum networking applications. Distributed quantum computing architectures require innovative memory management strategies to synchronize information across multiple quantum nodes, addressing issues related to entanglement distribution, communication delays, and the coordination of quantum information.

Educational initiatives and collaborative research efforts play a vital role in preparing for the integration of quantum principles into memory technologies. Training a workforce with expertise in quantum information science, quantum computing, and materials science is essential for advancing the field. Collaborations between academia, industry, and research institutions foster the exchange of ideas, the development of practical solutions, and the exploration of novel approaches to quantum memory. Quantum information science programs and research centers provide the intellectual and technological infrastructure necessary to prepare for the integration of quantum principles into memory technologies.

In conclusion, preparing for the integration of quantum principles into memory technologies requires a holistic and multidisciplinary approach. It involves deepening our understanding of quantum information theory, harnessing the power of quantum entanglement and coherence, reimagining memory architectures to accommodate quantum states, advancing materials science for diverse qubit technologies, implementing robust quantum error correction, exploring innovative solutions for qRAM, optimizing quantum-classical interfaces, and addressing the challenges posed by quantum networking and distributed quantum computing. The collaborative efforts of researchers, educators, and industry professionals pave the way for the realization of efficient and practical quantum memory technologies, ushering in a new era of information processing with the potential to transform computing paradigms and solve complex problems previously deemed insurmountable.

Decentralized approaches to memory management.

Decentralized approaches to memory management signify a departure from traditional centralized models, introducing a paradigm shift in the way computing systems allocate, access, and optimize memory resources. In the context of decentralized memory management, the emphasis lies on distributing memory-related responsibilities across multiple entities within a system, fostering adaptability, scalability, and improved fault tolerance. This departure from a centralized approach is motivated by the growing complexity of modern computing environments, characterized by distributed systems, cloud computing, edge computing, and the proliferation of interconnected devices. To comprehend the nuances of decentralized memory management, it is essential to delve into the underlying principles, architectural considerations, challenges, and potential benefits inherent in this transformative approach.

At the core of decentralized memory management is the notion of distributing memory-related tasks among individual nodes or entities within a computing system. Unlike centralized models where a single memory manager governs the allocation and deallocation of memory resources, decentralized approaches empower individual nodes with the authority to manage their own memory space. This distributed autonomy aligns with the principles of decentralization, where each node operates independently, contributing to a more flexible and scalable system architecture. This architectural shift is particularly relevant in distributed systems, where a multitude of interconnected devices collaboratively execute tasks, share data, and contribute to overall system functionality.

One key aspect of decentralized memory management is the concept of local autonomy, wherein each node independently manages its own memory resources based on its specific requirements and workload characteristics. Local autonomy introduces adaptability to varying memory demands, allowing nodes to dynamically adjust their memory allocations in response to changing workloads. This adaptability is crucial in scenarios where nodes operate in diverse environments, experience varying workloads, or possess unique memory requirements. Decentralized memory management accommodates this heterogeneity, promoting a more resilient and responsive system architecture.

The implementation of decentralized memory management often involves the use of distributed data structures and algorithms. These distributed structures enable nodes to collaborate, communicate, and share information about their memory usage patterns. Distributed algorithms facilitate coordinated decision-making processes, such as load balancing and memory allocation optimization, across the decentralized network. These mechanisms are essential for achieving efficient resource utilization and ensuring that each node contributes to the overall performance and stability of the system. Decentralized memory management leverages these distributed techniques to enhance the coordination and collaboration among nodes in a dynamic computing environment.

Scalability is a key advantage offered by decentralized memory management, particularly in large-scale distributed systems. As the number of nodes within a system grows, the centralized management of memory resources can become a bottleneck, hindering scalability and introducing performance limitations. Decentralized approaches, on the other hand, distribute the memory management responsibilities across the nodes, allowing the system to scale more effectively. Each node independently manages its memory, reducing the burden on a central entity and enabling the system to expand seamlessly to accommodate a larger number of nodes.

Fault tolerance is another inherent benefit of decentralized memory management. In decentralized systems, the failure of a single node does not necessarily lead to a catastrophic failure of the entire system. Since each node operates autonomously, the impact of a node failure is confined to that specific entity. Other nodes can continue functioning independently, and the decentralized nature of memory management allows the system to adapt to the loss of individual components without compromising overall stability. This fault-tolerant characteristic is particularly valuable in scenarios where system reliability is crucial, such as in distributed cloud environments or edge computing deployments.

Decentralized memory management also aligns with the principles of edge computing, where computing tasks are distributed across a network of edge devices rather than relying on centralized cloud servers. In edge computing scenarios, individual edge devices have limited resources and varying workloads. Decentralized memory management empowers these edge devices to autonomously manage their memory resources based on local demands, enhancing the efficiency of edge computing systems. This adaptability is essential for addressing the dynamic and resource-constrained nature of edge environments, where responsiveness and local decision-making are paramount.

Challenges, however, accompany the adoption of decentralized memory management. Coordination and consistency across distributed nodes become critical concerns. Ensuring that all nodes operate in harmony, without conflicts or inconsistencies in memory management decisions, requires robust communication protocols and distributed algorithms. The challenge of maintaining coherence in a decentralized environment necessitates careful consideration of data synchronization mechanisms, consensus algorithms, and strategies for handling concurrent memory access across distributed nodes.

Security is another significant challenge in decentralized memory management. The distribution of memory management responsibilities introduces new attack vectors and potential vulnerabilities. sibilities introduces new attack vectors and potential vulnerabilities.

Decentralized systems must implement robust security measures to safeguard against unauthorized access, data breaches, and malicious activities that could compromise the integrity of memory resources. Encryption, secure communication protocols, and access control mechanisms become essential components of decentralized memory management strategies to ensure the confidentiality and integrity of data stored and processed across distributed nodes.

The efficiency of decentralized memory management also depends on the design of effective load balancing mechanisms. In a decentralized system, nodes may experience varying workloads, leading to uneven memory usage patterns. Efficient load balancing algorithms are crucial for redistributing memory resources dynamically, ensuring that no single node is overloaded while others remain underutilized. Load balancing mechanisms need to adapt to the dynamic nature of distributed workloads, responding in real-time to changes in demand and ensuring optimal resource allocation across the decentralized network.

Furthermore, the development of decentralized memory management architectures must address the complexities introduced by the diverse array of devices and platforms within modern computing ecosystems. Heterogeneity in hardware architectures, memory technologies, and operating systems across distributed nodes requires a standardized approach or middleware that enables seamless coordination and communication. The challenge lies in creating a unified framework that accommodates the diversity of devices while providing a cohesive and interoperable decentralized memory management solution.

Decentralized memory management also intersects with the concept of edge intelligence, where edge devices contribute to local decision-making and data processing. In edge intelligence scenarios, decentralized memory management becomes a key enabler for optimizing resource utilization and responsiveness at the edge. Edge devices, endowed with the autonomy to manage their memory resources, can adapt to local requirements, process data locally, and contribute to overall system efficiency. Decentralized memory management aligns with the principles of edge intelligence by empowering edge devices to make autonomous decisions about memory allocation, enhancing their ability to process data locally and respond to real-time demands.

The future evolution of decentralized memory management involves exploring advanced technologies, such as blockchain, for enhancing coordination and trust among distributed nodes. Blockchain, with its decentralized and secure ledger capabilities, could play a role in providing a tamper-resistant record of memory management decisions, ensuring transparency and accountability in a decentralized environment. This integration could contribute to the development of more secure and auditable decentralized memory management systems, addressing concerns related to trust and accountability in distributed computing environments.

In conclusion, decentralized approaches to memory management herald a new era in computing architectures, aligning with the distributed and dynamic nature of modern computing ecosystems. By empowering individual nodes with the autonomy to manage their memory resources, decentralized memory management offers adaptability, scalability, and fault tolerance. This approach is particularly relevant in the context of distributed systems, edge computing, and decentralized networks, where diverse devices collaborate to execute tasks. While challenges such as coordination, security, load balancing, and heterogeneity must be addressed, the potential benefits of decentralized memory management position it as a transformative strategy for optimizing resource utilization and responsiveness in the evolving landscape of computing.